PRAISE FOR *THE SAVVY ALLY: A Guide for Becoming a Skilled LGBTQ+ Advocate*

"This is it. You found it—the very best guide on how not to make mistakes with LGBTQ+ employees, customers, students, congregants, patients, and family members. If you want to be an effective ally for LGBTQ+ people, buy and read *The Savvy Ally*. I very enthusiastically endorse this book."—**Brian McNaught**, named "The Godfather of Gay Diversity Training" by the *New York Times*

"This is a beautiful book. A necessary book. An unputdownable book. Please read this book."—**Alison Smith**, Lambda Literary Award Winner and author of *Name All the Animals*

"An ideal, practical, effective, and thoroughly 'user friendly' DIY instructional guide and manual, *The Savvy Ally: A Guide for Becoming a Skilled LGBTQ+ Advocate* is an especially and unreservedly recommended addition to family, personal, professional, community, college, and university library LGBTQ collections and supplemental curriculum studies lists."—**Midwest Book Review**

"If you want to support LGBTQ+ people but no one has ever taught you how, this is the book for you. Written in an accessible and entertaining style, *The Savvy Ally* is filled with useful scenarios, tips, and examples to help you transition from well-intentioned bystander to effective and informed advocate." —**Robyn Ochs**, named by *Teen Vogue* as one of "9 Bisexual Women Who are Making History"

"Once in a while, a book comes along that resonates with my heart and my life's passion/mission. This is *The Savvy Ally* book by Jeannie Gainsburg. It contains all the relevant aspects and more on how to be an ALLY, excuse me, a SAVVY ALLY as Jeannie's badass humor and personality came through the reading for me. I love it so much!"—**Loan Nguyen**, PFLAG New York City Program Coordinator

"If you have LGBTQ+ friends, family, colleagues, service users, or are simply keen to be more knowledgeable about the subject of gender equity, *The Savvy Ally* is the best reference guide you are ever likely to read. Jeannie Gainsburg is a skilled and professional ally, as well as a tremendous author."—**Matt McAvoy**, senior editor, MJV Literary Author Services

"This is such an amazing book about how someone who is not part of the LGBTQ+ community can be a helpful advocate to those who are. . . . I highly recommend this book to everyone."—*SMS Nonfiction Book Reviews*

"This book is long overdue, and I loved reading it! It is a call to action in a positive, optimistic, and engaging way—a masterful blend of information, personal stories, humor, and serious content. This is much more than just an informative book. It is designed to build skills that can be translated into ongoing, meaningful action. If you want to be an effective LBGTQ+ ally, buy this book. It won't just sit on your shelf. You'll use it every day!"—**Mike Streeter**, executive director, Workforce Diversity Network

"In her book, *The Savvy Ally*, Jeannie Gainsburg informs and empowers readers to consider how they might be more open and engaging toward those who might be different. It is a resource I have recommended many times."—**Hunter O'Hanian**, Stonewall National Museum & Archives Executive Director

"I love the compassionate sentiment that is weaved through this book that being an ally doesn't mean you have to be perfect; it means being able to acknowledge when a mistake is made and then trying your best to be better. If you truly want to be an ally, *The Savvy Ally* will lead the way through real-life examples, questions that make you go hmmm . . . , and 'what if' scenarios. Thank you, Jeannie Gainsburg, for supporting my ally journey!"—**Kimberly Braithwaite**, senior human resource manager, Barilla America Inc., and one of *Profiles in Diversity Journal's* 2019 Women Worth Watching

"*The Savvy Ally* provides a successful foray into the confusing and ever-changing world of being an ally to the LGBTQ+ community. The thoughtful definitions, various analogies, and personal examples used to clarify issues are always helpful and often brilliant. Clearly, Gainsburg's many years of 'operating in solidarity with' the LGBTQ+ community have provided her with the necessary insight to create such a useful tool. I am grateful for such a perceptive and kindhearted book!"—**Matthew Burns**, dean of students, University of Rochester

"*The Savvy Ally* is a read for everyone. It is one of the best tutorials I've read that offers key insights into LGBTQ communities while offering practical guidance and action-oriented tips that will help allies become more culturally competent, respectful, and impactful in their interactions, both personally and in business."—**Joseph L. Searles Jr.**, corporate diversity relations director, Excellus BlueCross BlueShield

"*The Savvy Ally* is a book I will recommend again and again for its thoughtful approach to gaining knowledge, skill, and confidence. It's a much-needed tool in our box!"—**Kelly Clark**, director, Q Center, Binghamton University

"I was really hesitant to read a book written about the LGBTQ+ community by someone who does not identify as LGBTQ+. I read the first few pages with skepticism, ready to poke holes in the book. And, I have never been so happy to be proven wrong! Jeannie's book is filled with great information for anyone who wants to understand what it means to be an advocate for LGBTQ+ people and how to act as an ally. It's also educational for those within the community—I found myself saying 'huh! I didn't know that!' multiple times as I was reading. I loved the book so much that we offered the book as a virtual book club at work during pride month this June. My colleagues had rich and meaningful discussion and we would highly recommend it!"—**Cara Pelletier**, senior director of diversity, equity & belonging at Ultimate Kronos Group

"Jeannie Gainsburg has written a brilliant guide to what we all need to know and do to be better allies for LGBTQ+ people in all aspects of our lives. It's a treasure trove of practical ideas, sprinkled with the perfect amount of humor." —**Karen Catlin**, author of *Better Allies* and *Belonging in Healthcare*

THE SAVVY ALLY

A Guide for Becoming a Skilled LGBTQ+ Advocate

Second Edition

Jeannie Gainsburg

ROWMAN & LITTLEFIELD
Lanham • Boulder • New York • London

Acquisitions Editor: Mark Kerr
Acquisitions Assistant: Sarah Rinehart
Sales and Marketing Inquiries: textbooks@rowman.com

Published by Rowman & Littlefield
An imprint of The Rowman & Littlefield Publishing Group, Inc.
4501 Forbes Boulevard, Suite 200, Lanham, Maryland 20706
www.rowman.com

86-90 Paul Street, London EC2A 4NE, United Kingdom

British Library Cataloguing in Publication Information Available

Library of Congress Cataloging-in-Publication Data

Names: Gainsburg, Jeannie, 1963– author.
Title: The savvy ally : a guide for becoming a skilled LGBTQ + advocate / Jeannie
  Gainsburg.
Description: Second Edition. | Lanham : Rowman & Littlefield, [2023] | Revised
  edition of the author's The savvy ally, [2020] | Includes bibliographical references
  and index. | Summary: "The Savvy Ally: A Guide for Becoming a Skilled LGBTQ+
  Advocate is an enjoyable, humorous, encouraging, easy to understand guidebook
  for being an ally to LGBTQ+ communities"—Provided by publisher.
Identifiers: LCCN 2022049426 (print) | LCCN 2022049427 (ebook) | ISBN
  9781538169230 (cloth) | ISBN 9781538169247 (paperback) | ISBN
  9781538169254 (epub)
Subjects: LCSH: Sexual minorities—United States. | Sexual minorities—United
  States—21st century—Guidebooks. | Sexual minorities—Civil rights—United
  States—21st century—Guidebooks. | Lesbians—United States—21st century—
  Guidebooks. | Gays—United States—21st century—Guidebooks. | Bisexuals—
  United States—21st century—Guidebooks. | Transgender people—United States—
  21st century—Guidebooks. | Sexual minority community—United States—21st
  century—Guidebooks.
Classification: LCC HQ73.3.U6 G35 2023 (print) | LCC HQ73.3.U6 (ebook) |
  DDC 306.760973—dc23/eng/20221130
LC record available at https://lccn.loc.gov/2022049426
LC ebook record available at https://lccn.loc.gov/2022049427

To Scott Fearing,
for seeing and believing in the educator in me
long before I ever did

savvy *[sav-ee] adj., experienced, knowledgeable, and well-informed*

BRIEF CONTENTS

CONTENTS

AUTHOR'S NOTE

In 2019, I wrote *The Savvy Ally* because I saw a need for an accessible, encouraging, and action-oriented guidebook on how to be an ally to the LGBTQ+ communities. Now, three years later, I see a need for an updated version.

So much has changed over the past three years. LGBTQ+ language and cultural etiquette has changed, as it always does with time. But there has also been a huge political shift. With a record-breaking number of anti-LGBTQ+ bills introduced at the state level, it's reasonable to call 2022 the worst year in US history for LGBTQ+ rights and inclusion. Florida passed the Parental Rights in Education Act, aka the "Don't Say Gay" bill, restricting discussions of sexual orientation and gender identity in the classroom. More than a dozen other states are considering similar legislation. Fifteen states have restricted, or are considering laws that would restrict, gender-affirming medical care for transgender youth. The state of Texas is attempting legally to classify gender-affirming care as child abuse.

Knowing how to support LGBTQ+ people, advocate for LGBTQ+ inclusive spaces, and have effective conversations with people who think differently from the way you do is more important than ever. The second edition of *The Savvy Ally* offers the most up-to-date LGBTQ+ information and includes four entirely new chapters:

- "Pronouns: Sharing, Gathering, and Using," which provides pronoun etiquette and tips for gathering pronouns from others without making it awkward

- "Creating LGBTQ+ Inclusive Spaces in Different Settings," which recommends ally actions specifically for implementation in health and mental health settings, the workplace, faith communities, schools, and your home
- "Now What? Questions from Allies in the Real World," which features great questions I've fielded from allies over the past three years and my responses to them
- "Messing Up Properly," which offers steps for recovering gracefully after you've messed up and tips for getting it right the next time

I've also added a personal touch to this new edition by including illustrations that I doodled when I was procrastinating from writing.

Thank you for reading the second edition of *The Savvy Ally* and helping to make the world a better place.

—Jeannie

PREFACE

What is your purpose? Why are you here?
Start small and find out.[1]

—Nannie Helen Burroughs, *The 12 Things*
the Negro Must Do for Himself

For my fortieth birthday, my husband gave me a book that changed my life. Up until that point I believed in LGBTQ+[2] equity and inclusion, but I hadn't done a thing to help create a more inclusive world. In February 2003, inspired by that book, I launched myself into a career as an ally to the LGBTQ+ communities. Here is a brief summary of my life before, during, and after I read that book—and why I became motivated to write this one.

I grew up in New Jersey without any out LGBTQ+ friends or family members. I would later discover that I'd had plenty of LGBTQ+ friends—I just didn't know it. Despite this dearth of out and authentic LGBTQ+ people in my early life, the word *gay* wasn't avoided or considered naughty in my childhood home.

When I was ten years old, my mother leaned across the table at Serendipity, a quirky restaurant in Manhattan, and said to me, "Did you know that all of the waiters here are gay?" My conclusion: Gay men are friendly, clean, polite people who bring you fantastic food. These were clearly superior human beings.

At age fourteen, I was an avid fan of the TV sitcom *Soap*. Billy Crystal stole the show as Jodie, a bright, funny gay man who was one of the first-ever out and proud LGBTQ+ characters on television.

A few years ago, I discovered evidence that my early environment had made me a tolerant child. While cleaning out my childhood desk, I found a note that I had passed in eighth-grade science class (circa 1977) with my best friend; in it, we were discussing gay people. My friend argued that gay people were "gross." I countered with this thorough and articulate rebuttal: "What is your problem? Live and let live!"

Finding evidence that as a young teen in the 1970s I'd had a very chill attitude about gay people made me incredibly happy, but I certainly was no ally at that point. As a teenager, I couldn't understand why folks got their knickers in a knot over whom people loved, but I hadn't done anything to promote inclusion, understanding, and acceptance. I didn't know the word *ally* and I didn't know that, as someone who had no connection to the LGBTQ+ communities, there could be a role for me in supporting them. My budding passion and ally efforts would lie dormant for another quarter of a century.

All sorts of events related to the LGBTQ+ communities were brewing as I approached my fortieth birthday. Marriage equality was newly being discussed in the media. James Dale lost his lawsuit against the Boy Scouts of America, allowing the organization legally to discriminate against gay scout leaders. My young children had started school, and I was disheartened to find that gay slurs were still extremely prevalent among elementary school children.

Then one night, I was in bed reading the book my husband had given me for my fortieth birthday: Geoffrey Ward's and Ken Burns's *Not for Ourselves Alone*, the companion book to the Burns's documentary on the battle to secure the right for women to vote in the United States. I was awed, thankful, and inspired by the indomitable women who had gone before me and fought for my right to vote. I started doing something that I often find myself doing when I read history: imagining myself back in that time period and wondering how I would have behaved if I had lived then. I convinced myself that I would have fought alongside Susan B. Anthony, Nannie Helen Burroughs, and all those other amazing women.

Suddenly it hit me: What a hypocrite I was being! Here I was fantasizing about how I would have behaved more than a hundred years ago, while social justice battles were happening right now, in my own lifetime, and I was sitting them out. I asked myself, what will I tell my grandchildren if they ever ask me if I was involved in the fight for LGBTQ+ rights? When I reflect back on my life, will I know that I have left the world a better place? How have I gotten so caught up in my daily life that I have lost track of the big picture?

The next morning, I looked up the word *gay* in the phone book (yes, I really did), found our local LGBTQ+ center in my new hometown of Rochester,

New York, and called to ask if I could volunteer. I began my volunteer work by answering phones at the office and training to be a public speaker. It seemed odd to me that the agency's staff wanted me to be a member of their Speakers Bureau when I knew almost nothing about the LGBTQ+ communities, but they did. Back in 2003, they had very few speakers who were not part of the LGBTQ+ communities, and they informed me that my voice as an ally was incredibly important.

I messed up frequently with my language and assumptions. The center's staff and volunteers were very kind, patient, and forgiving of my blunders, but I wished I had a guidebook to tell me what to say and what not to say, with concrete tips about what I could actually do to make the world a more inclusive place. That book didn't exist.

I volunteered at the center for three years. This work was truly life changing. It launched me into a career as an activist for LGBTQ+ inclusion and an educator on effective allyship.

In 2006 I was hired as the center's education and outreach coordinator. In 2013 I was promoted to education director, a role I held for more than five years. Since that first phone call, I've met the most amazing people, learned so much about the LGBTQ+ communities and myself, and come to understand the powerful role that allies can play in the fight for LGBTQ+ rights, inclusion, and acceptance.

This book, *The Savvy Ally*, is the book I wanted and needed when I first began my work as an ally. It is with so much appreciation and gratitude to the many people who encouraged, educated, and supported me that I can now offer it as a guide for others.

NOTES

1. Reprinted from Nannie Helen Burroughs, *The 12 Things the Negro Must Do for Himself*, circa early 1900s.
2. A definition of *LGBTQ+* is coming up in chapter 2. Jump ahead if you'd like it now.

1

GETTING STARTED

 A journey of a thousand miles begins with a single step.[1]

—Lao Tzu

THANK YOU

I begin my book with a heartfelt thank you. The world needs more allies. Whether you're already fired up about being an ally to the LGBTQ+ communities and are currently out there doing ally stuff or you're just a little ally-curious, thank you for picking up this book and for your interest in creating a more equitable, safe, and inclusive world.

WHAT YOU CAN EXPECT FROM THIS BOOK

This book is focused on *how* to be an ally to the LGBTQ+ communities, not *why* to be an ally. There are many great books, movies, videos, and blogs out there that focus on the realities of living in our world as an LGBTQ+ person, the history of LGBTQ+ discrimination, and why allies are so important. They have been created with the purpose of motivating non-LGBTQ+ individuals to get involved. This book is not one of them. If you've picked up this book, it's my hope that you are already on board with the idea that the world needs to be more LGBTQ+ inclusive and you want to know how you can help.

This book is a collection of the tools and skills that I have discovered over the past twenty years to be most useful in being an ally to the LGBTQ+ communities. It includes pointers for having respectful and effective conversations, the most common places that allies get tripped up or stuck, and best-practice solutions for creating spaces that are LGBTQ+ inclusive. The book is divided into four main sections dealing with the following topics: (1) becoming knowledgeable allies, (2) building skills for having respectful conversations, (3) taking action to create more LGBTQ+ inclusive spaces, and (4) allying responsibly. My goal in writing this book was to help create allies who are more active, who are kind to themselves, and who find ways to make allyship a sustainable part of their everyday life, not a frenzied burst of action followed by exhaustion or disillusionment. This book helps you navigate an often confusing and intimidating world of changing LGBTQ+ terms and cultural practices and offers suggestions for creating positive change with your words and actions. It's not as daunting as it may seem. You've got this!

DEFINING ALLY BROADLY

An ally is a person who is not a part of a particular marginalized group but who stands up and advocates for the rights of people in that group. Typically, when we see the word *ally* in the context of LGBTQ+ advocacy, we think only of the person who is straight (i.e., heterosexual) and not transgender. However, we *all* can be LGBTQ+ allies, even if we are a part of the LGBTQ+ communities. If you are a lesbian, you can be an ally to bisexual/pansexual people who face challenges that may be different from what you experience. (For example, the very existence or legitimacy of bisexual/pansexual people is often questioned.) If you are a white transgender man, you can support and advocate for transgender women of color, who are more likely to be the victims of violence and discrimination than any other group under the LGBTQ+ umbrella.

One of my favorite post-training reactions comes from LGBTQ+ participants. It's basically: "Wow! I learned so much about the LGBTQ+ communities! I didn't know how much I didn't know!" You may be an expert on your own identity and community and yet know very little about others under the LGBTQ+ umbrella or how to be an ally to other communities. This book is for us all.

BRINGING MY FRIENDS ALONG FOR THE RIDE

Throughout my ally adventure (thank you to comedian Sofie Hagen for motivating me to find alternative words for *journey*, which I find I use way too often),[2] LGBTQ+ community members and other allies generously shared their stories and experiences with me to help me understand concepts. With their permission, I have included quotes, stories, and experiences from my friends and colleagues to help bring concepts to light with voices from the LGBTQ+ and allied communities. When they desired it, I've paid tribute to these people by using their real names; I've used aliases for those who preferred anonymity. Thank you to all who have shared your personal experiences. You have made this book explode with personality, warmth, and humanity. It feels so right and so good to bring you all along with me for the ride.

PRACTICE MAKES PRETTY DARN GOOD

This book is not about how to be a perfect ally; it's about how to be a pretty darn good one. In an interview with *VolleyballUSA* magazine, three-time Olympic gold medalist Karch Kiraly advises: "Focus on just being good, play after play. Trying to be perfect often leads to poorer and less consistent performance."[3] Telling ourselves that we must perform perfectly sets us up to fail. It puts so much pressure on us that instead of elevating our game, it typically has the opposite effect.

My colleague Noah, a straight, white, transgender man, has gotten closer to becoming a perfect ally than anyone else I know. He is dedicated to social justice, he reads voraciously on the topic, he understands the nuances of advocacy work, and he is incredibly thoughtful and intentional in his language. He is my go-to guy whenever I need someone to discuss a social justice issue or concern. Here are his thoughts on perfect allies:

> I am far more interested in the Intentional Allies, folks who work hard toward the goal of advocating frequently but not every second of every day, than the Perfect Allies, folks who respond to every comment every time. I think living and acting intentionally is a far more manageable and sustainable experience. . . . Sustained 50 percent is better than a burst of 100 percent followed by burnout.

This book aims to help us become and remain pretty darn good allies by embracing our vulnerability, forgiving ourselves when we mess up, and working to be better.

THE POWER OF THE ALLY

Social justice movements need allies. Our numbers alone can help shift cultural norms and public perceptions of marginalized groups. But allies offer more than just bodies. Here are some of the valuable gifts that allies bring to social justice movements.

Allies Can Help Validate a Cause

You may be reading this book because you have an LGBTQ+ child, parent, or friend, and that's wonderful. I applaud you for seeking more ways to support them. The best-known ally organization in the nation is PFLAG, which was started by a gay man's mom. I don't have an LGBTQ+ child, and at the time that I began my work as a volunteer, I didn't have any local LGBTQ+ friends or acquaintances either. Because of this, many people asked me why I was getting involved. Think for a moment about the powerful statement made by this question. The implication is that no one would be involved in a particular social justice issue if it weren't about themselves, their family members, or their friends. Initially I was concerned that I wouldn't be welcome because I didn't have an LGBTQ+ family member. In the end, I found great value in sharing that I did not, as a way of validating the fight for LGBTQ+ equity and inclusion on its own merits.

Allies Can Be a Cultural Bridge

Because allies are not a part of the marginalized group, they often have a keen understanding of the myths, stereotypes, misunderstandings, and fears that get in the way of acceptance and that hold people back from getting involved (e.g., unflattering and inaccurate media portrayals of LGBTQ+ people, no personal connections to the LGBTQ+ communities, and the fear of saying something offensive). These obstacles may be the very same things that initially held *us* back from becoming active allies. But the more we learn about LGBTQ+ individuals and communities, the better we become at changing hearts and minds outside those communities. We can help to bridge the gap between these two worlds and aid in understanding and communication.

Allies Can Take the Heat Off of LGBTQ+ People

People who are part of historically marginalized communities should not have to be the ones always taking on the emotional labor of educating others. In the same way that white people should be educating other white people about systemic racism and appropriate language, people who are not part of the LGBTQ+ communities should be stepping up and educating others about LGBTQ+ inclusion and respectful LGBTQ+ language choices. Allies are not directly impacted by well-meaning but hurtful LGBTQ+ related comments or ouchy word choices; therefore, we are better positioned than our LGBTQ+ friends to provide safe, nonjudgmental spaces where folks can listen, share, ask foolish questions, use outdated terms, and mess up royally without feeling like boneheads while they figure it all out.

Allies Can Be Possibility Models

The wonderful Laverne Cox, transgender advocate, actress, and star of the television series *Orange Is the New Black*, came up with the phrase "possibility model." In an interview with *RadioTimes*, she said, "I hate the term 'role model.' It's presumptuous to think that anyone should model their life after you, but I do like the term 'possibility model.'"[4]

I love this sentiment. One of the most amazing things I'm able to do through my work is to be a possibility model for others. I was pleasantly surprised to find out how many ally wannabes there were in my midst. When I began talking about the work I was doing, I discovered that many of my friends and acquaintances were also fully on board with LGBTQ+ rights and inclusion and just didn't know what needed to be done or how to get involved. One of the projects I took on for our center was facilitating our bike ride fundraiser. Through this ride, I assembled a large crew of new allies. They were able to access communities previously unreached by LGBTQ+ advocates and talk about why they rode, in turn becoming possibility models for others.

Allies Can Get Special Access

Because I am not a part of the LGBTQ+ communities, part of my growth as an ally was learning to navigate conversations about my identity and understanding when it was important to share it, and when it wasn't. It became apparent early on that others often assumed I was a lesbian. (Not shocking. I worked for an LGBTQ+ center and I wore comfortable shoes.)

FUN FACT

You can't really identify a lesbian by her shoes. (See chapter 7 on gaydar.)

Well, I wasn't a lesbian and I didn't "become" one either. Fifteen years working at an LGBTQ+ center and I didn't "catch the gay." I am living proof that it's not contagious. (Yes, that's a joke.) Often it was easier and more comfortable to simply let people assume that I was a member of the LGBTQ+ communities. However, there were many times when my voice as an ally was critical.

I learned that as an ally, I have access to systems of power and communities of people that LGBTQ+ people often don't. Due to homophobia, biphobia, transphobia, and the fact that I am perceived as less threatening when I disclose that I am not LGBTQ+, I am able to have conversations around social change with people and in places that my LGBTQ+ friends cannot. I can spend energy bemoaning this pitiful situation or I can view it as an opportunity to give something back to a community of people who have welcomed me with open arms. I choose the latter.

WHAT'S YOUR STORY?

As I mentioned earlier, this book isn't about why you should be an ally; it's about how to be an ally. The rest of this book will be focused on actions for helping to make the world a better and more inclusive place. However, I always get the "why" questions as I do this work, and I suspect you do (or you will) as well. Why are you so passionate? Why *this* social justice movement? Why are LGBTQ+ rights so important to you? Your responses to these questions can be a powerful tool for creating change, and I encourage you to think about your answers. Here's one of mine.

I once asked my grandmother how the Holocaust happened. She was an elderly Jewish woman, and I thought she would be able to explain it to me. I wanted to know the details, like why the Jewish people didn't run, hide, or rip the Star of David from their clothing. But my grandmother had grown up in

Brooklyn, and she couldn't explain it to me any better than the history books could.

It wasn't until I read *Schindler's List*[5] that I began to understand the process of systematic oppression that had taken place: starting with the name-calling and scapegoating, moving gradually into discrimination and segregation, then to acts of violence, and eventually to genocide.

For many people, the Holocaust must feel like ancient history. But for others—like me, in my early sixties—it was shockingly recent. After hiding in a friend's attic for more than two years, Anne Frank was killed a mere eighteen years before I was born.

One of my biggest fears is that I *will* be able to explain to my grandchildren exactly how something like this could happen. How first we allowed doctors to refuse care to LGBTQ+ people because it went against their religious beliefs. How we then removed safe access to bathrooms and other facilities for transgender people. How we banned teachers from saying the word *gay*. How we began arresting parents for providing health care to their transgender teens. How there were mass shootings in LGBTQ+ spaces, until, finally, I had people hiding in *my* attic.

I refuse to allow this to become my future story. It's why I do the work that I do. It's why I wrote this book. Allies are a mighty and necessary force for any social justice movement. If you are inspired to be a part of that force, or are part of the force already, this book will give you effective tools to help create a safer and more inclusive world. If the fire to create change is not yet burning within you, I am honored that you are giving me the opportunity to light the match.

NOTES

1. From Lao Tzu, *Tao Te Ching*.

2. Sofie Hagen, *Happy Fat: Taking Up Space in a World That Wants to Shrink You* (London: 4th Estate, 2019), 250.

3. Don Patterson, "40 Keys to Volleyball Greatness," *VolleyballUSA* (summer 2014): 39.

4. "*Orange Is the New Black*'s Wonder Woman Laverne Cox on Being a Transgender Trailblazer," *RadioTimes*, July 26, 2015, https://www.radiotimes.com/news/2015 -07-26/orange-is-the-new-blacks-wonder-woman-laverne-cox-on-being-a-transgender -trailblazer/.

5. Thomas Keneally, *Schindler's List* (New York: Simon & Schuster, 1994).

Part I

BECOMING KNOWLEDGEABLE ALLIES

2

CAUTION

Identities Being Defined!

 It's "I-dentity" not "YOU-dentity." Respect people's right to self-define.[1]

—Robyn Ochs

I have added a glossary of some of the basic LGBTQ+ terms at the back of this book for you to use as a reference. Identity words are incredibly important, and I will share more about why that is later in this chapter. However, I have found that focusing too heavily on a large glossary of terms has the opposite effect than one might hope. People can get so intimidated by the enormous number of terms and identities that, instead of having conversations, they are completely silenced by their fear that they are accidentally going to say something wrong, outdated, or insulting.

Instead, in this book, I am choosing to share tips for how to navigate respectful conversations with LGBTQ+ individuals even if you don't know or remember *any* of the proper terms. So, when you have a moment, feel free to look at the basic glossary of LGBTQ+ terms and identities that I have provided at the back. Read the warning first and then proceed with caution. Do become familiar with the words. Do not walk through the world with your glossary in hand, labeling people. Cultural words and identity words vary in meaning depending on the user, and they can also change over time.

With all of that said, there are three terms I would like to focus on in this chapter to ensure we are all on the same page so you can get the most out of this book. They are *cisgender*, *LGBTQ+*, and *queer*.

CISGENDER

The first term—*cisgender*—is one I already had to dance around and not use in chapter 1, so it's definitely time to define it. This word is an excellent one to add to your vocabulary if it's not there already. From here on I use it throughout the book.

A cisgender person is an individual whose sex assigned at birth matches their gender identity, or who they know themselves to be. In other words, if the doctor or midwife said, "It's a girl!" when you arrived on the planet, and, as you grew, the word fit for you—perhaps so well you never even thought about whether it fit or not—you are cisgender. It's a word that means "not transgender."

The word *cisgender* was added to the *Oxford English Dictionary* in 2013. For those of you who are word nerds and get excited by etymology, the prefixes *cis* and *trans* originally come from Latin. Cis means "on this side of" and trans means "across" or "on the far side." So, a very simplified way of thinking about this is if the sex you were assigned at birth is on the same side as your gender identity, or these two components of your identity align, then you're cisgender, or cis for short. Here's a diagram showing a cisgender woman.

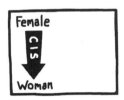

If the sex you were assigned at birth is across from your gender identity, or more accurately these two components of your identity don't align, then you're transgender, or trans for short. Here's a diagram showing a transgender man.

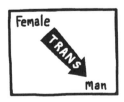

Those of us who have lived our entire lives as cisgender people, without ever feeling like we needed a term for what we were, may wonder why this term is necessary. This is a great question and one that's important for savvy allies to know and understand.

Imagine if we only had the word *gay* but not the word *straight*. We'd probably end up saying things like, "He's not gay. He's normal." Which is really offensive! The same is true with the words *transgender* and *cisgender*. If we only have a word for transgender people, but not for people who aren't trans, then people who aren't trans become the default or just "regular." Which, of course, implies that trans folks are "irregular." Which is also really offensive!

In the *Advocate* article "The True Meaning of the Word *Cisgender*," transgender scholar K. J. Rawson explains:

> Because straight folks don't typically experience their heterosexuality as an identity, many don't identify as heterosexual—they don't need to, because culture has already done that for them. Similarly, cisgender people don't generally identify as cisgender because societal expectations already presume that they are. . . . It's an incredible and invisible power to not *need* to name yourself because the norms have already done that for you. You don't *need* to come out as heterosexual or cisgender because it is already expected.

Having a word for people who aren't transgender helps folks understand that cis and trans are just different ways to be. One is not more normal, natural, or regular than the other. Norm-busting words like *cisgender* make the invisible visible.

HELPFUL HINT

If you've just discovered that you're cisgender, it doesn't mean you now have to walk around telling everyone that you're cisgender. (More on when and where to share this information coming up in chapter 9.)

LGBTQ+

You've probably seen many versions of the LGBTQ+ initialism and perhaps wondered which version you should use in order to be respectful. Here is a brief history of the evolution of the initialism in the United States and why I've chosen to use *LGBTQ+* in this book.

Back in the day, from about the 1940s to the 1980s, the word *gay* was used to represent anyone who wasn't straight. By the 1990s, the initialism *GLB* had taken hold in an effort to better represent the people in these communities. *GLB* stands for *gay, lesbian,* and *bisexual*. In the late 1990s, the *T* was added for *transgender*, making the most commonly used initialism *GLBT*.

Then someone had a brilliant idea. "Hey! Why do men always get listed first? Let's put women first for a change." And the initialism changed to *LGBT*. Which is cool. If I ran the world, I would change up the order of the letters every five years or so, just to keep it fair: "Congratulations to our bisexual friends! It's your turn at the front!"

Although you'll still occasionally see the initialism *LGBT*, by 2012 many people had begun to add a *Q*, in an attempt to be even more inclusive, making the initialism *LGBTQ*. The *Q* can stand for *queer*, or *questioning*, or both. I'll talk more about the word *queer* in a moment. *Questioning* is included in the initialism to help people remember and embrace the fact that, for many folks, identity is ever-changing. Understanding who we are and defining our attractions can be a long process and can change over time. Many social and support groups include the word *questioning* in the list of people who are welcome to join them so that individuals know they can attend the group even if they haven't gotten it all figured out yet.

After that, the initialism really started to grow! Some folks added another *Q* to fully represent both *queer* and *questioning*. Some folks added an *I* for *intersex*. Some added an *A* for *asexual*, or several *A*s for *asexual*, *agender*, and *androgynous*. Some added *2S* for *Two-Spirit*. Some added a *P* for *pansexual*. Others added two *P*s for *pansexual* and *polyamorous*. (If you're unfamiliar with any of these identity terms, please take a look at that glossary at the back of the book.)

But the reality is that *LGBTQQIAAA2SPP* is large, intimidating, and—most importantly—ever-changing. In addition, what nonprofit LGBTQ+ center can afford the ink to print that whole thing out on its brochures? (Yes, that's also a joke.) So, people started to search for ways to shorten the initialism while still being inclusive. Ta-da! Introducing the plus sign! The plus sign was added not to devalue the identities that didn't get included but to make the initialism more

---

POP QUIZ

Queer is a reclaimed word that . . .

  A. Was historically used as a slur against LGBTQ+ people and should never be used.
  B. Some people love, and others hate. Proceed with caution.
  C. Is now okay for everyone to use.

Answer: B

user-friendly and always relevant. It's also there to remind folks of the beautiful array of people who make up these diverse communities. *LGBTQ+* stands for lesbian, gay, bisexual, transgender, queer/questioning, plus so much more!

Everyone gets to decide for themselves which initialism to use. But many, at least in the United States, have settled on LGBTQ+. (At least for now.)

QUEER

Historically the word *queer* was used in an offensive and hurtful way, and there are folks who will never feel comfortable using it. Typically, these tend to be older folks who experienced the use of the word *queer* in a derogatory way, but sometimes it's younger folks too. Some LGBTQ+ people, however, have reclaimed this word and love it! The word *queer* can be used as an identity to define a person's orientation, gender, or both. So basically, anyone who is not straight and cisgender might embrace this term.

Reasons I have heard that explain why an individual might refer to themselves as *queer* include:

- A person might be several of the identities in the LGBTQ+ initialism, and none of the letters L, G, B, or T alone works for them. For example, they may be a bisexual transgender woman.
- A person might use the term *queer* because, although they are proud to be a part of the LGBTQ+ communities, they don't feel like they should have to specifically state their orientation and/or their gender identity.
- A person might find that their identities are ever-changing and evolving.
- A person might not yet have found an appropriate identity term that fits for them.

So how do we navigate a world where people have such different opinions about the word *queer*? How do we know who loves the word and who hates it? How can we have conversations with LGBTQ+ people without giving offense? We will get to that in chapter 6.

WHY DO THERE HAVE TO BE SO MANY IDENTITY WORDS?

A very common question is: "Why do we need all of these identity words; Can't we just all be human?" I do love the sentiment behind this question, and typically it's asked by people with kind intentions who are trying to be respectful. But unfortunately, it's just not that simple. Understanding and being able to explain why there need to be so many identities is a great task for a savvy ally!

So, let's begin dissecting this question by thinking about who is asking it. Typically, this question comes from someone who has already figured out their identity or identities and has their word or words locked in place. Often, if the asker is straight and cisgender, they've never even had to think about the fact that their identity words are readily accessible, because their identities have always matched societal expectations.

Interestingly, this question can and does also come from folks within the LGBTQ+ communities. A straight transgender man who became one of our agency's very best facilitators admits that before he started his work as an LGBTQ+ educator, he also used to ask this question. He looked at relatively new identity words like *genderqueer*, *pansexual*, *nonbinary*, and *agender* and thought, "Really? Enough already! This is getting ridiculous." He now understands that, because he had found his identity words (*straight* and *transgender*), his hunt was over. These words fit for him, and, in general, they were understood and accepted words in the English language. He was now in a place of relative comfort with his identity words as he observed others still seeking their words.

Every single word was once new. Words are created when there is a need. Here is the story of someone whose identity word had not yet been created in her language and the impact it had on her understanding of herself.

Dee is a transgender woman who grew up in the Philippines. She knew from an early age that she felt different, but she wasn't sure why. As she looked out into the world to see if there was anyone else like her and to try to find out who she was, she landed on the word *bakla*. It was the only word she could find in her language. Dee told me that *bakla* was a term used for a person who was assigned male at birth but expressed themselves, according to Filipino culture, in a very feminine manner. There were no separate Filipino words for a gay man, a transgender woman, and a cross-dressing man; they all just got lumped together and labeled *bakla*. So, the understanding was that a cisgender gay man was the

FUN FACT

Many people refer to *LGBTQ+* as an acronym. However, an acronym is an abbreviation that is pronounced as a word, like MADD (Mothers Against Drunk Driving) or DARE (Drug Abuse Resistance Education). *LGBTQ+* is actually an initialism because each letter is stated individually.

same as a transgender woman. What this meant for Dee was that she hung out at school with the gay guys and got labeled by others as *bakla*, but the term never really fit for her. When she was introduced to the English word *transgender*, a light bulb went off in her head—Dee had found her identity word!

According to trans advocate Alex Myers, "Adding more labels to the acronym isn't about making sure all the snowflakes know they are special. These labels save lives. These labels create a powerful sense of understanding and self-acceptance. The fact that the acronym has become a target for mockery only indicates the amount of work that still needs to be done around LGBTQIA+ civil rights."[2]

I hope I live to see the day when we all can just identify as human, but the reality is that we have a lot more work to do before we get there. We will know we're there when legal rights and protections are in place for everyone, when people stop making assumptions that everyone is straight and cisgender, when it's as easy for someone to come out as any of the identities under the LGBTQ+ umbrella as it was for me to come out as a straight cisgender person, and when no one gives a damn how anyone else identifies. We are definitely not there yet. There's lots more savvy ally work to be done.

NOTES

1. Reprinted with permissions from Robyn Ochs, "It's I-dentity Not You-dentity," RobynOchs.com, WordPress, April 27, 2021, https://robynochs.com/2021/04/27/its -i-dentity-not-you-dentity/.

2. Alex Myers, "Why We Need More Queer Identity Labels, Not Fewer," *Slate*, January 16, 2018, https://slate.com/human-interest/2018/01/lgbtq-people-need-more -labels-not-fewer.html.

3

COMING OUT
AS LGBTQ+

 *A snail only hides in its shell because the world outside feels hostile. If a snail recoils at the sight of you, it's not because the snail is cowardly or lying or deviant or withholding, it's because you've scared it.*[1]

— Jacob Tobia, *Sissy: A Coming-of-Gender Story*

WHY THE BIG REVEAL?

"**M**om, Dad . . . please sit down. I've got something to tell you. I know this is going to come as a surprise, but for a long time now I've known something about myself and it's time that I shared it with you. . . . I'm, um . . . straight."

Nope. It never happens. Straight cisgender people don't have to come out. They are pretty much just out. Let's think about that for a moment. Why is that? Straight cisgender people don't have to come out because we meet all of society's expectations of who we "should" be. (Please notice the quotation marks here.) I was assigned female at birth and that fit for me. I never questioned it. My parents expected me to grow up to be straight, and I did. How do I know that my parents expected me to grow up to be straight? Because everything I ever heard from them regarding a future partner and every book they ever read to me was heterosexually oriented. Straight cisgender people don't ever have to come out because our orientation and gender are correctly assumed; we have met expectations and we are on the "right" course.

What this means for our LGBTQ+ friends, of course, is that unless they grew up in a super-inclusive household, in a completely isolated bubble (where they didn't go to school, had no contact with other children, weren't a part of any faith community, didn't play on any sports teams, didn't watch popular movies, and didn't read popular books), they got the impression, as they figured out their identities, that they were on the "wrong" course.

As the education director at the LGBTQ+ center where I worked, I was in charge of training all of our volunteer Speakers Bureau members. Therefore, I had the privilege of hearing hundreds of coming-out stories. One of the things that struck me was that every speaker had an extremely difficult time coming out to their parents. This was true even when their parents had always let them know that they would be loved no matter what, had made a point of talking positively about LGBTQ+ people, and had LGBTQ+ friends who were welcomed into their homes. What these speakers shared with me was that the negative messages they received about being LGBTQ+ from the outside world were so strong that it made them doubt their parents' positive messages about LGBTQ+ people and statements of unconditional love.

Living in a liberal state like New York, it's not uncommon for straight, cisgender people to be under the impression that we're in a pretty good place now regarding LGBTQ+ rights, inclusion, and acceptance, and that our work is done. It's not. We'll be done when the coming-out process is no longer a process.

THE COMING-OUT PROCESS

Our society's limited expectations of and assumptions about who people are and who they should be gives LGBTQ+ people two choices that they must constantly make as they go about their daily lives: They must either come out or live a lie. Please bear with me while I repeat that; I don't want anyone to miss it: Our society forces LGBTQ+ people to constantly either come out or lie. Most LGBTQ+ people do not come out to shock people or because they want to be "in your face" with their identity. They come out because we as a society have a limited and narrow view of who people are and who they should be, and LGBTQ+ people do not fit those expectations. This is not because there is a problem with LGBTQ+ people. This is because there is a problem with our society.

What does it look like when you don't fit into society's expected identity boxes and how do you come to terms with that and lead a healthy and happy life? It's a process. Having a basic understanding of that process is essential for allies. It helps us understand why sometimes anger is directed toward straight cisgender people for no apparent reason at all, why having positive LGBTQ+ role models is so critical, why an LGBTQ+ person might tell hurtful gay jokes, and why being supportive and kind when someone comes out to you is so very important.

In order to understand the process, we are going to look at a developmental model of coming out. There are many models out there in the world, but one of the first, developed in 1979 by therapist Vivienne Cass,[2] is the model that most of the others have sprung from. As is true with all developmental models, it will ring true for some people and it will not for others, so please understand that I am not claiming that all LGBTQ+ individuals feel this model resonates with them. It doesn't. However, my experience has been that this model resonates with a heck of a lot of LGBTQ+ people and that it's a very useful tool for understanding.

Here is my personal synopsis of the six stages of coming out as LGBTQ+, adapted from Cass's model, followed by an example of how a person might behave in each of the stages.

Identity Confusion

Identity confusion is the stage where the individual feels different. They may not even be thinking along the lines of LGBTQ+ identities yet. They just know that they are not like the others. The big question is, "Who am I?"

Identity Comparison

In the identity comparison stage, the person asks themselves, "Might I be [gay, lesbian, transgender, etc.]?" and begins to look out into the world and compare themselves to what they know about these people.

Remember when professional basketball player Jason Collins came out as gay? There was a great deal of pushback from people who wondered, "Why did he have to come out? Couldn't he just be a basketball player? Why is his sexual orientation important?" The identity comparison stage is why having a professional athlete like Jason Collins publicly come out is so important.

Think about a teenage boy in this stage trying to figure out if he might be gay. He looks out into the world to see what it means to be a gay man, what that looks like, and how it's received. If he looks out and he sees only negative images and stereotypes of gay men—think Axel Foley as the diseased Ramon in *Beverly Hills Cop* or Mr. Antolini, Holden Caulfield's predatory teacher in *The Catcher in the Rye*—he will typically think one of two things. He might think, "That's not me," in which case he'll go back into the identity confusion stage and wonder, "If I'm not gay, why do I feel so different?" He might also think, "I'm pretty sure I am gay, but being gay is clearly bad. I am never telling anyone." And he will move into the stage of identity tolerance, feeling pretty crummy about who he is.

Now let's think about what happens if he looks out into the world and he sees the out gay athlete Jason Collins or the out gay actor Neil Patrick Harris. Truth be told, because of all those societal expectations that he should be straight, he probably is still not jumping up and down with glee about his identity, but his path toward self-acceptance is likely to be a lot smoother. With powerful, bright, and healthy gay possibility models like Collins and Harris, and better media portrayal of gay men, like Lieutenant Sulu in the *Star Trek* reboot, he is more likely to move rapidly through this stage of identity comparison and also through the next stage of identity tolerance.

Identity Tolerance

The word *tolerance* gets thrown around a lot in social justice circles and is often confused with *acceptance*, but the two are actually pretty different. We tolerate things that we dislike but have no control over, like traffic or a bad cold. Tolerating your identity is not a good or healthy place to be. The identity tolerance stage is when the person has come out to themselves but is unlikely to come out to others. They may think of their identity as their dirty little secret that nobody else ever needs to know. This is the stage where suicidal ideation and suicide attempts are likeliest.

Identity Acceptance

In the stage of identity acceptance, the individual begins to realize that they are not the only LGBTQ+ person in the world and that they are going to be okay. This is the stage where many people begin to seek out others like themselves and make their first attempts at coming out. They may come out to a total stranger to test the waters because it feels safer, or they may come out to a trusted friend or family member. (Perhaps one who is wearing a big rainbow pin! Just sayin'.) How their first coming-out reveal is received may affect whether they move into identity pride, hang out in identity acceptance, or move back into identity tolerance.

NOT-SO-FUN FACTS

It's been known for many years that the attempted suicide rate for gay, lesbian, and bisexual people is three to four times higher than it is for those who identify as straight.[3] In 2015, the largest survey of transgender individuals ever done showed that the attempted suicide rate for transgender people is over 40 percent.[4] Over 40 percent of the more than twenty-five thousand transgender people from all fifty states surveyed in this study have attempted suicide! Compare that with the 4.6 percent rate for the general public[5] and it's pretty clear that cisgender allies have a lot of work to do to support our trans friends. It's important to note that this study also revealed that when transgender individuals have support and, if desired, access to medical care for transitioning, the rate of attempted suicide drops down to the same rate as the general population. Once again, this is not a problem with LGBTQ+ people, this is a problem with our society.

Identity Pride

Identity pride is the stage I like to call the loud and proud stage. I've heard people who are in the identity pride stage described as being obnoxious, aggressive, angry, and over the top. It's important for allies to understand where these loud and proud behaviors and attitudes are coming from and to appreciate what the person has survived.

Identity pride is the stage where the person is finally out to the world and it feels *so* good! In many cases, it means that the person has come out to some folks during the identity acceptance stage and the world has not ended. In fact, they may have been surprised by the support they received. In the identity acceptance stage, they may have met other supportive LGBTQ+ people. Now, in the identity pride stage, they are sloughing off that oppressive cloak of self-hatred, self-doubt, and fear and stepping out into the world as their authentic, out, and proud selves. The aggression and anger that sometimes comes with this stage stems from having had to lie for so long about who they are, an impulse to protect their new authentic selves, and a vow not to go back into the closet and hide who they are ever again.

A participant in one of my workshops had a light bulb go off when I described the identity pride stage. She said, "Oh wow! This makes so much sense! I had a customer come into my shop recently, and she said, 'I'm a lesbian. Okay? Do you have a problem with that? 'Cause if you have a problem with that, I'll go somewhere else.' And I thought to myself, 'What the heck? Did I do something to make her feel unsafe or unwelcome?' This makes total sense now!"

For a person in the identity pride stage, their identity as LGBTQ+ is likely to be at the forefront of all of their other identities. They may spend less time with their straight cisgender friends during this time. They may be intolerant of other LGBTQ+ people who are not living out and authentically. If they are a student, every writing assignment is likely to be about their LGBTQ+ identity. If they are in the workplace, they may suddenly add a boatload of rainbow paraphernalia to their cubicle. Typically, you know when someone is in the stage of identity pride: You can see the rainbows flowing from the back of their heads.

Identity Synthesis

With time, patience, love, and support, most LGBTQ+ individuals will move into the stage of identity synthesis. In this stage they are, of course, still proud to be LGBTQ+, but it's not everything they are about. I have a friend who says that when he was in the identity pride stage, he was a Capital-G Gay professor. Now in the stage of identity synthesis, he's gay, a professor, a father, a dog owner, a basketball player, a wine enthusiast, and so on. Being gay is just a part of who he is.

Is there still anger and aggression in this final stage? There certainly can be—and for good reason. However, the anger is typically more appropriately focused on people who are being disrespectful or discriminatory, not on the entire straight cisgender population.

In Summary

To sum things up, let's look at how differently an LGBTQ+ person might respond to a coworker's question, "Hey! I'm going to the Pride parade this Saturday. Anyone wanna come?" depending on where the LGBTQ+ person is in their process of coming out:

Identity Confusion: "I don't think so, thanks."
Identity Comparison: "I don't think so, thanks."
Identity Tolerance: "Seriously? No way! I'm no homo."
Identity Acceptance: "Um . . . I've got other plans on Saturday, but thanks for asking." (And then a text later in the day: "Actually, I would like to go with u to the parade. LOL")

Identity Pride: "Hells yeah!!! I'm psyched!!! I'm buying rainbow tutus for everyone!!!"

Identity Synthesis: "I'm pretty sure I can. Let me check with my partner and I'll let you know. Thanks."

FROM THEORY TO REALITY

What I've just shared is a theoretical developmental model. Now let's look at the realities of coming out in the real world. Typically, folks do not move seamlessly, in a completely linear fashion through the six stages of the Cass model to the final stage of identity synthesis, and then—*ding!*—they're done! The Cass model is a tool that can be helpful to understand the coming-out process, but when we look at people's real-life experiences, there are some key points to keep in mind.

Coming Out Is a Lifelong Process

Coming out for LGBTQ+ people is not a single event. Folks do not leap from the closet on their official coming-out day with glitter flying and Diana Ross's "I'm Coming Out" blasting in the background—"Ta-da! I'm out!"—never to return to the closet ever again. (I find this unfortunate because that would be pretty fabulous.) Coming out is a lifelong process.

My friend Jonathan was buying flowers for his husband at the grocery store a few years ago. Very kindly, just making conversation, the cashier said, "Oh, those are beautiful. Are they for your wife?" All Jonathan had done was pop into the market to purchase flowers, and now he was faced with a decision about whether to come out to the cashier or not.

The decision to come out or not, at any given moment, depends on many factors, not the least of which is safety. Lesbian comedian Sabrina Matthews recalls one of these moments: "I remember flying through Dallas/Fort Worth Airport on National Coming Out Day with my National Coming Out Day T-shirt on because I'm proud . . . and my sweatshirt over that, because I'm smart."[6]

The idea that people can create safe and welcoming spaces with their language is an incredibly important one. As allies, we should strive to model inclusive language at all times and educate others about its importance. In chapter 6, we'll look at language choices that won't force people into the come-out-or-lie position.

The Process Is Not Always Linear

Some folks find that they move in a very linear fashion through the six stages of the Cass model. Others jump around a bit, skip stages, go back, and generally travel through them like an Upstate New York driver is forced to drive in March, skidding and swerving down a pothole-filled street. People can actually move across several stages on the very same day depending, for example, on the setting. Let's think about a lesbian college student who's in the identity synthesis stage on campus. She's out to all her college friends and she speaks freely about her identity. Then she returns home for Thanksgiving to a family that has indicated that being LGBTQ+ is not okay, and she slides back into the identity tolerance stage, hiding her identity and feeling unhappy about who she is. People may spend a lifetime jumping around in the different stages, depending on whom they are with and how open and accepting the environment feels.

It's So Much Fun, Some Folks Do It Twice!

Okay, I'm actually kidding about it being fun, but some folks definitely go through the process of coming out twice or even more times than that. I know several straight transgender men who came out first as cisgender lesbians. Most of them didn't even know the word *transgender* at their first coming out, so they didn't have that identity word to latch on to. (Remember our earlier discussion about the importance of all of those identity words?) So, as they began looking out into the world during the identity comparison stage, they grabbed hold of the term *lesbian*. They knew they were attracted to girls/women, and *lesbian* fit a lot better than *straight*. Many of these men got all the way into the identity pride stage before they heard the term *transgender*, met some transgender people, and eventually realized that the reason they felt so different wasn't their sexual orientation but instead their gender. Then they had to backtrack and come out again with their new identity as straight transgender men. My friend Sean, a bisexual trans man, who travelled a long, winding road of self-discovery around both his sexual orientation and gender, jokes about how at one point or another in his life, he has been every single letter of the LGBTQ initialism.

It's Not Just for LGBTQ+ People

The Cass model was originally based on cisgender gay men and cisgender lesbian women. However, it resonates with lots of other folks both within the LGBTQ+ communities and outside of the LGBTQ+ communities.

My friend Todd is Deaf. His parents, wanting only what they felt was best for him, insisted that he learn to read lips and speak so that he could fit into the hearing world. He grew up in a rural town, so he didn't know there was a Deaf community and, as a child, was never exposed to sign language. When he moved to Upstate New York, he met other Deaf people. He shared with me that he went through every one of the Cass model stages as a Deaf man. When he hit that pride stage, he said that it felt so amazing to be with other people like himself, to find community and understanding, and to embrace American Sign Language (ASL) as his language. Hearing friends and coworkers, who didn't understand this fantastic feeling of connection and community, felt that he had gotten a bit "aggressive" with the whole Deaf thing and that he needed to tone it down a bit. Todd was "flaunting" his Deafness. Sound familiar?

Even some family members and friends of LGBTQ+ people find that this model rings true for themselves. My friend Wanda, a cisgender lesbian, grew up in Puerto Rico. When she was age eighteen, her mother woke her up at five o'clock one morning, handed her a plane ticket, and sent her to a mental health institution in New York to have her lesbianism "fixed." She didn't even get a chance to say good-bye to her siblings. Over time, Wanda's mom went through a bit of a metamorphosis after receiving new information, meeting new people, and, finally, having interactions with her daughter, who was clearly so much happier and healthier as an out lesbian. Wanda's mom moved slowly from the stages of confusion, comparison, and tolerance into the stage of acceptance of her daughter's identity. Several years later, Mom was in her pride stage, marching alongside her daughter in our local Pride parade! I believe Mom has toned it down a bit recently and is less likely to "flaunt" her pride for her daughter, but she still loves a good drag show.

The first response from someone to whom a friend or family member has just come out is likely to be different from how they feel years, months, or possibly even days later. Friends and family members may need to go through their own coming-out process as supporters and allies.

Coming Out Is Not Always the Immediate Goal

I hope that someday we will live in a world where everyone can live authentically and safely in all aspects of their lives, but we're not there yet. Unfortunately, many people are in environments where it's not safe to come out. Therefore, we shouldn't think of coming out as an absolute, essential, and immediate goal for everyone. If a young person comes to you, for example, and shares that they're thinking of coming out to their parents, consider asking the youth how their parents are likely to respond. If there's a reasonable chance that this youth will end up without any financial support or homeless, as a result of their parents' non-acceptance, then perhaps coming out shouldn't be the goal at that time. That conversation should wait until the youth is less dependent on their parents for basic needs or until the youth has a solid safety net and a support system in place.

RESPONDING WHEN SOMEONE COMES OUT TO YOU

A Better Metaphor for Coming Out

Before I offer some tips on what to say and what not to say when someone comes out to you, I'd like to share a quote from Jacob Tobia, author of the book *Sissy: A Coming-of-Gender Story*. They wrote:

> Instead of The Closet, I'd like to propose a more humane metaphor. What if we talk about queer/trans people coming out of our shells? . . . When a person hides in The Closet, we act as if it is their responsibility to come out. But when a snail hides in its shell, we don't delegate responsibility in the same way. A snail only hides in its shell because the world outside feels hostile. If a snail recoils at the sight of you, it's not because the snail is cowardly or lying or deviant or withholding, it's because you've scared it. . . . The Closet is a metaphor that sets queer and trans people up to feel that we are somehow dishonest or immoral for concealing our identities; that it is somehow our *lack of courage* that is to blame.[7]

Adjusting our thinking in this way (i.e., blaming the hostile environment if an LGBTQ+ person doesn't feel safe coming out, rather than blaming the person for lacking courage) will guide us well in our response when people do come out to us. It will also help remind us that some environments, situations, and people are going to feel safer to the LGBTQ+ person than others.

What to Say

Coming out as LGBTQ+ is often scary, and it's a big deal. So, what does that mean if someone comes out to you? Typically, it means that this person trusts you immensely. It's a huge compliment. Therefore, a great thing to say, if you are so inclined, is, "Thank you." Keep in mind that saying, "Thank you for trusting me enough to share this with me" is better than saying, "Thank you for being honest with me," which implies that the LGBTQ+ person was being dishonest before.

After thanking them, I would recommend mostly listening. Let them take the lead on what they want to talk about. They may, in fact, not want to talk about anything more. It may just be a huge relief to tell someone and know that they are supported.

If there is an awkward silence, you could throw in one or two of these comments as well:

> "I'm so glad you can be yourself around me."
> "How can I support you?"
> "Hey! Let's celebrate!"

It's also important to keep confidentiality in mind. Coming out is the LGBTQ+ person's job, not yours. You should *never* out the person to others. If it doesn't come up naturally in the coming-out conversation, you may want to say something like, "I want to make sure I'm protecting your privacy and keeping you safe. I won't share this with anyone unless you want me to." This statement is better than asking "Who else knows?" which is a bit intrusive.

If the individual has come out as transgender and is asking you to use a new name and pronoun, it will be critical to discuss when and where the new name and pronoun should be used. Sometimes people will ask close friends to support them and affirm their identity by using their new name and pronoun in private, but they'll use their old name and pronoun in public because they're not ready to come out to everyone yet or they don't feel safe doing so. Getting clarity on how the person would like you to navigate those situations is important and shows how committed you are to supporting them and keeping them safe.

What Not to Say

If someone comes out to you, do try to avoid asking, "Are you sure?" or implying that it may just be a phase. Even if you truly think that this may just be a phase, saying it aloud is unlikely to be received well. If it *is* a phase, the person will figure it out in their own time. Your love and support during that time will be valuable. If it's not a phase, you're likely to lose the person's trust with these comments.

Another question to avoid asking is when they "decided" to be LGBTQ+. Just as I didn't choose or decide to be straight or cisgender, LGBTQ+ people don't choose their identities. The only thing they're choosing is to live and love authentically.

A great point by Dannielle Owens-Reid and Kristin Russo, from their book *This Is a Book for Parents of Gay Kids*,[8] is to avoid saying "I always knew." First of all, you may think you always knew, but you actually just made a correct guess, possibly based off of harmful stereotypes and assumptions. Secondly, hearing that you always knew may make the person feel foolish or cowardly for waiting so long to come out to you, diminish the importance of the information they wanted to share with you, cause them to wonder what they did to make it so obvious, and make them worry that others can also tell.

Here's a response that just needs a slight tweak. "I love you anyway." Anyway? "Anyway" implies that being LGBTQ+ is something bad. So, hack out that word "anyway." "I love you" will do just fine.

Finally, you should avoid asking questions about a person's anatomy or sexual behaviors. There's an interesting phenomenon that sometimes happens when people think about LGBTQ+ individuals and the LGBTQ+ communities: Their heads go right to the person's body parts and/or what they're doing in the bedroom. If this happens to you, remind yourself that being LGBTQ+ is not about body parts or the bedroom, it's about who people are and whom they love. So, when someone comes out to you, please know that it doesn't give you a free pass to ask intrusive questions about their body or sex life. Asking a gay man who has just come out to you, "Have you slept with a guy yet?" or asking a trans woman, "Are you planning on having surgery?" is not okay. Just because someone comes out to you does not mean that they are required to be an open book. If you're curious about what types of surgeries are available for transgender people, do some online research. If you're curious about what LGBTQ+ people actually do in the bedroom, take my pop quiz on the next page!

If someone comes out to you and you're not sure if a question is okay or not, the "switch it" technique is useful: Switch the person's LGBTQ+ identity for straight or cisgender and try the question again in your head. Is the question polite, supportive, or useful, or is it offensive, intrusive, or motivated by curiosity? Never in my sixty years of living has anyone ever asked me, "Do you think being cisgender might just be a phase?" or, "How do you know you're straight if you've never slept with a woman?" Our society believes I am on the "right" course and therefore no one has ever questioned my sexual orientation or gender. Using the "switch it" technique, it becomes clear that these are not respectful questions to ask anyone.

Another great thing to keep in mind that may help to steer you away from inappropriate questions is that sexual orientation and sexual behaviors are completely separate things. One has to do with whom we are attracted to and the other is what we actually do. Think about when you first knew whom you

POP QUIZ

What do LGBTQ+ people do in the bedroom?

A. Have sex
B. Read books
C. Sleep
D. Occasionally vacuum and change the sheets
E. All of the above

Answer: E

A friend of mine described a gender and sexuality workshop he participated in once where everyone in the room got an index card. On one side, they wrote down their sexual orientation and gender. On the other side, they wrote down a favorite sexual activity. They then put all of the cards on a table with the "sexual activity" side up. The facilitator asked the participants to look at the sexual activities and figure out who was gay, lesbian, bisexual, transgender, straight, and cisgender. Guess what happened? They couldn't do it. They had no idea. Humans can be very creative in the bedroom, and no one group has cornered the market on any one sexual activity. Are there straight couples who engage in anal sex? Yup. Are there gay couples who have never engaged in anal sex? Yup. It's disrespectful and inaccurate to make assumptions about or to define a group of people by what we think they are doing in the bedroom.

were attracted to. I had a pretty solid idea by the time I was in third grade. Was I having sex yet? No. I didn't need to have sex to know that my little nine-year-old heart went pitter-patter every time I looked at Danny Fox.

Thinking you could have responded better when someone came out to you? Good thing there are no expiration dates on apologies! Reconnect with your LGBTQ+ friend, family member, or colleague now and make it right.

FUTURE FANTASIES

I hope I live long enough to see the Cass model and other LGBTQ+ identity development models disappear. They won't be needed because our societal expectations will have shifted. Parents, teachers, friends, and faith leaders will read stories to children about all kinds of people and families, use language that doesn't assume sexual orientation or gender, and have no expectations about who a person is or who they will be. There will be no fear, shame, or despair for anyone as they figure out who they are and whom they are attracted to. LGBTQ+ centers will close down or become museums. Books like this one will no longer be needed. Students will read about conversion therapy (therapy aimed at turning gay people straight) and people like CeCe McDonald and Matthew Shepard in their history books and say, "Can you believe stuff like that used to happen back then?" (If you aren't familiar with CeCe McDonald or Matthew Shepard, there's some ally homework for you.) In this future world, it will be as easy to come out as LGBTQ+ as it was for me to come out as a straight cisgender person—that is, it won't need to be done at all. Parents will simply remain open to the possibility of their child being anyone just as they remain open to the possibility that their child may be right- or left-handed. The entire "process" of coming out will disappear, not because we've fixed our LGBTQ+ people but because we've fixed our society.

NOTES

1. Reprinted from Jacob Tobia, *Sissy: A Coming-of-Gender Story* (New York: G. P. Putnam's Sons, 2019), 102.

2. Vivienne Cass, "Homosexual Identity Formation: A Theoretical Model," *Journal of Homosexuality* 4, no. 3 (spring 1979): 219–35.

3. Laura Kann, Emily O'Malley Olsen, Tim McManus et al., "Sexual Identity, Sex of Sexual Contacts, and Health-Related Behaviors among Students in Grades 9–12—United States and Selected Sites, 2015," *Centers for Disease Control and Prevention Morbidity and Mortality Weekly Report, Surveillance Summaries* 65, no. 9 (August 12, 2016): 19–22.

4. S. E. James, J. L. Herman, S. Rankin et al., The Report of the 2015 U.S. Transgender Survey (Washington, DC: National Center for Transgender Equality, 2016), https://transequality.org/sites/default/files/docs/usts/USTS-Full-Report-Dec17.pdf.

5. Ibid.

6. Rich Tackenberg (director), *Coming Out Party* (Studio City, CA: Ariztical Entertainment, 2003), DVD.

7. Jacob Tobia, "A Very Dramatic (First) Coming Out," *Sissy: A Coming-of-Gender Story* (New York: G. P. Putnam's Sons, 2019), 102.

8. Dannielle Owens-Reid and Kristin Russo, *This Is a Book for Parents of Gay Kids* (San Francisco: Chronicle Books, 2014).

4

ORIENTATIONS, IDENTITIES, BEHAVIORS—OH MY!

Binaries are for computers.

—Anonymous

If you have ever asked (or, let's face it, been too embarrassed to ask):

"What the heck does nonbinary mean?"
"Can transgender people also be gay?"
"How can I tell if someone is gay?"
"How can someone be asexual but still have sex?"

Then this is the chapter for you. In this chapter, we'll take a look at the various components that make up who we are as sexual and gendered beings and answer these and many other questions that can be incredibly confusing.

Whether we have had to think long and hard about our sexuality, our gender, and our identities (as have most LGBTQ+ folks) or we have given very little thought to these things because we never had to (as is the case with most straight cisgender people), we are all represented on the diagram of the components of sex, gender, and sexuality that I'm about to discuss. This diagram, based on the work of Michael G. Shively and John P. DeCecco, shows the five components that make up our sexual and gendered selves: biological sex, gender identity, gender expression, attraction, and intimate behaviors.[1] Even though only three categories are depicted for each of the five components, please think of each component as a continuum with billions of people represented with points, and even arrows if they're more fluid, all over the spectrum.

Toward the end of this chapter, for your reading pleasure, I've mapped myself out using this diagram. I've also included diagrams from three LGBTQ+ community members who were kind enough to map themselves out and offer their diagrams as well. Think about where you fall on each component and map yourself out too. I encourage you to do this either in private or, for the more adventurous, perhaps at the dinner table during your next big family gathering.

A BASIC DIAGRAM OF THE COMPONENTS OF SEX, GENDER, AND SEXUALITY

Biological Sex

The first component that makes up human sex, gender, and sexuality is biological sex. Our biological sex has to do with our reproductive system, hormones, chromosomes, genitalia, and secondary sex characteristics. Despite the fact that bodies are biologically varied and complex, the only assessment we typically get is a doctor or midwife—or, if your mom's timing was really off, cabdriver—looking between our legs and boldly assigning us a sex, based solely on the outward appearance of our genitals. These assignments are either *male, female,* or *intersex*. For some people, that sex assignment fits (cisgender folks and some intersex folks), and for some it doesn't (transgender folks and some intersex folks).

Here is a diagram showing biological sex as a continuum:

Female - - - - - - - - - - - - - - - - - - Intersex - - - - - - - - - - - - - - - - - - - Male

Intersex individuals are folks whose biological sex characteristics (i.e., genitals, reproductive organs, chromosomes, and/or hormones) do not fit typical binary notions of male or female bodies. (Please note the respectful use of the word *typical* rather than *normal*.) People who fall under the intersex umbrella have all sorts of natural variations and have existed throughout time. The old term *hermaphrodite*, which has a much narrower definition, is outdated, stigmatizes natural body variation, and should no longer be used. Please cross that word out in your head and replace it with *intersex*.

A few examples of people who fall under the intersex umbrella are:

- People who have genitalia that are not typical, and to whom the doctor or midwife is unable to assign a sex of *male* or *female* at birth.

- People who were assigned *male* or *female* at birth, later have fertility issues as adults, have genetic testing done, and find out that they have atypical chromosomes.
- People who were assigned female at birth, never menstruate, and find out as teenagers that instead of ovaries they have undescended testicles.

One of my favorite quotes about natural biological variation comes from Alice Dreger, professor of medical humanities and bioethics at Northwestern University: "There isn't really one simple way to sort out males and females. . . . And the science actually tells us sex is messy. Or as I like to say, humans like categories neat, but nature is a slob."[2]

Don't believe her? Think about the challenges the International Olympic Committee has been experiencing as it tries to sort athletes into "true" male and "true" female categories so they can compete. It can't be done. Physical examinations, chromosome testing, and hormone-level assessments have all been put in place over the years in an attempt to fit athletes into two binary boxes of males and females, but many athletes still can't be categorized that way. Sex-verification testing (which identifies sex chromosomes) and testosterone-level testing have both proven to be inaccurate and discriminatory. Many athletes deemed "male imposters" were later found to be intersex.

Starting in the 1960s, doctors had the ability to perform cosmetic surgery on infants to "normalize" the appearance of their genitals. It quickly became common practice to perform surgery, almost immediately after birth, on babies who had genital variations, obviously without their consent. More often than not, the surgeons crafted their genitalia to look like vaginas, because it was easier to surgically construct a vagina than a penis. (This is still true today.) The thinking back in the 1960s was that gender was completely dependent on socialization, not biology—nurture rather than nature. Therefore, the belief was, if you surgically crafted a vagina on a two-day-old infant, dressed the baby in pink, gave the baby a girl's name, and purchased dolls for the baby, all would be well. But as it turns out, our gender identity, which we typically know at a very young age, is not influenced by the color of our clothes and the toys we are given as children.[4]

FUN FACT

Most of us know our gender identity between the ages of about three and five. Many transgender individuals can date those first feelings of not being like the other kids to kindergarten or earlier.

POP QUIZ

What percentage of the population is born intersex?

A. Approximately 1 in 700 people, comparable to the number of people born with Down syndrome.
B. Approximately 1 in 400 people, comparable to the number of people born Deaf.
C. Approximately 1 in 60 people, comparable to the number of people born natural redheads.

Answer: C

I used to believe that being intersex was extremely rare—a common misunderstanding. What I have learned is that the number of folks who fall under the intersex umbrella is remarkably large. It's estimated that intersex individuals make up about 1.7 percent of the population, making it as common as being a natural redhead.[3]

Why is the general perception that being intersex is extremely rare? One reason is that before we had the ability to do genetic testing, most of the people who were assigned *intersex* were only the ones who had atypical genitalia at birth. Another reason is because, historically, there has been a lot of shame and secrecy around intersex individuals and their bodies.

Although this practice of immediate, nonconsensual surgery continues today in some places, most medical facilities have stopped performing cosmetic surgeries on intersex infants. Instead, many medical providers now focus on educating and supporting the parents of intersex infants. It's incredibly difficult to raise a child who doesn't have a sex assignment in our binary world.

In the past ten years or so, thankfully, we've seen an increase in intersex visibility and acceptance. Many of those 1960s babies who had surgery performed on their bodies are pissed, and they are speaking out about what happened to them. Some of them were never even told that surgery had been performed on

HELPFUL HINT

The next time you see a parent with a newborn, instead of asking, "Is it a boy or a girl?" try, "What a beautiful baby! What's the baby's name?"

their bodies and many of them now have bodies that don't match their gender identity. Their bravery in sharing their stories helps destigmatize the intersex community and informs the search for smarter solutions for the future.

If you're interested in this topic, I would highly recommend the documentary film *Intersexion*,[5] in which intersex individuals share their stories, the POPSUGAR interview on YouTube with Emily Quinn,[6] and the book *As Nature Made Him*, the true story of a boy who was forced to live life as a girl after a botched circumcision.[7]

Gender Identity

The second component that makes up our sex, gender, and sexuality is gender identity. This is the answer to the question, "Are you a boy or girl?" or "Are you a man or woman?" The answer may be: "I'm a man," or "I'm a woman," or perhaps "Um . . . no." Many people believe that there are only two options when it comes to gender identity: You're a boy/man or a girl/woman. However, just like our beautiful array of varied bodies discussed in the previous section, there is also a beautiful array of gender identities.

JUST FOR FUN

Whenever someone announces the gender of a baby with, "It's a boy!" or "It's a girl!" my friend Rowan thinks to himself, ". . . for now."

Those of us who are men or women (whether we're cisgender or transgender) fit into the gender binary (i.e., relating to two things or two options). Folks who are nonbinary do not. Nonbinary individuals may describe themselves as

FUN FACT

Many people think that being nonbinary is a relatively new phenomenon. But, like all LGBTQ+ people, nonbinary individuals have existed throughout time and within all cultures and societies. Check out Out & Equal's article "Nonbinary Gender Identities: A Diverse Global History" to learn more.[8]

having no gender, having a different gender from man or woman, having both genders, having multiple genders, having gender fluidity, and more. Some of the many identities that fall under the nonbinary umbrella are genderqueer, gender-fluid, agender, and Two-Spirit.

Here is a diagram showing gender identity as a continuum:

Woman - - - - - - - - - - - - - - - - - - Nonbinary -Man

People will fall in different places all over this continuum. Visualize the billions of dots and arrows, please.

HELPFUL HINT

If you're starting to get that overwhelmed feeling, please remember that you don't need to know or even necessarily understand all the identities under the sun to be a good ally. Just have a thirty-second dance party (thank you, *Grey's Anatomy!*) and celebrate the diversity of all the wonderful people on this planet.

Gender Expression

For those of us who were assigned the sex designation of either *male* or *female* at birth and, as we grew, found that assignment matched our gender identity, we may be feeling all "ho-hum" right now. Well, hang on to your rainbow beanies! This third component gets pretty exciting for almost all of us.

Gender expression has to do with how we express our gender to the world. We do this with our clothing, hairstyles, activities, movements, and mannerisms. Some of these may be conscious choices we make for ourselves, like what we choose to wear and how we style our hair. These may also be unconscious things that we do or say that others pick up on, like the way we gesture or how much space we take up in a room. Society categorizes gender expression as feminine, masculine, or androgynous (defined as neither feminine nor masculine, or as a blending of the two).

Here is a diagram showing gender expression as a continuum:

Feminine - - - - - - - - - - - - - - - Androgynous - - - - - - - - - - - - - - - Masculine

We may express our gender differently from day to day. Our gender expression may change over time as we age. We may even exhibit behaviors that are labelled by our culture and society as feminine and ones that are labelled as masculine at the same time. For example, picture a woman with long red nails under the hood of her car changing her oil.

Did you read that last sentence about the woman changing her oil and experience a bit of anger or frustration? Did you think to yourself, "Why is changing the oil in your car considered masculine behavior? Who gets to decide this stuff?" I feel your anger and I second it! This stuff irritates the heck out of me. Who *does* get to decide this stuff? I have no idea. Similarly, I have wondered, in countries where all nouns are labelled as either masculine or feminine (for example, a table in French is feminine), what do they do when there is a new thing? When the telephone was invented, was there a gender committee that got to decide whether it was masculine or feminine? This is such odd stuff.

An educated guess can help us figure out where *some* of the masculine and feminine labels came from. Because of biology, women traditionally took on the tasks of nurturing the babies, cooking, and tending the home. Men, unfettered by pregnancy and nursing, took on the hunting and the heavy labor. So, it's easy to understand how these roles became gendered. But how, when, and why did we decide to gender things like musical instruments and colors?

Even though this irritates many of us, if I asked you to create a list of colors, behaviors, clothes, activities, and mannerisms that are considered feminine and masculine you could probably do it easily. We all know this stuff and are inundated with it daily.

Also of note is the fact that lists of what's considered masculine versus feminine vary greatly depending on culture and society. What is considered masculine behavior in some cultures and societies may be considered feminine in other places of the world. Think about a man walking around with a satchel, considered a masculine behavior in London. Pick that guy up and plop him down in rural Mississippi and that look is going to be considered pretty feminine. In some countries, men walk around holding hands with other men; it's a sign of friendship. In other countries, two men holding hands are likely to be the target of nasty comments or even violence, as this behavior is considered extremely unmasculine.

It's clear that this stuff is culturally and socially defined, not innate, and can change over time. And, in my humble opinion, it's pretty nonsensical—but holy smokes is it powerful! It has affected *all* of us, whether we're part of the LGBTQ+ communities or not. Most likely, every single one of us was told at some point in our lives (or at many points), "Boys don't do that," or, "Girls

FUN FACTS

Cheerleading was originally a men's sport. It wasn't until World War I, with so many men off fighting in the war, that women were finally able to break into the "masculine" sport of cheerleading.[9] In the early 1900s, pink was considered an appropriate color for boys and blue was considered an appropriate color for girls.[10] At the time, pink was thought to be a bolder color, and blue was considered daintier. High-heeled shoes were originally worn only by men.[11]

don't do that." I remember many moments during my childhood where I was "guided" toward doing the more feminine thing. In third grade, when we got to choose a musical instrument to play, I chose the drums; I was promptly told I had to choose something else because drums were a "boy instrument." I was told that the flute and the clarinet were good choices for girls. I didn't yet know the word *badass*, or that I aspired to be one, so I complied. I played the clarinet (very poorly) for the required amount of time and then immediately quit. I could have been the next Karen Carpenter, but I was restricted by gender norms!

The societal and cultural pressure to stay in our rigidly defined gendered boxes, known as gender policing, was very real when I was growing up and is still very real today. Every single one of us has been affected by it and all of our children are affected by it. Gender policing limits our creativity and our ability to live life as our authentic selves. It's at the heart of so much pain, fear, self-hatred, homophobia, biphobia, and transphobia.

Many homophobic/biphobic/transphobic actions and behaviors (e.g., name calling, bullying, and violence) are precipitated not by the target's sexual orientation or gender identity, but by their gender expression. It is gender policing taken to an extreme level. Think about an eight-year-old boy who plays the flute, who doesn't like sports, and whose favorite shirt is pink. That kid is likely being picked on at school, and he's probably being called "gay." That kid may not have a clue what his sexual orientation is yet. He is being picked on for not behaving "masculine" enough.

A few years ago, here in upstate New York, two straight, cisgender guy friends were sitting at a bar drinking beer. Two other guys in the bar picked up on something about these two friends and their gender expression and decided that they were a gay couple. When the two friends left the bar, they were jumped by the other guys, verbally abused with homophobic slurs, and severely beaten.

These two straight, cisgender men were victims of homophobia-related violence based not on their sexual orientation, but on their gender expression.

Gender expression is the component where most of us have personal experience being somewhere along the continuum, rather than at one end or the other. It's likely that almost everyone expresses, at any given time, a blending of masculine and feminine mannerisms, hairstyles, clothing, activities, and movements. At this moment, as I write, I am sporting a feminine, long hairstyle; a masculine sweatshirt; and feminine leggings, and I'm sitting with one leg up on my desk in an extremely "unladylike" manner. I'm blending, my friends!

JUST FOR FUN

In her Netflix comedy show, *Nanette*, Hannah Gadsby says, "There is too much hysteria around gender . . . 'A man in a dress? That's f-ing weird!' No, you know what's weird? Pink headbands on bald babies. *That's* weird. I mean seriously, would you put a bangle on a potato?"[12]

Let's take a look at the first three components that I've just presented:

Biological Sex

Female - - - - - - - - - - - - - - - - - - Intersex - Male

Gender Identity

Woman - - - - - - - - - - - - - - - - - Nonbinary - Man

Gender Expression

Feminine - - - - - - - - - - - - - - - Androgynous - - - - - - - - - - - - - - Masculine

Question: What do they all have in common?

Answer: They are all solely about us.

Now we are about to move into territory relating to others: attraction and intimate behaviors. These two components often get confused and conflated with the other three components, but they are completely separate parts of our identity.

Attraction (Also Known as Orientation)

Attraction has to do with who (if anyone) makes our hearts go pitter-patter. Sometimes this component is labelled *sexual orientation*, but I refer to it simply as "attraction" because not all orientations and attractions are sexual. Our attractions may be sexual or romantic (also known as *affectional*). Some people feel that romantic and affectional attraction are two distinct types of attractions, but most consider them to be the same. For the sake of clarity, I will refer to them as the same and will use them interchangeably in this book.

Generally, sexual attraction has to do with people we want to engage in sexual activities with (passionate kissing, sexual intercourse, oral sex, etc.). Romantic or affectional attraction has to do with people we want to engage in emotional and affectionate behaviors with (holding hands, snuggling, talking on the phone for hours, etc.). For those of you who are sexually and romantically attracted to the same types of people and can't tease these types of attraction apart, you may now have a big, old question mark over your head, but it's important to know that for some folks these two types of attraction are distinctly different.

If you haven't already, you are likely to begin to hear people separate these different types of attractions. For example, a woman may describe herself as heterosexual and biromantic. For her, this might mean that she wants to engage in sexual behaviors only with men, but she wants to engage in romantic/affectional behaviors with both men and women. A man may define himself as being asexual and heteroromantic. For him this might mean that he has no interest in engaging in sexual behaviors with anyone, but he wants to engage in romantic/affectional behaviors with women.

People may potentially be attracted to no one, to anyone, or to very specific types of people. Please note the use of the word *potentially* in this last sentence. I am straight. That doesn't mean that I am attracted to every man I see. I simply have the potential to be attracted to individual men.

Some of the many ways that people define their sexual attractions are gay, lesbian, bisexual, pansexual, asexual, and straight. Some of the many ways that people define their romantic attractions are homoromantic, biromantic, panromantic, aromantic, and heteroromantic.

Here is a diagram showing attraction or orientation as a continuum:

Potentially Attracted to   Potentially Attracted to   Potentially Attracted to

Men - - - - - - - - - - - - - - - Both/Anyone/No one - - - - - - - - - - - - - - Women

POP QUIZ

What does pansexual mean?

   A. The person is potentially sexually attracted to Disney characters.
   B. The person is potentially sexually attracted to cookware.
   C. The person is potentially sexually attracted to anyone, regardless of gender.

Answer: C

Pansexual typically means that the person has the potential to be attracted to anyone. I have heard people describe their pansexuality as being attracted to "hearts not parts." How does being pansexual differ from being bisexual? A fine question! It may not differ at all. Remember how identities mean different things to different people? Well, two people with the same type of attraction may use different identity words to define that for themselves. So why did we need another term when we already had the term bisexual? For some folks, the word bisexual was too binary. Although the definition is changing, the term bisexual originally implied that a person was attracted to only men and women. What if the person is attracted to nonbinary people who aren't men or women? The word pansexual gets away from that binary thinking. Now, I have met many people who use the word bisexual but they define it this way: "I'm attracted to people who are like me and my gender and to people who are a different gender." That's how the bi—the two options—gets defined for them. The moral of the story, once again, is to listen to the terms that people use to refer to themselves and their loved ones and use those terms.

Intimate Behaviors

Intimate behaviors are what we actually do. These may be sexual behaviors or they may be romantic behaviors.

Here is a diagram showing intimate behaviors as a continuum:

With Men - - - - - - - - - - - - - With Both/Anyone/No one - - - - - - - - - - - - - With Women

We might think that what we do sexually and romantically will always align with our attractions, but this is not always the case. The two components, attraction and intimate behaviors, may not align for many different reasons. One reason is societal pressures: for example, the teenage boy who knows that he's gay (attraction) but is sleeping with as many girls as he can (behaviors) in an attempt to prove to others that he's straight. Another reason why these components might not align is that we don't necessarily act on all of our attractions at once. For example, a pansexual married woman who is having sex only with her husband has not suddenly become straight. Her attraction or sexual orientation has not changed; she is still pansexual.

The confusion over attractions and behaviors is at the heart of many of the misunderstandings about LGBTQ+ people. As I mentioned in chapter 3, when people hear anything having to do with LGBTQ+ identities, their heads often go right to sexual behaviors. It's at the core of the comment, "I don't mind gay people; I just wish they would keep it in the bedroom." It's also, I believe, at the core of most of the pushback against normalizing LGBTQ+ people and families and providing essential education around LGBTQ+ identities in US K–12 schools. Some parents and teachers are afraid that the conversation will be about sexual behaviors.

Take a look at the entire model with all five components.

Biological Sex

Female - - - - - - - - - - - - - - - - - - - Intersex - Male

Gender Identity

Woman - - - - - - - - - - - - - - - - - - Nonbinary - - - - - - - - - - - - - - - - - - - Man

Gender Expression

Feminine - - - - - - - - - - - - - - - - Androgynous - - - - - - - - - - - - - - Masculine

Attraction

Potentially Attracted to   Potentially Attracted to   Potentially Attracted to

Men - - - - - - - - - - - - - - - Both/Anyone/No one - - - - - - - - - - - - - - Women

Intimate Behaviors

With Men - - - - - - - - - - - - With Both/Anyone/No one - - - - - - - - - - - - With Women

The first four components (biological sex, gender identity, gender expression, and attraction) are always with us. They come with us everywhere. The idea that these parts of ourselves could be left at home when we go to work or school is comical. Can you imagine an employer asking an employee to leave the fact that they're hard of hearing at home? Or saying, "Being Jewish has nothing to do with work, so can you not bring that part of yourself into the office?" People can't leave these parts of themselves at home, and they can't leave their gender and sexual orientation at home either. All people can do with any of these identities if they feel unsafe or unsupported is hide them. A lesbian may switch pronouns when she talks with coworkers about her wife because she feels unsafe, but she's still a lesbian at work. The only one of these five components that can, and in most cases, should be left at home is intimate sexual behaviors. Let's say I'm a teacher, and my students ask me, "Hey, Ms. Gainsburg, what did you do over the weekend?" and I answer, "My husband and I discovered this great new sexual position." This is an example of being out with my intimate sexual behaviors. Not okay. But the response, "My wife and I saw this great movie" is an example of being out about my attraction or my relationship status, which is, or should be, just peachy.

PUBLIC SERVICE ANNOUNCEMENT

We interrupt this book to bring you this important message: Please vote for politicians who support the rights of LGBTQ+ people and value their safety.

At the time of this book's publication, teachers, who are women, saying, "My wife and I saw this great movie" is *not* so peachy in Florida. In 2022, the Parental Rights in Education Act (aka the "Don't Say *Gay*" bill) passed in Florida, prohibiting (in grades K to 3) and limiting (in grades 4 to 12) conversations about LGBTQ+ people and families in public school classrooms. Currently, more than a dozen other states have proposed similar bills.

Mark election days on your calendar and get your butt to the polls. Your vote matters. Thank you.

Understanding the differences between attractions and behaviors and being able to explain these differences to others is a critical role that a savvy ally can play as we create a safer and more inclusive world.

WHERE DO I FALL?

And now, for your reading pleasure, and as promised, I will map myself out using this basic diagram of the components of sex, gender, and sexuality. I'll admit, the first time this model was shown to me I thought to myself, "I'm so plain vanilla. This is going to be boring. I'll be all on one side of this diagram." However, it was actually a pretty eye-opening experience.

POP QUIZ

Picture someone you have never met walking down the street. There is only one component that we see or "know" about someone. Which one is it?

A. Biological sex
B. Gender identity
C. Gender expression
D. Attraction
E. Intimate behaviors

Answer: C

Gender expression is the only component we see or "know" about people. We do not see the person's genitals, chromosomes, or hormone levels. We don't know how they identify their gender unless they tell us. We don't know their orientation or whom they are attracted to. And if they are just walking down the street, we are not seeing their intimate behaviors. All we see and pick up on is the person's gender expression. We see their hair, clothes, jewelry, whether or not they have tattoos, and the way they move, and very often we think we can fill in the other components. We make assumptions about people's biological sex, their gender identity, whom they are attracted to, and, let's face it, probably also what they are doing in the bedroom, based solely on their gender expression. For example: We may see a woman in high heels, makeup, a dress, and long hair (gender expression) and we may assume that she has a vagina and ovaries (biological sex), identifies as a woman (gender identity), is attracted only to men (attraction), and is sexually and romantically active only with men (intimate behaviors). Sometimes we're right, but lots of times we're wrong—and, unless we're the person's lover or doctor, typically we will never know.

The way that humans make sense of the world is by putting things and people into categories. It's something we do naturally. In this case, try to fight it. Whenever you find yourself thinking, "I bet that guy is gay," or, "I think she may be trans," give yourself an imaginary dope slap.

Biological Sex

I've never had genetic testing, but I was able to reproduce and create two wonderful children, so I am going to guess and put myself around here:

Female - - - - - - - - - - - - - - - - - - - Intersex - Male

    X

Gender Identity

I've never questioned my gender identity. The doctor said, "It's a girl!" and that always fit for me. So, I am going to put myself here.

Woman - - - - - - - - - - - - - - - - - Nonbinary - - - - - - - - - - - - - - - - - - - Man

    X

Gender Expression

Here is where things get more interesting for me. I have spent a great deal of my life looking at women who, in our society and culture, are considered very feminine (e.g., high heels, lacey clothing, and makeup) and thinking to myself: "I feel as far from that as I do from being a dude, but I know I am a woman. What the heck?" Until I saw this diagram, I didn't have the language to make sense of this. When this diagram was drawn out for me by a friend on a napkin in a coffeehouse, I definitely had one of those light bulb moments. I am a woman and I have always known that. It's my gender expression that has had me confused.

When I think honestly about my gender expression, I realize that mine is all over the place and that it varies depending on the situation and on my surroundings. For example, I tend to express more femininity when I dress formally to facilitate a workshop or go out to dinner, but when found in my natural habitat, my gender expression is much more masculine. Therefore, I map myself like this:

Feminine - - - - - - - - - - - - - - - Androgynous - - - - - - - - - - - - - - - - Masculine

       X ←——————————————————→ X

Attraction

When I first saw this model, the only orientation I was aware of was sexual orientation, and I placed myself solidly in the "attracted to men" section. Since that time, my understanding of attraction has grown. As I began to learn about affectional attraction, I suddenly remembered some crushes I'd had on girls and women. These crushes confused me at the time because I knew I didn't want to have sex with these women. However, I looked up to them, was incredibly flattered by their attention, and, if I'm honest with myself, wouldn't have minded some PG-rated hand-holding or snuggling with them. So, I map myself like this:

Potentially Attracted to   Potentially Attracted to   Potentially Attracted to

Men - - - - - - - - - - - - - - Both/Anyone/No one - - - - - - - - - - - - - Women

   X (Sexually)

      X (Romantically)

Note: I am currently running into a *major* design flaw with this model, which is why sexuality and gender educator Sam Killermann developed the "-Ness" model. (More on this coming soon.)

Intimate Behaviors

Okay, here we go. I know you are all dying to know what straight people actually do in the bedroom. Well . . . although I sometimes get a hamstring cramp, one of my favorite sexual positions is where I take my right leg and . . . oh, wait—this is the one I'm *not* supposed to share, right? (Just making sure you're paying attention.) Let me just say that my intimate behaviors have all been with men.

With Men - - - - - - - - - - - - - With Both/Anyone/No one - - - - - - - - - - - - - With Women

 X (Sexually)

 X (Romantically)

Now let's take a look at a few more diagrams and how some folks from the LGBTQ+ communities have mapped themselves out. I didn't ask these folks to separate their attraction by sexual and romantic attraction unless they wanted to. I also didn't ask them for information regarding their intimate behaviors.

Darlene is a pansexual cisgender woman. Her pronouns are she/her/hers. Here is how she has mapped herself out.

Biological Sex

Female - - - - - - - - - - - - - - - - - - - Intersex - - - - - - - - - - - - - - - - - - - Male

       X

Gender Identity

Woman - - - - - - - - - - - - - - - - - Nonbinary - - - - - - - - - - - - - - - - - - - Man

          X

Gender Expression

Feminine - - - - - - - - - - - - - - - - Androgynous - - - - - - - - - - - - - - Masculine

  X

Attraction

Potentially Attracted to   Potentially Attracted to   Potentially Attracted to

Men - - - - - - - - - - - - - - - Both/**Anyone**/No one - - - - - - - - - - - - - - Women

            X

Take a look at where Darlene placed her "X" under the gender identity component. Although both Darlene and I use the term *woman* to refer to ourselves, I've placed my "X" directly under *woman*, whereas Darlene's "X" is shifted a bit more toward nonbinary. This is a great reminder that people don't all fit neatly into three categories. We're limited by the words we have to describe ourselves, in this case *woman*, *man*, and *nonbinary*, but as a whole, we're actually spread out all over the continuum. Remember in chapter 2 when I argued that we need more words, not fewer? There you go.

Patrick is a straight transgender man. His pronouns are he/him/his. Here is how he has mapped himself out.

Biological Sex

Female - - - - - - - - - - - - - - - - - - - Intersex - Male

X ════════════════════════════════▶ X

Gender Identity

Woman - - - - - - - - - - - - - - - - - - Nonbinary - - - - - - - - - - - - - - - - - - - Man

X

Gender Expression

Feminine - - - - - - - - - - - - - - - Androgynous - - - - - - - - - - - - - - Masculine

X

Attraction

Potentially Attracted to   Potentially Attracted to   Potentially Attracted to

Men - - - - - - - - - - - - - - - Both/Anyone/No one - - - - - - - - - - - - - - Women

X

I like how Patrick mapped out his biological sex with an arrow showing movement. He was assigned *female* at birth. However, he chose to physically transition with hormonal therapies and surgeries, making his current body much more male.

Alex is a pansexual, transmasculine, nonbinary person. Their pronouns are they/them/theirs. Here is how they have mapped themselves out.

Biological Sex

Female - - - - - - - - - - - - - - - - - - - Intersex - - - - - - - - - - - - - - - - - - - Male

       X

Gender Identity

Woman - - - - - - - - - - - - - - - - - Nonbinary - - - - - - - - - - - - - - - - - - - Man

                    X

Gender Expression

Feminine - - - - - - - - - - - - - - - Androgynous - - - - - - - - - - - - - - Masculine

                                 X

Attraction

Potentially Attracted to   Potentially Attracted to   Potentially Attracted to

Men - - - - - - - - - - - - - - Both/**Anyone**/No one - - - - - - - - - - - - - - Women

       X

HELPFUL HINT

You may be wondering what's up with the word *transmasculine*. Transmasculine relates to an individual, typically one who was assigned female at birth, whose gender identity and/or expression falls in the man and/or masculine area of the gender spectrum. In Alex's case, their trans-masculinity relates to both their gender identity and expression.

AN ADVANCED DIAGRAM OF THE COMPONENTS OF SEX, GENDER, AND SEXUALITY

I mentioned previously that I ran into a major design flaw as I was mapping myself out. The main reason I chose the basic diagram to highlight in this chapter is that it's fairly simple. If you are helping other folks understand the different components that make up our sex, gender, and sexuality and it's the first time this information has been presented to them, this basic diagram is a good one to use. However, it definitely has some flaws.

One flaw with this basic diagram is that it sets up a linear continuum, with "female/woman/feminine/attracted to men/with men" on one side and "male/man/masculine/attracted to women/with women" on the other. The implication is that anything other than these two sides is "the middle." Why is that a problem? Well, for one thing, it makes the two ends seem like the norm, with all of that "unusual" stuff in the middle.

Another weakness with this basic diagram is that some things in "the middle" can be really different from other things in "the middle," but there's no way to demonstrate that. For example: both asexual (usually defined as having no sexual attraction) and pansexual (usually defined as having the potential to be attracted to anyone) are in the middle in this basic diagram, but they are *very* different orientations.

Sam Killermann has created an advanced diagram that he calls the "-Ness" model.[13] In this model, the components are mapped out on a sliding scale. Although his diagram is not perfect either, it solves the problems associated with "the middle" because there *is* no middle. For example, under the component of attraction, a person can map out how much they are attracted to women and how much they are attracted to men using arrows of different lengths. Therefore, our asexual friend and our pansexual friend can map themselves very differently using this advanced diagram.

An asexual person might map themselves like this:

Sexually attracted to . . .

⊘—→ Women and/or Feminine and/or Female People

⊘—→ Men and/or Masculine and/or Male People

And a pansexual person might map themselves like this:

Sexually attracted to . . .

⊘————————————→ Women and/or Feminine and/or Female People

⊘————————————→ Men and/or Masculine and/or Male People

The "-Ness" model also gets away from the idea that the two sides are opposites, which is how it appears in the basic diagram. Male and female, man and woman, masculine and feminine—these are not opposites. As Killermann says, "Being more of one thing needn't require you to be less of another."[14] If I am hunting (an activity we tend to think of in our society as masculine), it doesn't make me less feminine. In the basic model, moving more toward the masculine side pulls you away from the feminine side. In the "-Ness" model the levels for each can be represented independently, like this:

Gender Expression

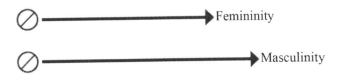

Another flaw with the basic diagram that I ran into while mapping myself out is that it doesn't distinguish between the different types of attractions or orientations. Killermann's "-Ness" model has two attraction scales, one for sexual attraction and one for romantic (or affectional) attraction. So, a gay man who is biromantic could make that distinction like this:

Sexually attracted to . . .

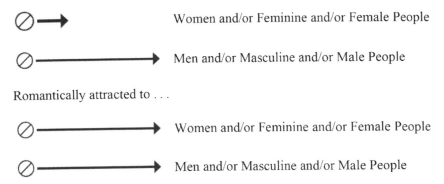

As allies, we should think about which diagram will help someone with their understanding of sex, gender, and sexuality the most. In general, I find that the basic diagram is best for folks who have never thought much about this topic, while the advanced model is better for higher-level, more nuanced conversations. If you're jazzed by this topic and want to know even more about sexuality and especially gender, I strongly encourage you to pick up Sam Killermann's book *A Guide to Gender: The Social Justice Advocate's Handbook*. It's a super-informative and extremely fun read.

ANSWERS TO OUR QUESTIONS

Now that we've reviewed the different components that make up our sex, gender, and sexuality, let's go back to the four questions from the beginning of this chapter and get some answers.

What the Heck Does *Nonbinary* Mean?

Nonbinary (sometimes written with a hyphen, *non-binary*) describes people who don't fit into the two typical binary gendered options of man or woman. Nonbinary people may describe themselves as having no gender, having a different gender from man or woman, having both genders, having multiple genders, and more. Shortened versions of the word *nonbinary* are *NB* and *enby*.

Can Transgender People Also Be Gay?

Absolutely. *Transgender* has to do with gender and *gay* has to do with attraction or orientation. They're completely separate things. A transgender person can be gay, straight, lesbian, pansexual, asexual, or bisexual, just as cisgender people can be any of those things.

Now when you see the letters *LGBT*, you know these identities are orientation-orientation-orientation-gender. The *Q* or *Queer* can be either an orientation or a gender, or both (see table 4.1).

The idea of a gay transgender man or a lesbian transgender woman can really confuse people. I've often been asked, "If a trans man was assigned female at birth and is attracted to men, why the heck didn't he just stay a woman?" The thinking behind this, I believe, is that this man would have fit into our society much better as a straight woman than he does as a gay trans man. Why would he put himself through all the trouble of transitioning and then living a potentially

Table 4.1. Identity Terms and Types

Identity Term	Lesbian	Gay	Bisexual	Transgender	Queer
Type of Identity	Orientation	Orientation	Orientation	Gender	Either/Both

difficult life as a gay trans guy in a homophobic and transphobic world? The answer is that living a life where you cannot be your authentic self *is* a difficult life, and it's incredibly painful. We can't simply choose our gender or orientation because it makes life easier. A gay trans man knows himself to be a man and he would like to be intimate with men as a man. Although what I am about to write confuses orientation with behavior, I am going to say it anyway because many people have found this helpful: *Very* simply put, one is who we sleep with (orientation) and one is who we sleep as (gender identity).

How Can I Tell If Someone Is Gay?

This one is easy. You can't. All you can see is someone's gender expression. The management is not responsible for any conjectures made by the reader. Assume at your own risk.

How Can Someone Be Asexual but Still Have Sex?

An asexual person has little or no interest in sexual activities with others. That tells us nothing about what they're actually doing sexually. They may be in a relationship with someone who enjoys sex and they may choose to engage in sexual behaviors for their partner's pleasure. Not having sex is celibacy (behavior); not having sexual attraction is asexuality (orientation).

FUN FACT

Asexuality (or the shortened version *ace*) can be used as an identity term, but it's also an umbrella term for a spectrum of identities. A few of the many identities under the asexual umbrella are *demisexual*, a person who experiences sexual attraction only after they've made a connection or an emotional bond with someone, and *graysexual*, a person who falls in the gray area between asexual and sexual or someone who experiences sexual attraction only occasionally.

Want to know more about asexuality? I recommend Hippie Calico's YouTube video "Asexuality: The Invisible Orientation"[15] and Angela Chen's book, *Ace: What Asexuality Reveals about Desire, Society, and the Meaning of Sex*.[16]

KEY ALLY TAKEAWAYS

- All we typically see or "know" about people is their gender expression. Don't attempt to fill in the rest (i.e., biological sex, gender identity, attraction, and intimate behaviors). As allies, we should focus on what we need to know about a person—often, simply how someone would like to be addressed or referred to—in order to be respectful.
- Being out in the workplace or at school means living authentically and not having to lie or be deceptive. It doesn't mean talking about sexual behaviors. It's not a "bedroom issue." People are LGBTQ+ 24/7.
- Without gender policing, we would all live much freer and more authentic lives.

NOTES

1. Michael G. Shively and John P. DeCecco, "Components of Sexual Identity," *Journal of Homosexuality* 3, no. 1 (1977): 41–48, https://www.tandfonline.com/doi/abs/10.1300/J082v03n01_04.

2. Christopher Clarey, "Gender Test after a Gold-Medal Finish," *New York Times*, August 19, 2009, https://www.nytimes.com/2009/08/20/sports/20runner.html.

3. Hida, "How Common Is Intersex? An Explanation of the Stats," Intersex Campaign for Equality, April 1, 2015, https://www.intersexequality.com/how-common-is-intersex-in-humans/.

4. Jason Rafferty, "Gender Development in Children," American Academy of Pediatrics, September 18, 2018, https://www.healthychildren.org/English/ages-stages/gradeschool/Pages/Gender-Identity-and-Gender-Confusion-In-Children.aspx.

5. John Keir (producer) and Lahood Grant (director), *Intersexion: Gender Ambiguity Unveiled* (Kilbirnie, Wellington, New Zealand: Ponsonby Production Limited, 2012), DVD.

6. POPSUGAR, "What It Means to Be Intersex with Emily Quinn," YouTube, June 14, 2017, https://www.youtube.com/watch?v=FwnfOnUweew&ab_channel=POPSUGAR.

7. John Colapinto, *As Nature Made Him: The Boy Who Was Raised as a Girl* (New York: HarperCollins, 2000).8. CV Viverito, "Nonbinary Gender Identities: A Diverse Global History," Out & Equal Workplace Advocates, https://outandequal.org/wp-content/uploads/2021/02/Nonbinary-History.pdf.

9. Lisa Wade, "The Manly Origins of Cheerleading," *HuffPost*, December 31, 2021 (updated March 2, 2013), https://www.huffpost.com/entry/cheerleading-history_b_2372103.

10. Jeanne Maglaty, "When Did Girls Start Wearing Pink?" *Smithsonian Magazine*, April 7, 2011, https://www.smithsonianmag.com/arts-culture/when-did-girls-start-wearing-pink-1370097/.

11. News 18, "Did You Know Men Were the First to Wear High-heeled Shoes?" *Smithsonian Magazine*, September 16, 2020, https://www.news18.com/news/lifestyle/did-you-know-men-were-the-first-to-wear-high-heel-shoes-2881163.html.

12. *Hannah Gadsby: Nanette,* directed by Madeleine Parry and John Olb (Netflix, 2018), https://www.netflix.com/title/80233611.

13. Sam Killermann, *A Guide to Gender: The Social Justice Advocate's Handbook*, rev. and updated ed. (Austin, TX: Impetus Books, 2017), ch. 13.

14. Ibid., 249.

15. Hippie Calico, "Asexuality: The Invisible Orientation," YouTube, https://www.youtube.com/watch?v=R9tSal4YyII&ab_channel=HippieCalico.

16. Angela Chen, Ace: What Asexuality Reveals ab*out Desire, Society, and the Meaning of Sex* (Boston: Beacon Press, 2020).

Part II

Building Skills for Having Respectful Conversations

5

PRONOUNS

Sharing, Gathering, and Using

*It is very unfair to judge of any body's conduct,
without an intimate knowledge of their situation.*[1]

—Jane Austen (using singular *they*
in her novel *Emma*)

WHY ARE PRONOUNS SO IMPORTANT?

I get asked this question all the time, and I'll admit that I'm slightly amused by it. It's kind of like asking, "Why are names so important?" Pronouns and names are important to all of us. Getting them correct is one of the most basic ways that we can show respect to a person.

The question typically gets asked by people who are always referred to correctly. These folks rarely even notice the pronouns that are being used for them because they're always the right ones. They'd understand immediately why pronouns are so important if people used the wrong ones for them. Pronouns aren't just important to trans folks. They're important to us all. A better question is, "How can we ensure that we're using the correct pronoun for everyone?"

In this chapter, I'll offer some best practices for sharing your pronouns, gathering pronouns from others without making it awkward, and using people's pronouns in respectful ways.

SHARING YOUR PRONOUNS

I've lived in the world for sixty years, and never once has someone used the wrong pronoun for me. Some might say that's reason enough to not add my pronouns to my email signature or wear a pronoun pin on my shirt at a conference. My pronouns are obvious. By displaying them I'm certainly at risk for being called *woke*, and not in that early-twentieth-century, Black American, complimentary way, but in that newer, "virtue-signaling," derogatory way. I'm aware that my readers may also fear that they'll be called *woke* if they display their pronouns. Here's a story that may help.

Ari (pronouns *they/them*), a participant in a workshop that I facilitated, recently began a new job. The company that they work for had no systems in place that offered employees the opportunity to share their pronouns. All of Ari's new coworkers immediately assumed that Ari's pronouns were *she/her* based on their appearance. Because the company didn't acknowledge pronouns in any way, Ari wasn't sure if it would be safe for them to let their coworkers know their real pronouns. What Ari ended up doing was sharing their pronouns (and their conundrum) only with the coworkers who displayed *their* pronouns in their email signatures. To Ari, the colleagues who displayed their pronouns weren't virtue-signaling; they were ally-signaling. These colleagues ended up supporting Ari by leading the way in using the correct pronouns for Ari, encouraging others to use Ari's correct pronouns, and starting the conversation about creating systems at work where everyone was offered the opportunity to share their pronouns to eliminate the problem for future employees.

Sharing pronouns, even if they're obvious, is not political correctness gone awry. Don't allow your fear of being called *woke* scare you away from this powerful and impactful ally action

Here are a few more reasons why sharing your pronouns, even if they're obvious, is a great thing to do.

1. When allies share their pronouns, it normalizes the behavior, making it easier for others to do it too. How awkward and "othering" would it be if the only people walking around with pronoun pins or pronouns on their name tags were the ones whose pronouns weren't obvious?
2. Creating a culture where people display their pronouns helps to avoid those embarrassing moments when we're not sure how to refer to someone. If everyone displays their pronouns, we'll nail it every time!

3. Establishing a protocol where everyone is offered the opportunity to share their pronouns avoids having to single someone out by asking them directly.
4. As demonstrated in the story about Ari, displaying your pronouns lets others know that you support all kinds of people, whether or not they conform to society's gendered expectations.
5. It's a great conversation starter! I've gotten into some wonderful conversations with people who've asked, "She/her? Isn't that obvious? Why are you wearing that on your shirt?"

Now that you have some excellent reasons why to share your pronouns, here's some information on how to do it respectfully. Simply state what pronouns you use; don't assign a gender to them. In other words, you should say, "My pronouns are he/him/his," rather than, "I use masculine pronouns." Along these lines, you should refer to pronouns like singular *they*, *ze*, and *per* as "gender-neutral pronouns" rather than "nonbinary pronouns." People are nonbinary; pronouns aren't. You should also avoid saying things like, "I'm a she." Just say, "My pronoun is she."

Here are some great places to display your pronouns: in your email signature, on your name tag or ID badge, on your desk or door nameplate, on a pin or bag tag, next to your name on your video conferencing platform, on your business card, and on your social media pages.

GATHERING PRONOUNS FROM OTHERS

There's a lot of discourse about the importance of asking people for their pronouns, but very little information on how to do it well. I realized, as I was writing this chapter, that I've *never* come right out and directly asked someone, "What are your pronouns?" Asking people directly about their pronouns puts people on the spot, making it very uncomfortable for them if they don't want to share. It can also offend some people who think that their pronouns should be obvious. There are better ways to gather people's pronouns that are more tactful and less likely to cause anxiety.

One-on-One

In a situation where we're talking one-on-one with someone, we typically don't need to know their pronouns because we use the gender-neutral pronouns *you*

POP QUIZ

When I share my pronouns, should I share one, two, or three forms (for example, "she," "she/her," or "she/her/hers")?

- A. I should only share one. Why waste ink?
- B. I should share two. It's what all the cool kids are doing.
- C. I should share three. It normalizes the behavior for those who use new pronouns, like *ze and per*, and who often need to educate others about how to conjugate them properly.
- D. There doesn't seem to be a consensus regarding which is best.

Answer: D

Although this may change over time, currently there doesn't seem to be a consensus or an official recommendation regarding how many forms of your pronoun you should share.

When people first began sharing their pronouns, most everyone was sharing three forms. More recently, the number of pronoun forms that people share tends to be a matter of personal choice. If you use more than one pronoun, for example, "he/they," then it makes sense to share only one form, because "he/him/his/they/them/theirs" is extremely long and clunky. (Information on how to respectfully refer to people who use two pronouns coming up.) If you use only one pronoun, I do like the idea of sharing three to normalize the behavior for folks who need to educate others about how to use their pronouns, for example if their pronouns are ze/hir/hirs. However, it would be neglectful of me not to tell you that recently some savvy youngsters told me that all the cool kids actually *are* sharing only two pronouns. Sharing three is apparently so 2020.

and *yours* as we talk with them. For example, you might say to the person ahead of you in line at a coffee shop, "I love your Marvin the Martian tattoo. Did you know that the reason Marvin wants to destroy Earth is because it obstructs his view of Venus?" We may be tempted to try to figure out people's pronouns in situations like this where we don't need to know them. Humans naturally categorize to create order and make sense of the world. But in this situation try to fight it. Asking a stranger at a coffee shop about their pronouns is unnecessary and intrusive.

The desire to gather information that we don't need reminds me of a goofy behavior I exhibited when my friends first started using cell phones. Having grown up with only landlines, I was used to knowing exactly where people were when I talked with them on the phone. They were in their homes. If I knew them well, I could even picture where they were sitting or standing in their house or apartment as they spoke with me. When cell phones became a thing, I was completely discombobulated. I couldn't picture where my friends were when they were talking to me, and it was disorienting. Right after "Hello," I'd immediately ask, "Where are you?" Eventually I realized that asking people where they were when they talked to me by phone was intrusive, and I forced myself to curb my curiosity. Some of us may have this same feeling of disorientation when we don't know someone's pronouns, but we shouldn't gather pronouns simply to curb our curiosity or so *we* feel more oriented.

In a Small Group

Now let's imagine we're talking with a small group of people at a social event. In this situation, it's helpful to know people's pronouns. For example, if we want to say, "Jay has really impressed me with [fill in pronoun] Looney Tune expertise. My Marvin the Martian trivia failed to wow [fill in pronoun]. [Fill in pronoun] [*is/are*] the real aficionado!" We can, of course, continue to use "Jay" and avoid pronouns all together, but that's extremely repetitive and difficult to do in a long conversation. That would require me to say, "Jay has really impressed me with Jay's Looney Tune expertise. My Marvin the Martian trivia failed to wow Jay. Jay is the real aficionado!"

So, here are some tips for gathering pronouns in a small group setting like this. Start by offering your pronouns first. Have you ever called someone on the phone and not known who you were speaking with? Perhaps someone unexpected picked up and you didn't recognize their voice. Or, for example, when I call my auto repair shop. I know the folks who work there but I can't always tell them apart by their voice. When this happens to me, instead of asking, "Who is this?" which is rather abrupt, I offer my information first. I say, "Hi! This is Jeannie. Who am I speaking with?" In this same vein, offering your pronouns first makes the interaction less jarring and much more polite.

In a small group setting, I would say, "Hey! I'm Jeannie. My pronouns are she/her/hers." This way I'm setting the example of sharing my pronouns as part of my introduction. Often others will follow suit.

If you want to be more direct, after you introduce yourself and offer your pronouns, you can add, "How may I refer to you?" "How may I refer to you?" is a better question than "What are your pronouns?" It's clear what you're asking because you've just shared your pronouns, but it gives the other person an out if they don't want to share theirs. They can simply say, "You can call me

Jay." If this is the response you get, it's probably best to just use the person's name and avoid pronouns altogether.

If you've joined a group that's already mid-conversation and the people in that group seem to know each other already, listen to the pronouns they're using and mirror those.

HELPFUL HINT

This whole delicate dance of gathering pronouns would be completely unnecessary if everyone at this social gathering was wearing pronoun pins. Just sayin'.

In Large Numbers

Finally, let's discuss how to best gather pronouns when we're in environments with large groups of people, for example in the workplace or at a school. In these situations, the best way to gather pronouns is to offer *everyone* the opportunity to share. This avoids having to single anyone out whose pronouns are unknown, and it indicates that your workplace, medical center, school, or faith-based organization is an LGBTQ+ welcoming and inclusive place.

Here are three suggestions for creating opportunities where everyone can share their pronouns if they'd like to.

1. Ask at work meetings when someone new joins your team. Just as we don't ask employees to share their names at every staff meeting, it's also unnecessary for employees to share their pronouns at every staff meeting. However, when someone new joins your team and you're asking folks to share their names and titles, that's a great opportunity to ask everyone to share their pronouns, too, if they feel comfortable doing so. If it's the first time you're implementing this practice at your workplace, offer your information first so you can model what you're asking. For example, "Hey everyone. I'm José. My pronouns are he/him/his. I'm the director of operations."

   Do keep in mind that sometimes people will misunderstand what you're asking, even if you've modelled it first, and they'll share their identities instead of their pronouns. For example, "Hi. I'm Kesha. I'm a straight woman and I'm the volunteer coordinator." In these situations, it's important for you to clarify what you're asking, or others may start sharing their identities too, which will create a very uncomfortable environment. In the workplace, no one should ever be asked how they identify. So, if this happens to you, simply say something like, "Thanks Kesha. Let me just remind folks that sharing your identity isn't necessary. Just let us know your pronouns, if you feel comfortable sharing them."

2. Ask on forms. At schools, workplaces, medical facilities, mental health centers, and other service agencies, a wonderful place to ask folks for their pronouns is on forms. Add an optional category of "pronouns" right under "name." Give examples of the information you're seeking, in case people are confused. For example, "Pronouns (optional) _____ (for example, *she/her, he/him, they/them*)."

3. Offer pronoun pins or stickers. In a setting like a social event or a faith-based gathering, where name and pronoun go-arounds and forms aren't typically used, you can offer pronoun stickers or pins as people enter your space. If you're asking people to fill out name tags for the event, encourage them to add their pronouns under their name. Leave a few examples on the table.

No matter what setting you're in, it's important to remember that sharing pronouns should always be optional. Think of the sharing of pronouns as an opportunity, not a requirement. We shouldn't force people to share their pronouns, and we shouldn't question folks if they choose not to share.

My colleague Noah, a transgender man, remembers a time in his life when being forced to share his pronouns would have made him feel incredibly uncomfortable:

> I vividly recall the anxiety (hello, depression) around that feeling of not having told anyone I was trans let alone started transitioning. But I definitely knew I wasn't a girl and to state that would have been a rejection of myself and what I knew was true. That would've been a really hard time to say my pronouns because they definitely weren't "she/her," but I didn't feel like they could be "he/him" yet either. Making pronouns optional made it so I didn't have to lie/disrespect myself or feel self-conscious about how masculine I did or didn't look and feel.

One final note on gathering pronouns is to keep in mind that pronouns and identities are not interchangeable. There are nonbinary folks who use the traditional pronouns *he* and *she*. There are binary folks who use gender-neutral pronouns like *they*. We shouldn't assume a person's gender based on their pronouns.

USING PRONOUNS CORRECTLY

In this section I'll discuss how to use pronouns correctly. Since most, if not all, of us received lessons in elementary school on how to use *she* and *he* properly, I'll focus only on the proper use of gender-neutral pronouns.

Singular *They*

There are many gender-neutral pronouns, but the one that's currently used most often in the United States is singular *they* (i.e., using *they* to mean one person). Because singular *they* refers to one person, it would seem like the correct way to use it would be, "They is coming for dinner." But this is incorrect. Singular *they* should be used the same way you would use it if you were referring to a group of people. For example, "They are coming for dinner."

Here are my five favorite reasons why everyone should embrace singular *they*. Yes, even you folks who have worked yourself into a tizzy because you believe it isn't grammatically correct.

1. It's now generally acceptable in written English and in speech to use *they* to refer to one person. Both the *Merriam-Webster Dictionary* and the *Oxford English Dictionary* have expanded the definition of *they* to refer to

a person whose gender is not known or to refer to a single person whose gender identity is nonbinary.

2. Singular *they* has been used in written English since 1375. Geoffrey Chaucer, William Shakespeare, and Jane Austen all used it.
3. It's an award winner! *They* was chosen as the word of the year in 2015 by the American Dialect Society and in 2019 by *Merriam-Webster*. How many words do you know that have won medals?
4. You probably use it already without even realizing it. If you find someone's cell phone, do you really say, "Somebody left his or her cell phone. I hope he or she gets it back"? Or do you say, "Somebody left their cell phone. I hope they get it back"?

And here's the most important reason of all . . .

5. It's some people's pronoun. So, it's the respectful thing to do.

One final matter worth discussing while we're on the topic of singular *they* is whether or not we should use it to refer to everyone. Some people believe that a great way to get around the entire issue of figuring out which pronouns to use for people is to simply use singular *they* for everyone. I do like this idea and I hope someday our world will be ready for a big change like this, but I don't think we're there yet. We currently live in a very binary world regarding gender, and most people like and are comfortable with their gendered identity words. I believe we'd end up offending more people by using singular *they* for everyone than we would if we continued to fumble along using our current imperfect system of trying to figure out their actual pronouns. I know several binary transgender folks (i.e., transmen and transwomen) who hate being referred to as *they*. These folks have shared with me that they've worked hard and gone through a great deal in order to have people refer to them as *he* or *she*. Having someone use *they* as their pronoun feels offensive.

With that said, there are some situations where using singular *they* for everyone is appropriate and unlikely to offend. These situations are when we know absolutely nothing about a person or we're talking about a person in general. An example of the first situation, where we know nothing about a person, is if someone says, "Would it be okay to bring my friend to your dinner." It would be appropriate to respond, "Of course! Do they eat fish?" An example of the second situation, where we're talking about a person in general, is a school district writing, "A student who is late to school must sign in at the office and bring a note from their parent or guardian."

POP QUIZ

You're at a deli counter waiting to place your order. The person standing next to you is ahead of you in line, but the server asks you what you'd like first. The best way to let the server know that the person next to you should place their order first is to:

    A. Look at the person's gender expression (i.e., what clothes they're wearing, how they've styled their hair, whether or not they're wearing makeup) and make your best guess as to what their pronoun is. For example, "I believe she was here first."
    B. Avoid pronouns. For example, "I believe this person was here first."
    C. Use singular *they*. For example, "I believe they were here first."

Answer: B

As I mentioned earlier, during long conversations it can be challenging to avoid using pronouns. However, during brief interactions with strangers, like this one, it's quite manageable. In situations like this, it's best to avoid both pronouns and gendered words, like *lady* and *sir*. (More on ungendering our language coming up in chapter 6.) If you've gotten into a brief conversation with the person next to you and you want to say something a bit less formal, you can say, "I believe my friend here was first."

Neopronouns

Neopronouns are gender-neutral pronouns that have not yet been officially recognized in the language in which they're used. In other words, you won't find them in the dictionary. The prefix *neo* means new. A few examples of neopronouns are *ze*, *ve*, *per*, and the Spanish gender-neutral pronoun *elle*. Singular *they* isn't considered a neopronoun because it has been added to the dictionary and is recognized in English.

The use of neopronouns is currently not very common. A 2020 Trevor Project survey of forty thousand LGBTQ+ youth found that only 4 percent of LGBTQ+ youth use neopronouns, meaning 96 percent use the more common *she*, *he*, and/or *they*.[2] With that in mind, it's not necessary to memorize a list of all the neopronouns and how to conjugate them. A better way to show respect is to wait until you meet someone who uses a neopronoun and then put the time and energy into learning how to pronounce it and how to use it in its different forms.

Check out the Practice with Pronouns website.[3] It helps you practice neopronouns with fun sentences like, "_____ stays inside _____ office at all times, only communicating with us through sealed envelopes that are spat out from under the door like a sunflower shell through teeth."

More than One Pronoun

More and more often I meet people who use two or even three pronouns, for example *she/they* or *he/they/she*. There are several reasons why a person might use more than one pronoun. Here are a few.

1. Some folks feel that both or all the pronouns they use fit them equally well.
2. Some folks, like gender-fluid individuals, feel that different pronouns fit for them at different times.
3. Some folks feel that a gender-neutral pronoun fits best for them, but they offer the more common *he* or *she* pronoun because they don't mind it and they know that it's easier for others to use.
4. Some folks feel that a gender-neutral pronoun fits best for them, but they use it only in certain settings (e.g., in LGBTQ+ spaces or when they're with their friends) because they don't like having to constantly educate others on how to use it or why they use it.
5. Some folks feel that the more common pronouns, like *she* or *he*, fit best for them, but they want to promote and encourage the use of gender-neutral pronouns to help normalize them and pave the way for others to comfortably use them.
6. Some folks use pronouns in English and pronouns in other languages to represent their intersectional identities and/or to indicate that they're bilingual, for example *she/ella*, *he/él*, or *they/elle*.

I have two best-practice tips for respectfully talking with and about someone who uses more than one pronoun. The first is to ask the person how they would like you to navigate the use of their pronouns. Asking is a good thing to do if you have a relationship with the person or you're in a setting where it feels appropriate. You might say something like, "How may I use your pronouns in a way that's most respectful to you?" Some people will tell you they don't care which you use. Some people will ask you to mix it up and use both or all of their pronouns. And some people will ask you to use a specific pronoun or different pronouns depending on the setting, the environment, and/or their sense of themselves at any given time. Gender-fluid folks, whose pronouns can change frequently, sometimes wear pronoun bracelets or pins to help guide others in which pronoun to use.

Best-practice tip number two is for when you're in a setting where asking doesn't feel right. In this case, it's best to mix it up and use both or all of the person's pronouns. You're least likely to offend the person by using both or all. Many people, when they encounter a person with pronouns like "she/they," will only use the more common pronoun "she," because it's easier and they know that they're less likely to make a mistake. However, most folks with multiple pronouns truly appreciate it when others make the effort to use their gender-neutral pronouns too.

Mixing up the use of people's pronouns doesn't mean you need to change pronouns every time you use one. Although alternating every time is feasible in writing, when speaking most people find this difficult. For example, "He just saw the new Star Wars movie. Let's ask them what she thought of it." I don't know about you, but *my* brain doesn't work fast enough to pull that off. But do try to mix up the use of their pronouns every few sentences or with each new conversation.

MESSING UP PROPERLY

Despite our best efforts, our knowledge of pronoun etiquette, and our newly practiced skills, we are still bound to mess up occasionally. It's inevitable. Knowing how to recover gracefully after you mess up, without calling too much attention to your mistake, is extremely important. In chapter 14, you'll learn the best ways to respond after you've misgendered someone (i.e., used the wrong pronoun or gendered word for a person), as well as some tips for getting it right the next time.

NOTES

1. Reprinted from Jane Austen, *Emma* (London: John Murray, 1815), 133.
2. The Trevor Project, "Pronoun Usage among LGBTQ Youth," July 29, 2020, https://www.thetrevorproject.org/research-briefs/pronouns-usage-among-lgbtq-youth/.
3. Practice with Pronouns, https://www.practicewithpronouns.com.

6

LGBTQ+ ETIQUETTE TIPS, COMMON BLOOPERS, AND OUTDATED TERMS

The only real mistake is the one from which we learn nothing.[1]

—Henry Ford

In this chapter, you'll learn some simple language tips that will allow you to respectfully navigate conversations with and about LGBTQ+ people and create safer spaces. In the first section, I offer some LGBTQ+ etiquette tips for having respectful and inclusive conversations. In the second section, I share the most common LGBTQ+ etiquette bloopers[2] or cultural faux pas. In the final section, I list some outdated terms and better language choices. If you've already got these tips down, then take them out into the world. These are great pointers for savvy allies to share with others to help create more respectful and inclusive environments for everyone.

LGBTQ+ ETIQUETTE TIPS

Tip #1: Ungender Your Language

In workshops, when I recommend that people ungender their language, invariably someone will make a comment like this: "I asked the man about his wife, and he just corrected me and let me know that he had a husband. It was no big deal."

It may have been no big deal for the asker, but we have no idea whether it was a big deal for this married man. What went through *his* head before he shared that he was actually married to a man? Annoyance? Discomfort? Anxiety? Was he concerned for his safety? Did he look around to see who else was listening? It *is* possible that it was no big deal for this man, but it's a pretty big deal for many.

One of my workshop participants who pushed back on this tip was an elementary school teacher. I tried the "switch it" technique with her, changing the scenario to a school setting with young children. I asked her to think about saying "Merry Christmas" to her class as they left for winter break, rather than "Happy Holidays." I told her that she may have a student who feels comfortable raising their hand and saying, "My family celebrates Hanukkah." However, she may also have a student who's thinking, "Does my teacher think that everyone celebrates Christmas? Perhaps Hanukkah isn't as important or as valued as Christmas. Maybe my teacher doesn't like Jewish people. I'd better not let on that I celebrate Hanukkah."

Sometimes the "switch it" technique works extremely well and light bulbs go off. Unfortunately, in this case the light bulb did not go off. This teacher told me that she still says "Merry Christmas" to her class because that's what most of her students celebrate. Bummer. (See chapter 8 for a discussion on planting seeds and how people learn.)

Back to our ungendering language tip: If you're not wearing a big rainbow button on your shirt (which I highly recommend, by the way), this is the next best way you can indicate to an LGBTQ+ person that you are aware that LGBTQ+ people are out there among us and that you support them. Seriously, LGBTQ+ people and their loved ones are looking and listening for these indicators.

Several years ago, I was sitting next to a woman on a plane when we got into a conversation about where we each were going.

"I am continuing on to Denver. My daughter is getting married," she said.

I said, "Oh wow! Congratulations! Are you pleased with her choice in a partner?"

The woman hesitated for a moment and then said, "Yes. I am. And I'm really pleased that you used the word *partner*. She's marrying a woman."

If I had asked, "Are you pleased with her choice in a husband?" she might have corrected me or she might have simply said, "Mm-hmm" and turned back to read her emergency-landing card in the seat-back pocket. The point is that by using the word *partner*, I told her with my language that I was open to hearing her tell me that her daughter was marrying anyone under the sun.

The assumption that everyone is straight (also known as *heteronormativity*) is extremely common and not necessarily meant to be hurtful—and we are all guilty of it, myself included. Remember my friend Jonathan from chapter 3, the man who was buying flowers for his husband at the grocery store? Let's look closer at what happened when that cashier said, "Oh, those are beautiful. Are they for your wife?"

If Jonathan had been purchasing the flowers for his wife, he might have simply said, "Yes," and moved on, completely unaware that this question could cause stress or fear for anyone. But Jonathan was purchasing the flowers for his husband, so he was now backed into a corner by the cashier's language. He had three options:

Lie: "Yes. They are for my wife."
Deflect: "I think you just dropped my tomato."
Come out: "No, actually they're for my husband."

For many LGBTQ+ people, this is an anxiety-filled moment. What if they're out to their friends but not to their parents? Should they be telling the grocery store cashier their orientation when their parents don't even know? What if an incredibly homophobic person is standing in line behind them, listening in? Might that person harass them or even become violent in the parking lot?

It's so unfair that LGBTQ+ folks are constantly forced into situations where they have to decide whether or not to come out. By using ungendered language, we avoid putting people on the spot, we create safer environments, and we let people know that we are aware that straight and cisgender are not the only ways to be.

Great words to remove from your vocabulary if you have no idea who someone is or how they like to be referred to include *husband, wife, girlfriend, boyfriend, ladies, gentlemen, guys, Mr., Mrs., Miss, Sir,* and *Ma'am.*

HELPFUL HINT

Karen Catlin, author of the book *Better Allies,* brought to my attention the fact that in the 2022 Winter Olympics, "ladies" figure skating was finally rebranded to "women's" figure skating. Catlin explains in her book why the term *lady* can come across as patronizing. "Because 'lady' is still related to nobility in some cultures, it can make modern women feel as though they're being reminded of a time when women were quieter, gentler, and more 'well-behaved.' The male equivalent is 'gentleman,' but aside from messages of welcome, this word has largely dropped from common usage. (Ever heard someone shout, 'Hey, watch it, gentleman'? Me neither.)"[3]

POP QUIZ

What would have been the best way for this cashier to have made small talk with Jonathan?

  A. "Oh, those are beautiful flowers. Are they for your wife or husband?"
  B. "Oh, those are beautiful flowers. Are they for your partner?"
  C. "Oh, those are beautiful flowers. You're going to make someone's day with those."

Answer: C

Answer A is more inclusive, but it still puts Jonathan on the spot, forcing him to think about whether or not he should come out. Also, the language implies that everyone is binary and that everyone identifies as a man or a woman. As we discussed in chapter 4, not everyone does. Answer B is better than A but could potentially still cause anxiety because Jonathan is still being asked to share personal information. Answer C is best. If Jonathan wants to have a conversation about who the flowers are for, he can. However, it also gives him an out not to share his personal relationship information in public. He can simply smile and say, "Yup."

I'm cisgender and I have the privilege of moving through the world and having people pretty much always guess correctly when they assume my gender. But I'd like to share that I hate being referred to as *Ma'am* or *Mrs. Gainsburg*. I can't even imagine how hurtful it would be if I were also being misgendered with these terms. In other words, it would be so much worse if I were being referred to as *Ma'am* or *Mrs. Gainsburg* and I were actually a man. I would love for all professional offices to have a form that allows me to choose how the staff refers to me. These questions on forms are great for learning how to respectfully address *everyone*.

How might we gather information on how people would like to be addressed when a form isn't feasible? Let's look at a situation with a police officer pulling someone over. Police officers are typically trained to say *Sir* and *Ma'am*, as in, "Good evening, Ma'am. Do you know why I pulled you over and am about to hit you with a big, fat ticket?" Now, I know that there are people who like to be referred to as *Sir, Ma'am, Mr.,* or *Mrs.* For many folks, this is a sign of respect. So how do we navigate a world where some people want others to refer to them with formal gendered language and others will be made super happy by ungendered terms? Once again, whenever possible, we ask—and we ask *everyone*, not just the folks we look at and are not quite sure.

Here is what a more inclusive interaction might look like with this police officer and me:

Police officer: Good evening, I'm Officer Thomas. How may I address you tonight?

Jeannie: You can call me Jeannie.

Police officer: Do you know why I pulled you over and am about to hit you with a big, fat ticket, Jeannie?

Voilà!

Great ungendered words to add to your vocabulary if you have no information about people, their loved ones, or how they like to be referred to are *partner* or *partners* (let's be mindful of our polyamorous friends), *loved one* or *loved ones*, *special person* or *people*, *significant other* or *others*, *important person* or *people*, *folks*, *colleagues*, *team*, *friends*, *everyone*, and (if you can pull it off) *y'all*.

FUN FACT

In 2021, Disney theme parks, in both the United States and Japan, switched their standard greeting of "Ladies and gentlemen, boys and girls" to "Dreamers of all ages."[4] Their goal: to make all guests feel welcome, regardless of their gender identity.

Changing the language you've used all your life is hard. It's going to take time and effort. Here are a few suggestions for effectively ungendering your language without being too hard on yourself. First, take language tweaks one at a time. Perhaps you're a teacher and you want to stop saying *guys* to refer to all of your students. Focus on that one tweak until you have it down, and then move onto another. Second, remember that catching yourself using a gendered term is the first step toward change. It's when you don't even realize that you're using the gendered term that you may need to enlist the help of a friend to notify you when you use it. When you catch yourself using *guys*, for example, that's good! Stop yourself and say something like, "Oops. I'm trying to get rid of that word. I meant friends." Finally, be kind to yourself while you're under construction. And remember, when it comes to language, we're always under construction!

FUN FACT

I grew up in New Jersey, home of the expression "youse guys." (Not a Jersey-related fact I'm proud of.) I was initially resistant to stop using *guys* to mean everyone, as it was a part of my heritage. Here are a few things that people said or asked me that helped me change my mind.

- "If you're looking for a restroom and you pass one that says, 'guys,' are you going in?" (Thank you, Karen Catlin, for this question. My answer is typically "No." That's obviously the men's room. The only reason I'd go in there is if it's empty and the line is really long for the women's room. See chapter 10 for a discussion of ungendering single-stall restrooms.)
- "If we used the term *gals* to refer to everyone, do you think that would fly in our society?" (My answer: "Definitely not. Who are we kidding?")
- "Ask a straight man how many *guys* he's slept with, and you'll see pretty quickly that *guys* is not a gender-neutral word." (My response: "Bahahaha! True!")

One final note I'd like to share before we move on from this tip is to clarify that the goal of ungendering language is not to neutralize gender or create a genderless world. It's to create a gender-friendly world. "A gender-friendly world," as author Lee Airton states, "isn't a world without gender. It's not a palette of grays and beiges, or a sea of shapeless bodies in tunics and bowl cuts."[5] A gender-friendly world will allow all people to express their gender in all its glory.

Tip #2: Mirror Terms

This is one of my favorite tips, as it's a wonderful way to show respect to all, not just people in the LGBTQ+ communities: Listen carefully to the terms that people use to refer to themselves, their loved ones, their relationships, their ability, their size, their race, their religion, and the like, and mirror those terms. It's so beautifully simple and will take you so far.

Imagine someone says to me, "As a *queer* woman, I find it difficult when people make faulty assumptions and assume that I am straight." If I respond with, "I know I am guilty of making those errors myself. Since you're a *lesbian*, I would love to hear what suggestions you have for me so that I can change my language," then I've just demonstrated to this woman that I'm not listening. I'm making assumptions and labelling someone according to my glossary of terms.

Ugh! Didn't I warn myself to use that darn glossary with caution? Most likely I thought to myself, this is clearly a woman who likes other women; therefore, she must be a lesbian. I'll use that term. However, this individual used the word *queer* to refer to herself. I should have listened and mirrored that term.

The mirroring of terms is also important when people are talking about their loved ones and family members. If I invite a friend from work to my house for a party and, as he walks in, he says, "This is my *husband*, Javier," and I respond with, "Hey everyone! This is Marc's *partner*, Javier," then once again, I'm not listening or using my respectful communication tip of mirroring terms. I should have mirrored Marc's language and introduced Javier as his husband.

One final point to note here is that if we have a most excellent conversation with someone and we use their terms and identities, we should not assume that the next person we talk to uses the same terms. In other words, now that I know the woman in the first scenario uses the word *queer* to refer to herself, the next time I meet two women who are together as a couple, I should not refer to them as queer. But how *should* I refer to these two women if I don't know how they refer to themselves? I would avoid using an identity term altogether. I would simply say something like, "I met a great couple at your party last week."

POP QUIZ

Who does the queer woman in the above scenario have sex with? Does she have sex only with women? Does she have sex with men and women? Does she have sex with people regardless of their gender? Does she have sex at all? Choose all that apply.

A. She has sex only with women; otherwise, she would have said she was bisexual or pansexual.
B. We have no way of knowing unless we ask.
C. It's none of our business.

Answer: Both B and C

We have no way of knowing unless we ask (and let's not ask unless we know her really, really well), and it's none of our business (unless we are her doctor). All we know from what she's told us is that she's not straight. We don't know whom she is attracted to, whom she has sex with, or even if she has sex at all. We just know that she refers to herself as *queer*.

Combining Tip #1 and Tip #2

Now let's put what we learned in Tip #1 (ungender your language) together with what we learned in Tip #2 (mirror terms). You may be wondering why the use of *partner* was okay for me to use on the airplane but not okay in the example of Marc and Javier at the party. *Partner* or *partners* are great ungendered terms to use if you don't know the gender of someone's loved one or loved ones. But once you receive information about how someone refers to their loved one or loved ones it's respectful to mirror those terms. Here's a best-practice step-by-step guide:

> *Step 1:* Use ungendered terms when you know nothing about a person or their relationships.
> Example: "Please feel free to bring your partner or partners to my party."

> *Step 2:* Listen to how people respond.
> Example: "Oh, well thank you very much. I would love to bring my wife to your party."

> *Step 3:* Mirror terms that people use to refer to themselves and their loved ones.
> Example: "Wonderful! I am looking forward to meeting your wife."

Tip #3: Implement the "Switch It" Technique

The "switch it" technique, which I introduced in chapter 3, is a fantastic self-help tool that allies can use to determine whether or not a question or comment is respectful and appropriate. If you're not sure if a question you're about to ask an LGBTQ+ person is rude or intrusive, switch it! Ask yourself if you'd ever ask a straight and/or cisgender person the same question. Often this quick test can guide us toward more respectful conversations. Here are a few examples.

Are you thinking of asking your gay son what he thinks caused him to be gay? Switch that question and ask yourself if you'd ever ask your straight son what caused him to be straight. Straight people *never* get asked this type of question, because in our society and culture being straight is considered the norm or the "right" way to be. By asking your gay son this question, you're making it clear that you think being gay is the wrong way to be. So, don't ask.

Are you wondering if you should offer some "helpful" makeup tips to your coworker who just came out as a transgender woman? Switch it! I'm a cisgender woman. The last time I wore makeup[6] was at my high school prom in 1981. That means I've been makeup-free my entire working life. Not once has a coworker come up to me and said, "You know, Jeannie, if you wore a little lipstick, you'd look much more feminine." Not only has this never happened to me, but I would have been so offended if it did! Transgender people have as much variety in their gender expression as cisgender people. Let's offer our transgender coworkers the same respect that we offer to our cisgender coworkers by not making assumptions about how they want to look. Now, if your transgender coworker approaches you and says, "I love your makeup! Will you show me how you apply it?" she's asking for your help. Go have a blast with your makeup tutorial.

Tip #4: Use the Correct Name and Pronoun

This one probably seems obvious: Refer to people the way they want to be referred to. If you meet a new coworker whose name badge says "William," but they introduce themselves as "Bill," you're probably going to use the name "Bill." Easy-peasy. Now let's move on to a few situations that might be a bit more confusing.

Imagine you're supervising a transgender employee whose legal name is Jamal but who would like you to refer to them as Jasmine. What should you do? First, refer to them as Jasmine. Next, see if you can find out which pronouns Jasmine would like you to use by implementing the strategies we learned in chapter 5. Offer yours first, and then ask, "How may I refer to you?" Additionally, in a situation like this one, you should probably have a private conversation with Jasmine about how best to share Jasmine's name and pronouns, if they've changed, with the other employees. A final best-practice tip is to keep Jasmine's legal name confidential, on a need-to-know basis only.

I've worked with many transgender coworkers. Some had legally changed their names and some had not. It didn't matter to me as a coworker. I used the name they asked me to use. I never asked what their name used to be or, even worse, what their "real" name was. (*Hint:* These questions are rude.)

You might work at an agency or company that has policies stating that legal names be represented on all name badges, ID cards, and email addresses. It stinks, but it's a reality in some workplaces. If this is the case where you work, here are some recommended ally actions.

- Work with your employee or encourage the agency's leadership to work with the employee to come up with creative "duct tape patch-up job" solutions that will help to make sure the employee is addressed properly. For example: Add a ribbon to the bottom of the employee's name badge that says, "Please call me Bill," or, "Please call me Jasmine."

- Normalize the "Please call me _____" ribbon by adding one to your own name badge and encouraging others to do the same. This way transgender employees are not easily identified and do not stand out as obviously different.

- Look at long-term "big fix" solutions that can make your workplace more inclusive in the future. Talk to your leadership or administrative team about the current policy and let them know it's problematic for some employees. Ask if there are adjustments that can be made to the legal-name policies and the current confidentiality policies (i.e., policies put in place to protect employees' personal information). Be an advocate for change. (Read more about duct tape patch-up jobs and big fixes in chapter 10.)

We should also use a person's correct current name and pronouns when we refer to their past. We shouldn't do that thing in our heads where we think: "Hmmm. When my coworker Alice was five, she was a guy, so to be accurate I should switch back to Alfred and use the pronoun *he* when I talk about her as a young person." That is not cool, not respectful, and may be a safety issue for Alice.

If we say loudly in the cafeteria, "Hey Alice, when you were Alfred, did you play on any sports teams?" we've just outed Alice to everyone within hearing distance, potentially putting her at risk. Using her old name, also known as "dead naming," is probably also violating our company's confidentiality policies. The unfortunate reality is that we live in a very homophobic, biphobic, and transphobic world. In the LGBTQ+ communities, transgender women run the highest risk of being victims of violence. Transgender women of color are at the highest risk of all.[7] Your little slipup could have devastating consequences. Accuracy isn't a good enough excuse for being disrespectful with our language or for potentially putting someone's safety at risk.

I've often heard the comment, "This would be so much easier if they just legally changed their name!" I won't go into lengthy detail here describing the daunting, time-consuming, expensive, and sometimes humiliating process that trans folks must go through to legally change their names. I'll simply share a few eye-opening facts.

HELPFUL HINT

The correct and respectful way to talk about the actor Elliot Page is to say, "Elliot Page was so good in the movie *Juno*. He's a talented actor." Even though we know at the time the film was made Elliot was using a different name and pronouns, we should stay in the present with his current name and pronouns. (Notice how I was able to explain this concept without dead-naming Elliot?)

- In many states, the process for a person to change their legal name requires that the change, along with the person's current address, be published repeatedly in a newspaper for all to see. Many people are afraid to make their transition and their home address this public.
- In many states, a person must petition the court for a legal name change. A judge may reject the application, and many judges will reject the applications of transgender people.
- Separate name-change applications must be submitted for Social Security, driver's license, birth certificate, passport, and more. Each department has different requirements. The total cost is typically hundreds of dollars, a financial burden that can be prohibitive for many people.

There may be other, more personal reasons why someone may decide not to change their name legally. I know a transgender woman who believed it would be unsafe for her to bring her authentic self to work. She only felt safe being herself when she was at home or with friends. This unhappy situation doesn't make her any less trans than someone who has the support at work and the finances to be able to legally change their name. As allies we should always work hard to use a person's correct chosen name, regardless of whether it's been legally changed or not.

One final point to keep in mind is that who someone is in terms of their gender (gender identity) and how they dress or wear their hair (gender expression) are completely different things. We don't ever want to think to ourselves, "Huh. Jasmine is wearing a tie today. I should probably use her old name, Jamal." Just because Jasmine is choosing to dress in a way that our society considers masculine doesn't mean that her gender identity has changed. People express themselves in all different ways. It doesn't change who they are.

Tip #5: Focus on What You Need to Know

What do we really need to know about our coworkers, clients, and students in order to be respectful? Do we need to know how they identify? We may think the answer is yes, but most often, it's no. We don't need to know whether someone is a lesbian, a transgender man, a straight woman, or a nonbinary person. This isn't the information we should be gathering at school and at work. Do we need to know what our coworker's, client's, and student's anatomy looks like? This question is easier. The answer is, of course not. Do we need to know what our coworkers, clients, and students do in the bedroom? Pretty sure we all know the answer to this one.

In order for us to be respectful in our language, all we need to know about the people we interact with at work and school is how they would like us to refer to them. That's it. Unless we're in the field of health care, it's not important for us to know and it's not appropriate to ask how folks identify, what their anatomy looks like, and what they do in the bedroom.

Let's not assume folks' identities based on the pronouns they're asking us to use, either. There are cisgender folks who use singular *they* as their pronoun. There are nonbinary folks who use our traditional pronouns *he* and *she*. We can't tell someone's gender simply by learning their pronouns.

COMMON LGBTQ+ LANGUAGE BLOOPERS TO AVOID

"Just tell me what not to say." This plea is so common that even though I am not focusing heavily on vocabulary in this book, I decided to add a section on outdated terms and cultural faux pas. However, it's important to keep in mind that just as individuals embrace different identity terms and define them in a variety of ways, individuals also have differing opinions about what is offensive and what's not. So before diving into some common bloopers, I want to acknowledge that not everyone thinks these *are* bloopers. The recommended language tips in this chapter are simply the best choices to make if you have no other information about a person.

Getting Creative with the Word *Transgender*

People get very creative with the word *transgender* and the shortened version *trans*. Creativity is usually a good thing, but in this case it's ill-advised. Most of the creative variations of the word *transgender* are offensive.

The words *transgender* and *trans* are adjectives: words that describe a noun. The same is true for the words *gay* and *queer*, but the words *transgender* and *trans* seem to get misused the most.

Correct	Incorrect
A transgender man	A transgender
Trans folks	The transgenders
They are a transgender person.	They are a transgendered person.

I field a lot of questions about person-first language. Although person-first language (e.g., "people with disabilities" instead of "disabled people") has taken hold in some communities as the respectful way to refer to people, it hasn't really taken hold in the LGBTQ+ communities. For example, "a transgender person" is used by more transgender folks than "a person who is transgender."

Another creative variation of the word *transgender* is the incorrect word *transgendering*. People transition; they don't transgender.

Confusing the Terms *Transgender Man* and *Transgender Woman*

Many folks confuse the terms *transgender man* and *transgender woman*. They're unsure which is which. Here is a tip that helped me when I was first figuring this out: It would be very unusual for a person to embrace an identity term that had the wrong gender word in it. So, the identity is, very simply put, where the person is going, not where they came from. Let's look at the wonderful Laverne Cox. She was assigned male at birth, but she's a woman. My guess is she wouldn't want the words *male* or *man* included in any part of her identity. She is a transgender woman.

It's also important to point out that, although there are times that we might refer to Laverne Cox as a transgender woman, for example, "Laverne Cox was the first transgender woman to win a Daytime Emmy Award," in general, we should simply refer to her as a woman.

Talking about *Preferred* Pronouns

Avoid using the word *preferred* when asking about or talking about people's pronouns. Back in the day, when people first started asking others for their pronouns, almost everyone was using the verbiage *preferred pronouns*. But then folks started to push back on this language choice, and for good reason. The word *prefer* means having a fondness for something. Our pronouns aren't just something we're fond of. Like our names, pronouns are part of our identity. I'm not just fond of the pronoun *she*. If someone refers to me as *he*, it's not okay. So, remove the word *preferred* and just refer to people's pronouns.

Using the Word *Preference* Instead of *Orientation*

You should also avoid the word *preference* when talking about whom people are attracted to. I often hear people say, "That's his sexual preference." It's more respectful to say, "That's his sexual orientation." Once again, the words *prefer* and *preference* imply a fondness for something. Attraction or orientation is part of who we are. It's not a choice. Listen to the difference in these two sentences: "She's attracted to women" and "She prefers women." The second sentence sounds like, "Yeah, she prefers women, but if there are none around, anyone will do." Being intentional with your language and avoiding the words *prefer* and *preference* in these contexts is a great way for you to indicate to others that people don't choose their orientation or gender.

Using Language That Implies That Transitioning Is Completed

Avoid the phrase "completed transition" or any other language that implies that a transitioning person is "done," like a cinnamon roll in the oven. I have never had a single transgender person ever tell me that their transition was done. Transitioning is a lifelong process. Every trans person has their own unique decisions to make about that process, and these decisions may change throughout their lifetime. Their transitioning experience may or may not include legal name changes (on some or all documents), hormone therapies, and/or various surgeries. Each individual will decide for themselves what is right for them, what they can afford, and what new care is necessary as their body ages and changes.

Transitioning can be a daunting, time-consuming, and expensive process. Many individuals can't afford the hormone therapies or surgeries they need. Legal name changes are complicated and difficult to access for those who work a nine-to-five weekday job, and they can be a financial burden as well. Other reasons why a transgender person might not legally change their name have to do with safety, insurance coverage, age, and their support system.

For these reasons listed above, transgender-related policies contingent on a person's transition being "done"—which are not uncommon—are extremely unfair. For example, many states require transgender individuals to show medical proof that they've had specific surgeries before they can apply for a name change on their birth certificate. As allies we can help educate others about the

POP QUIZ

When should we change the name and pronouns, during everyday interactions, with a coworker who is transitioning?

A. When the coworker asks us to please use their new name and pronouns.
B. When the coworker asks us to please use their new name and pronouns and their name has been legally changed.
C. When the coworker asks us to please use their new name and pronouns, their name has been legally changed, they have completed a medical transition, and they are wearing their "Done!" sticker.

Answer: A

Ideally, the leadership and human resources department at your workplace will have met with the transitioning employee to create a workplace transitioning plan that includes decisions involving the sharing of their new name and pronouns with others. Our job as coworkers is to use the new name and pronouns when asked to do so. The legal status of a coworker's new name and their medical choices do not and should not matter to us.

Here comes the wonderfully useful "switch it" technique! Can you imagine saying these things to a coworker?

"Congratulations on your marriage! I hear you've asked us to use a new last name. Has your name actually been legally changed? If not, I think I'm gonna wait until that paperwork comes through before I stop using your old name."
"Hey, Tanya, my wife is thinking of having a hysterectomy. Do you still have your uterus?"

realities of the transitioning process, the fact that not all transgender people transition, and that a person's transition is never really "done."

Focusing on the Past

For many transgender individuals, the time before they transitioned was a painful one, when they were forced to express themselves in ways that felt wrong. Focusing on the past by using an old name or pronoun for a transgender person, asking what their name used to be, or asking to see a photo of them before they transitioned may be asking them to go back to a very unhappy place.

If you must refer to a transgender person's past, and you aren't outing them inappropriately by doing so, here are a couple of respectful communication tips for doing it correctly:

- Rather than saying, "When you were a boy . . ." or "When you were a girl . . . ," say, "Before you transitioned . . ."
- Rather than saying that someone was "born a boy" or "born a girl," refer to the sex they were assigned at birth. In chapter 2, when I defined the term *cisgender*, I didn't say, "A cisgender person is a person whose biological sex matches their gender identity." I said, "A cisgender person is a person whose sex assigned at birth matches their gender identity." If what we are referring to is the result of a doctor's peek between a newborn's legs and not a person's chromosomes, hormone levels, and reproductive organs, then saying "sex assigned at birth" rather than "biological sex" is not only more respectful, it's more accurate as well.

Asking a Gay Couple Which One Is the Man and Which One Is the Woman

This common question assumes that all relationships must mirror the masculine man/feminine woman structure that's typical of conventional straight couples. My friend Sam, a gay cisgender man, shares his feelings about this question beautifully:

> Huh? Are they asking who cleans the house or who is top and who is bottom in the bedroom? Are they asking if one of us pretends to be a woman, or wishes that he was? This is such a loaded question! It assumes that all legitimate couples fit into a binary gender-role division. All partnerships, whether they are gay or straight, bring together people who have a combination of skills, interests, styles, and personalities. The answer is, of course, that we're both "the man" because we are both men! But more importantly, we are both ourselves and not trying to match anyone's definition of what it means to be a man but our own.

OUTDATED TERMS AND BETTER LANGUAGE CHOICES

In this section, I'll share some outdated terms that are generally falling out of favor. There are still some LGBTQ+ people who use these terms to refer to themselves, and we should obviously mirror these terms back when we hear people use them for themselves. In general, however, it's a respectful starting point to swap the outdated term for the new term as listed here.

Use *Transgender* Instead of *Transsexual*

Transsexual is a dated term that is rarely used anymore, especially by younger people. Some folks dislike this word because it has the word *sexual* in it, which tends to reinforce the mistaken notion that all things LGBTQ+ are about sex. Others feel that the word *transsexual* is inaccurate because the term focuses on a person's sex rather than their gender. In addition, the term *transsexual* can hold a negative connotation because it was used, in the past, by mental health professionals to diagnose people with mental disorders. Most people now use the term *transgender* or the abbreviated version *trans*.

The word *transgender* can be used as an individual identity, but it can also be used as an umbrella term referring to a whole community. The word *transgender* is typically defined as relating to an individual whose sex assigned at birth doesn't match their gender identity. This can include people who are trans women, trans men, genderqueer, gender-fluid, agender, bigender, Two-Spirit, nonbinary, and more.

Use *Cross-Dresser* Instead of *Transvestite*

Transvestite is another outdated term. Cross it out in your head and replace it with *cross-dresser*. A cross-dresser is a person who enjoys wearing clothing that society doesn't consider appropriate for their gender. Cross-dressing is about a person's gender expression. It tells us nothing about their gender identity or their orientation.

Use *Gay* Instead of *Homosexual*

Many people dislike the word *homosexual* for the same reasons that people dislike the term *transsexual*: It has the word *sexual* in it, and it was used in the past by mental health professionals to diagnose people with mental disorders.

Use *Typical* Instead of *Normal*

When we are discussing gender identities, gender expressions, or biological sexes that are common or expected, it's respectful to use the word *typical*. Try

POP QUIZ

Which two countries were the first to declare that homosexuality was not a mental disorder?

A. The United States and Canada
B. New Zealand and Australia
C. Sweden and Denmark

Answer: B

The Royal Australian and New Zealand College of Psychiatrists Federal Council removed homosexuality from its list of mental illnesses in October 1973.

to avoid the word *normal*. The opposite of normal is abnormal, which has a pretty icky connotation.

Use *Intersex* Instead of *Hermaphrodite*

As we discussed in chapter 4, *hermaphrodite* is a dated and inaccurate term that pathologizes natural body variation. When talking about intersex individuals, also avoid words like *condition* or *disorder*. These words imply that being intersex is wrong or unnatural. Intersex people have beautiful and natural biological variations.

Use *Different Sex* or *Gender* Instead of *Opposite Sex* or *Gender*

Remember the advanced "-Ness" model that Sam Killermann created to get away from opposites? Instead of *opposite*, try *different*, as in, "I'm attracted to people of a different gender from me." If you're only attracted to men or women, you can simply say that. For example, a straight woman could change the sentence "I'm only attracted to the opposite sex" to "I'm only attracted to men."

Use *Are* Instead of *Identify As*

Many LGBTQ+ individuals dislike it when people say things like, "They identify as transgender." They find it more respectful when people say, "They are transgender." One reason is because, typically, we don't talk about straight cisgender people "identifying" as straight and cisgender; we just accept that they are. Secondly, when we say that someone "identifies" as something the connotation is that their identity is chosen and somewhat transient.

POP QUIZ

While reading this chapter, you realized that you have been guilty of one or more of these faux pas, and you feel like poop. You should:

A. Tell yourself you're a terrible person and a hopeless ally and close the book.
B. Tell yourself that it's okay to make these mistakes. You get a pass because you are an ally.
C. Remember that we all make mistakes. Forgive yourself but do put in the work to move forward.

Answer: C

Do forgive yourself; we all make mistakes. Do put in the work to move forward. Don't assume that you get a special pass just because you are an ally. You must hold yourself accountable for your language and behaviors just like everyone else.

One of the most horrendous examples I've encountered of a straight/cisgender person using what they considered to be their "special ally pass" happened at a workshop I was facilitating at a school for its teaching staff. My cofacilitator, a young trans man, had attended the school as a student, so several of the teachers in the audience knew him before he had transitioned. As I chatted with one of the teachers before the workshop, she continually referred to my cofacilitator using his old pronoun. When I said to her, "Oh, hey, I just want to remind you that he is now using he as his pronoun," she said, "Oh, it's okay for me to say that because we go way back!"

Even if we have lots of LGBTQ+ friends, allies don't get a special pass to be disrespectful or hurtful with our language. In fact, just the opposite is true. We should be modelling the most inclusive and supportive language we possibly can so that, like superstar Laverne Cox, we can be possibility models!

AVOID THESE TERMS ALTOGETHER

Gay Lifestyle

Living with fifteen cats is a lifestyle. Being gay is not. It's just who someone is. There's no gay lifestyle just as there's no straight lifestyle.

Tranny, Fag, and Dyke

Although these words may be thrown around jokingly within community, for example, gay men may jokingly call each other *fags*, these words are not okay for others to use. (See chapter 9 for a detailed discussion of why this is so.) As allies, we should help people understand that these words are incredibly offensive.

I'll end this chapter with this wonderful quote by American linguist John Mc-Whorter. "A mature societal take on language will understand that words are not simply what they mean in something called the dictionary and that words referring to issues societal or controversial—i.e., the interesting ones—will often need replacement about once a generation."[8]

NOTES

1. John Powell, *The Secret of Staying in Love* (RCL Benziger, 1974), 85.
2. * By "blooper" I mean an embarrassing error, not a funny mistake. It's not my intention to diminish the impact of LGBTQ+ faux pas and derogatory terms.
3. Karen Catlin, Better Allies: Everyday Actions to Create Inclusive, Engaging *Workplaces* (Second Edition) (Better Allies Press, January 2021), 120.
4. Jasmine Ting, "Disney Parks Switch to More Inclusive Messages," Paper Magazine, July 3, 2021, https://www.papermag.com/disney-parks-inclusion-2653650433.html?rebellitiem=5#rebelltitem5.
5. Lee Airton, *Gender: Your Guide: A Gender-Friendly Primer on What to Know, What to Say, and What to Do in the New Gender Culture* (Avon, MA: Adams Media, 2018), 151.
6. ** Not counting the times I've dressed in drag.
7. Human Rights Campaign, "Violence against the Transgender Community in 2018," https://www.hrc.org/resources/violence-against-the-transgender-community-in-2018.
8. John McWhorter, "How 'Woke' Became an Insult," *New York Times*, August 17, 2021, https://www.nytimes.com/2021/08/17/opinion/woke-politically-correct.html?action=click&module=RelatedLinks&pgtype=Article.

7

GAYDAR AND OTHER PROBLEMATIC ASSUMPTIONS

Take all of your identities, add them up, and you get you. There has likely never been another person, in all the 108 billion [people] of Earth's history, whose You Soup ingredient list has been the same as yours. . . . Yet many times in your life you're going to be viewed as a one-ingredient dish.[1]

—Sam Killermann, "You Soup: Understanding Diversity and the Intersections of Identity," 2012

All lesbians have short hair, wear flannel, play softball, and drive Subarus, true? All gay men have great fashion sense, sing show tunes, work out constantly, and say, "Guuuurrrrl!" a lot, right? Wrong. Some do, to be sure. And by the way, if you *are* a flannel-wearing, softball-playing lesbian with short hair who drives a Subaru, rock on! The purpose of this chapter is not to judge, mock, or disrespect anyone's gender expression or interests. The purpose of this chapter is to ensure that LGBTQ+ stereotypes are not applied to LGBTQ+ people and to reduce the harmful impact of myths, stereotypes, and misinformation about people in the LGBTQ+ communities.

GAYDAR

Let's start with our first goal: making sure that we are not assuming that all LGBTQ+ people dress the same, wear their hair the same way, and have the same interests. Many readers will have, no doubt, heard the word *gaydar*. Gaydar, which combines the words *gay* and *radar*, refers to the ability some people claim to have to accurately identify a gay person simply by looking at them or talking to them.

Here is the reality of how gaydar works: We observe someone's gender expression—what they're wearing, how they style their hair, whether or not they have tattoos or body piercings, how they walk, how they talk—and we draw conclusions about whom they are attracted to. I worked at an LGBTQ+ center for fifteen years and I'm here to tell you that my gaydar stinks. The reason it stinks is that there is as much variation of gender expression within the LGBTQ+ communities as there is within the straight cisgender communities. I have no idea who is gay, lesbian, asexual, bisexual just by looking at them—and, I'm sorry to say, you probably don't either.

We may see a guy walking toward us with a rainbow scarf, a Pride shirt, and purple hair and think to ourselves, "Gay—obviously." Then we miss the next three gay men who walk by us because they're wearing, respectively, a Coors tee, a suit and tie, and construction gear. And guess what? We may even be wrong about the dude in the Pride shirt!

No matter how amazing we think our gaydar is, the truth is that we can't tell someone's orientation just by looking at them—plain and simple. Let's not even try. As allies, it's respectful to just let people be their fabulous selves, no matter how they express themselves, without attempting to figure out their identities.

LGBTQ+ MYTHS AND STEREOTYPES

LGBTQ+ myths and stereotypes can be silly: for example, "All lesbians wear Birkenstocks." (Not true.) But they can also be incredibly hurtful: for example, "LGBTQ+ people are out to recruit others." (Definitely not true.) Both types of myths and stereotypes, the silly and the hurtful, have harmful and damaging impacts on people, both within and outside of the LGBTQ+ communities.

One way that myths and stereotypes can be damaging is by preventing LGBTQ+ people from seeing accurate and varied images of other LGBTQ+ people, which can delay the coming-out process. Even the silly stereotyping of LGBTQ+ people can be damaging in this way. Consider a young woman who

FUN FACT

When I first started working at our LGBTQ+ center, I was amused and pleased to note that I (the straight cisgender employee) was the only staff member who actually wore Birkenstocks.

is trying to figure out if she might be a lesbian, and the only thing she "knows" about lesbians is that they are all short-haired, flannel-wearing softball players. If this young woman has long hair and hates sports, she may think to herself, "That's not me, so I must not be a lesbian." Rather than moving forward in her coming-out process, she's likely to go back into the stage of identity confusion, as discussed in chapter 3. My friend Matt, who's a gay man, believed the myth that gay men weren't interested in fatherhood. He knew from a very early age that he wanted to be a father, and so he convinced himself that he must not be gay. His understanding of himself and his coming-out process were greatly delayed by this stereotype.

Now let's look at some myths and stereotypes that are beyond silly. Some extremely prevalent myths and stereotypes are downright hurtful and extremely dangerous. I run an activity in one of my workshops where participants write down all of the myths and stereotypes they can think of for lesbians, gay men, bisexual or pansexual people, transgender people, and straight cisgender allies. (Yes, there are ally myths and stereotypes too. We'll get to these in a moment.) Here are two very common and very harmful LGBTQ+ myths and stereotypes that make the list every time:

- Gay men are prone to pedophilia.
- If transgender women are allowed in women's restrooms, they'll behave in a sexually inappropriate manner.

These myths are so familiar that they're included in this list every time I run this activity, in locations all across the United States. Participants share that they were exposed to these myths by family members, friends, teachers, faith leaders, books, movies, and the media. Whether we believe them to be true or not, they are incredibly prevalent in our society, and we all seem to know them.

Some of us have done our homework and know that these harmful myths and stereotypes are false. Unfortunately, others, who don't know many LGBTQ+ people and have not researched the facts, often believe these myths and stereotypes to be accurate. (We'll discuss how to respectfully challenge these myths and stereotypes in chapter 8.)

Here are some real-life examples of the damage that these two harmful myths and stereotypes have caused in our society:

- Prohibitions on gay men becoming Boy Scout leaders.
- LGBTQ+ people being fired from jobs like teaching, where they work with children.
- Laws that keep transgender people out of restrooms that align with their gender identity.

Myths and stereotypes have a huge impact on individuals and devastating consequences for our society. As allies, we must listen for them in people's questions and concerns and address them. Start by doing your ally homework and checking out the facts:

- Did you know that the myth that gay men are prone to pedophilia has been widely debunked?[2]
- Did you know that in the eighteen states that have policies allowing people to use the restroom that aligns with their gender identity, there hasn't been a single reported incident of a transgender person behaving inappropriately in a public restroom? There have also been no documented incidents of cisgender boys dressing as girls or saying that they "feel like girls" in order to access the girls' locker rooms, a common parental fear.[3]

You don't need to know all the facts and statistics about LGBTQ+ people before you head out into the world as an ally, but it's worth having some data on the most common and hurtful myths and stereotypes in your savvy ally goody bag.[4] Fill it with more goodies as needed as you continue to have conversations with people about LGBTQ+ inclusion.

NOT-SO-FUN FACT

Here is what transgender folks want to do in the bathroom: pee and peace out. I know transgender people who dehydrate themselves when they go out to social events if they're not sure they'll have access to an all-gender restroom. They don't want to make other folks uncomfortable and they're worried for their own safety. Allies can help change this!

MYTHS AND STEREOTYPES ABOUT STRAIGHT/ CISGENDER ALLIES

When I ask participants to list some myths and stereotypes about straight cisgender allies, I often get a blank stare. *Are* there myths and stereotypes about straight cisgender allies? You betcha!

POP QUIZ

What is a common myth or stereotype about straight cisgender allies to the LGBTQ+ communities? Choose all that apply.

A. Allies always have an LGBTQ+ family member or very close friend who is LGBTQ+.
B. Allies are really LGBTQ+ themselves; they just haven't come out yet.
C. Allies are awesome!

Answer: A and B

(C is a fact.)

The two most common ally myths, in my experience, are that allies must have a close friend or family member who is LGBTQ+ or they wouldn't be involved (the "it's personal" myth) and that allies are really LGBTQ+ themselves; they just haven't come out yet (the "closet case" myth). Let me share with you a little bit about the impact that these two particularly prevalent myths had on me.

The first time I ever had any type of friendly relationship with out cisgender gay, lesbian, and bisexual people was in college. (I wouldn't meet an out transgender person until 2003, when I began my work at our local LGBTQ+ center.) I went to college in the early 1980s, and several of my varsity volleyball teammates were lesbians. Despite my camaraderie with these teammates, it never occurred to me that I had a place at any of the "Silence = Death" rallies that were taking place on campus to support LGBTQ+ people. I didn't have any close friends or family members who were LGBTQ+ and I had never heard the word *ally* in the context of social justice work, so I was pretty sure I wouldn't be welcome there. In other words, I was held back by the "it's personal" myth.

One day in the early 1990s, while I was in graduate school working toward my masters in social work, some members of the LGBTQ+ student club came into my classroom and invited all of the straight cisgender people to join their club. I attended their next meeting. A short while later, a fellow student teased me about my "fascination with lesbians." I knew she was implying that I was a closeted lesbian, which, I'll admit, freaked me out a bit. The "closet case" myth prevented me from returning to the club meetings or becoming really active for many years.

As I shared in the preface, it wasn't until I was forty years old that I finally picked up the phone and started volunteering at our local LGBTQ+ center, launching myself into what would become a decades-long career as a straight cisgender ally. Had those two myths about allies not gotten in the way, I likely would have started my work as an ally to the LGBTQ+ communities twenty years earlier.

How am I currently affected by these two ally myths? The "it's personal" myth is, at this point, just a fun one to bust. People often assume that I'm part of the LGBTQ+ communities or I have an LGBTQ+ child. I love sharing how and why I got involved and validating the importance of the fight for LGBTQ+ rights and inclusion on its own merits.

Honestly, I still struggle with the "closet case" myth. I don't care if I am mistaken for a lesbian or a trans woman or any other identity under the LGBTQ+ umbrella. It happens all the time. I *do* mind, however, when people assume that I am a closeted LGBTQ+ person or that I am confused about my own sexuality or gender. It's annoying and offensive to know that some people think they know more about me than I do and are waiting for me to figure out my "real" identity and finally come out.

Myths and stereotypes hold us all back. They are perpetuated by people both outside of and within the LGBTQ+ communities, and they are dangerous things. Listen closely, my friends. Behind almost every negative comment or concern about LGBTQ+ individuals, the savvy ally can find a hidden myth or stereotype. Hearing them is step one; debunking them is step two. (More on this coming up in chapter 8.)

INTERSECTIONALITY

For those who are unfamiliar with the word *intersectionality*, it basically means that we all have many identities that make us who we are and shape our experiences. Our age, race, body size, abilities, ethnicity, class, orientation, gender identity, and gender expression are part of who we are, and they're all interconnected. We can't simply add together the gendered experience of being a woman and the racial experience of being a person of color and come up with the lived experience of a woman of color. The ways that race and gender come together create unique experiences and societal challenges.

The word *intersectionality* was coined by Kimberlé Crenshaw in 1989. In her 2016 TED Talk, "The Urgency of Intersectionality," Crenshaw talks about how a legal case was the catalyst for creating this word. The case involved Emma DeGraffenreid, an African American woman who applied for a job at a car manufacturing plant but was not hired. DeGraffenreid believed this was a case of racial and gender discrimination, but the judge dismissed the suit. The judge's rationale was that the company had hired Black men for many of its industrial and maintenance jobs, proving that the company wasn't discriminating based on race. The company had also hired many white women for secretarial jobs, proving that the company wasn't discriminating based on gender. Crenshaw said:

> I was struck by this case. It felt to me like injustice squared. So first of all, Black women weren't allowed to work at the plant. Second of all, the court doubled down on this exclusion by making it legally inconsequential. And to boot, there was no name for this problem. And we all know that, where there's no name for a problem, you can't see a problem, and when you can't see a problem, you pretty much can't solve it.[5]

Crenshaw coined the term *intersectionality* to help frame DeGraffenreid's dilemma so that others could see and understand the problem. This was not simply a matter of adding up identities like a math equation and getting a simple answer. African American women like DeGraffenreid slipped through the cracks of the legal protections that were working for Black men and white women. The term *intersectionality* helps raise awareness that our many identities can cause multiple layers of discrimination.

Here's an example of intersectionality within the LGBTQ+ communities: Imagine an eighty-three-year-old gay man living in a senior-living facility. If we simply add the experiences of a gay man in his thirties and the experiences of an eighty-three-year-old straight man, we are unlikely to get an accurate picture of this man's life, his experiences, and the unique challenges that he has faced. Having lived through a time when he saw gay men arrested for their sexual orientation, diagnosed with mental disorders simply for being themselves, and forced to undergo electroshock therapy in an attempt to "fix" them, his level of distrust of medical and mental health professionals will be heightened by these lived experiences as a gay man *and* an older adult—more so than they're likely to be for a gay man in his thirties or an eighty-three-year-old straight man. This eighty-three-year-old gay man is less likely to make social connections at the senior-living facility and more likely to hide who he is and whom he has spent his life with. As professional senior caregiver Marsha Robinson says in the outstanding short film *Project Visibility*, his story would be missing.[6]

Roberto Valdes, a queer person of color, shares how intersectionality has impacted him:

> At various points in life, I've found myself placing my queerness in one box and my Blackness in another. In law school, for example, I was a member of the Black Law Student Association and OUTLaw, the law school's LGBTQ+ organization. But I never felt that an opportunity existed to discuss issues that specifically impacted queer people of color in either of those spaces. Within OUTLaw, there was a lot of interest in advancing marriage equality. But the same passion didn't apply to the fact that gay men of color in the United States are far more likely than gay white men to be diagnosed with HIV during their lifetime. I didn't feel that I could center the issues that disproportionately impacted LGBTQ people of color in either space without being seen as lacking an appropriate focus on the issues that were relevant to the organization.[7]

Why is a section on intersectionality included in a chapter that focuses on myths and stereotypes? Because a prevalent and hugely problematic myth is that there is one typical way to be an LGBTQ+ person: white, non-disabled, middle-class, hearing, non-religious, and between the ages of about sixteen and forty. But LGBTQ+ people come in all shapes, sizes, colors, ages, abilities, experiences, and backgrounds. They are grandparents, Deaf, Catholic, African American, single, homeless, low-income, cancer survivors, Republican, Muslim, polyamorous, war veterans . . . you get the idea. Their lived experiences are influenced by these intersectional identities.

Sam Killermann, on his website It's Pronounced Metrosexual, talks about how we're all like bowls of soup with multiple ingredients (race, ethnicity, gender, sexuality, disability status, socioeconomic status, faith, career, political beliefs, etc.), but we're often viewed as a one-ingredient dish. Can you relate to being reduced to only one or two of your many yummy ingredients? I highly recommend you check out Killermann's humorous blog post called "We're all snowflakes. But we're also all stereotypes. Let me try to help you understand that with a hot bowl of You Soup." He offers takeaways that will help you acknowledge and appreciate everyone's unique soup with all of their delicious ingredients.[8]

NOTES

1. Reprinted from Sam Killermann, "You Soup: Understanding Diversity and the Intersections of Identity," It's Pronounced Metrosexual, October 2012, https://www .itspronouncedmetrosexual.com/2012/10/individual-difference-and-group-similiarity/.

2. Here are a few good articles that bust the pedophilia myth: Gregory M. Herek, "Facts about Homosexuality and Child Molestation," Sexual Orientation: Science, Education, and Policy, https://psychology.ucdavis.edu/rainbow/html/facts_molestation.html; Olga Khazan, "Milo Yiannopoulos and the Myth of the Gay Pedophile," *Atlantic*, February 21, 2017, https://www.theatlantic.com/health/archive/2017/02 /milo-yiannopoulos-and-the-myth-ofthe-gay-pedophile/517332/; and Gabriel Arana, "The Truth about Gay Men and Pedophilia," *INTO*, November 16, 2017, https://www .intomore.com/impact/The-Truth-About-Gay-Men-andPedophilia.

3. Here are two good myth-busting articles on facility use: Amira Hasenbush, "What Does Research Suggest about Transgender Restroom Policies?" *Education Week*, June 8, 2016, https://www.edweek.org/ew/articles/2016/06/08/whatdoes-research-suggest abouttransgender-restroom.html; and Julie Moreau, "No Link between TransInclusive Policies and Bathroom Safety, Study Finds," NBC News, September 19, 2018, https:// www.nbcnews.com/feature/nbc-out/nolinkbetween-trans-inclusive-policiesbathroom -safety-study-findsn911106.

4. Here is a wonderful article on LGBTQ+ related stereotypes in general: Ashley Moor, "11 Stereotypes People Should Stop Believing about the LGBTQ Community," *Best Life*, April 16, 2019, https://bestlifeonline.com/worst-lgbtq-stereotypes.

5. Kimberlé Crenshaw, "The Urgency of Intersectionality," Speech given at TED-Women 2016, December 7, 2016, https://www.ted.com/talks/kimberle_crenshaw_the _urgency_of_intersectionality?language=en.

6. AAA Project Visibility, *Project Visibility* (Boulder, CO: Boulder County Area Agency on Aging, 2004), DVD.

7. Roberto Valdes, "I'm a Queer Man of Color. Here's How Intersectionality Impacts Me," *WHYY*, February 26, 2020, https://whyy.org/articles/im-a-queer-man-of -color-heres-how-intersectionality-impacts-me.

8. Sam Killermann, "You Soup: Understanding Diversity and the Intersections of Identity," It's Pronounced Metrosexual, October 2012, https://www.itspronounced metrosexual.com/2012/10/individual-difference-and-group-similiarity/.

8

GOOD TALK

The Art of Having Useful Conversations

Immerse yourself in someone else's story. Seek to understand other points of view. Learn to respond rather than react.[1]

— Scott Fearing, my friend and mentor

In this chapter, I focus on how we can have respectful and useful conversations with people who think differently from the way we do and how we can be effective agents for change. Allies are the perfect folks to be having "good talks" with others. People who are part of historically marginalized communities should not always have to be the ones doing the educating about their own communities. Allies can step in and take some of the weight off their backs. Also, people with big hearts who want to learn about the LGBTQ+ communities and how to support them are often fearful that they'll accidentally say something offensive in front of an LGBTQ+ person. For this reason, these big-hearted folks are more likely to ask questions and have candid conversations with allies than they are with members of the LGBTQ+ communities.

In the first section of this chapter, I talk about how humans learn. Next, I offer my favorite tips for having effective and worthwhile conversations with people who think differently from ourselves. Finally, I share a personal story about a night out with Lou, a man who thinks very differently from the way I do, and what I learned from him.

WE ARE ALL RESISTANT LEARNERS

Let's begin by examining how humans learn. All of us have a lump of knowledge, if you will, in our brains. This lump of knowledge is information that we have gathered over our lifetime to make sense of the world. This is stuff that we "know" to be true. I'm using quotation marks around the word "know" because the stuff in our lump of knowledge may or may not be accurate information.

Now let's look at what happens when we get a new piece of information that doesn't jibe with what we have going on in our lump of knowledge. Typically, we think about that new piece of information for a moment before dismissing it with a "nah." This is good, and this is as it should be. Think about the consequences of living in a world where everyone took new information, the second they got it, and replaced what they had known up to that point. Life would be absolute chaos.

Imagine a child trying to learn where babies come from, gathering disparate information from multiple sources.

> *Mom*: "When a mommy and a daddy love each other they kiss and make a baby." (Got it!)
> *Aunt Sophie*: "The stork drops the baby down the chimney." (Understood.)
> *Best friend's big brother*: "I heard the dad sticks the baby in the mom with his penis!" (Gross! But okay . . .)
> *Grandpa*: "You can buy 'em on Amazon, kiddo." (Wow! They really *do* sell everything.)

No, it's a wonderful thing that humans are resistant learners. We must be. There's a lot of bad information out there and we don't want to allow that stuff into our wonderful brains. We've worked hard to acquire our lump of knowledge, and we must protect it.

But let's say that over time, we continue to hear this new piece of information—perhaps in the media, perhaps during conversations with trusted and respected friends. Now we have some evidence that this new piece of information may be worth looking at more seriously. We ponder it. Perhaps we do a little research of our own. Eventually we may even decide that this new piece of information is right and valid—more right and valid even than the conflicting piece of information we've been holding in our own lump of knowledge. And then we do something amazing: We replace the old piece with the new piece.

The point is that learning is a process. Here, for your entertainment, is an embarrassing example of a time when I went through this process. You know that thing that people fill with leaves and push around their yard that looks like this?

 I managed to make it well into adulthood "knowing" that this thing was called a *wheelbarrel*. One evening over dinner, my sister Julie offered up a new piece of information: She claimed that the word was actually *wheelbarrow*. I immediately dismissed this new piece of information with a "nah." Here was my thought process: "What the heck is a barrow? Wheelbarrel makes sense! It's basically a barrel on wheels. The original wheelbarrels probably *were* literally barrels on wheels. In addition, I've lived for decades and never, to my knowledge, have I seen *wheelbarrow* written in any book, or I would have been aware of this ridiculous word. She must be wrong."

My learning process continued and included receiving affirmation from others that my sister was correct; pondering the likelihood of actually winning an argument with my sister, who is always right (super irritating, but true); and finally trudging over to the dictionary and looking the word up. (A funny side note is that when I recently shared this story with a twenty-four-year-old coworker, he also could not believe the word was *wheelbarrow* and the process started all over for him.)

Replacing information that we "know" is even harder when we've "known" it for a long period of time and when the people around us in our community also "know" it. If the people we trust (our parents, our friends, our teachers, our faith leaders, our media sources) have all taught us that being LGBTQ+ is a disease or is immoral, we are extremely unlikely to alter that assessment of LGBTQ+ people without a great deal of respectful conversation and getting to know many healthy, happy, well-adjusted, and kind LGBTQ+ people.

We should think about the conversations related to LGBTQ+ people, which we will doubtless take part in after reading this book, not as ways to change minds but as opportunities to exchange ideas and to plant seeds to ponder. This will not only help us with our messaging and tone, but it will also take the pressure off our shoulders to come up with that perfectly clear, informative, succinct, "angels singing in the background" response that will immediately change the mind of the incredibly stubborn person in front of us.

When I facilitate workshops, I'm frequently asked, "My [fill in the blank—usually a relative] is *so* homophobic! What can I say to change [his/her/their] mind?" The answer, of course, is that there *is* no one thing we can say to change someone's mind. What we *can* do is have respectful conversations where we share our thoughts and experiences in ways that open people's ears for listening to and learning from each other.

Try to avoid the common pattern of half listening, labelling the person or the behavior, then reacting. For example:

Person A: My son's teacher read his class a story about two dads. It made me uncomfortable. I'm worried my son—

Person B: OMG! Are you serious? That is *so* homophobic!

Instead, try to fully listen, ponder, then discuss. For example:

Person A: My son's teacher read his class a story about two dads. It made me uncomfortable. I'm worried my son will ask me questions about being gay or transgender and I won't know how to answer them.

Person B: Oh yeah. I get that. I also like being prepared with appropriate and well-thought-out responses when my kids ask me questions. I bet I can find some good resources for you about how to talk with your kids about LGBTQ+ people and families. Would you like me to take a look?

TIPS FOR HAVING RESPECTFUL AND USEFUL CONVERSATIONS

How do we have respectful and useful conversations with people who have opposing views and beliefs? Over the years, I've compiled a list of the most effective tips for having conversations in a way that everyone involved is less likely to get defensive and more likely to be open to new ideas. The first two tips are what I refer to as "prep work." They're best done before you begin the conversation. The final eight are tips to use while you're having your good talk.[2]

Put Yourself in the Hot Seat (Prep Work)

As you prepare for your good talk, think for a moment about your experiences as a learner. Ask yourself: If I'm the person whose lump of knowledge is being challenged, what will shut me down to the conversation and what will open my ears to new thoughts and ideas?

Think about a time when someone called you out on something you said or did—in other words, you said or did something that someone else found offensive and they brought it to your attention. Was the interaction effective? What worked and what didn't work in this interaction? When I ask participants in my workshops to answer this second question, I typically get a list that looks like this:

Didn't Work
Yelling
Calling me out in front of a bunch of people
Blasting me on social media
Labelling me and/or the behavior/comment (e.g., racist, sexist, homophobic)

Worked
Focusing on why the comment made them unhappy
Speaking to me in private
Sharing that they'd made a similar mistake once too (i.e., making themselves
   vulnerable)
Making it clear that they were having the conversation with me because they
   valued our relationship
Making it clear that they had faith in me that I would want to know and do
   better

When we yell, shame people in public, or label people or behaviors, we create a situation where the other person is likely to respond by becoming defensive and offended. Their ears are likely to close to anything else you have to say.
How would you respond if someone yelled at you for being homophobic? Put
yourself in the hot seat and focus on better ways to educate others.

Set Your Listen/Share Dial to at Least 50/50 (Prep Work)

Some good talks, like the one I describe at the end of this chapter, are simply
an opportunity for people to listen and learn from each other. Others, where
we have some information to impart, are more of an intervention, for example,
when someone uses an outdated word and we're suggesting better language
choices. In either situation, our listen/share dial should be set to at least 50/50.
In other words, even in situations where we've got some information to impart
(i.e., an intervention), we should be talking only about half the time.

I'm sure most of you have heard that, during interventions, the main focus of
the conversation should be on the impact of people's comments or behaviors,
not their intent, and I agree. However, that doesn't mean that the impact needs
to be the only thing that's focused on. Be kind to the person you're speaking
with and allow them the opportunity to share their perspective, ask questions,
and express their intent. There's a reason why people's first response after being told that they did something offensive is often, "Oh my gosh! I didn't mean
it that way!" Big-hearted people instinctively want to let others know that they

didn't mean to hurt anyone with their language or their behaviors. Allow them space and time to say it.

Assume Goodwill

If a person uses an icky, outdated term or makes a comment that rubs you the wrong way, assume that they didn't intend to be hurtful. This simple assumption will take you so very far in your efforts to have respectful conversations. In fact, it's the founding principle on which all of my educational efforts are built. Assuming that the person has simply not gotten the memo on the most updated and respectful terms—which is most likely true—will set the tone for a wonderful interaction.

"Assume goodwill" has developed a bad reputation, and that's because it's often misinterpreted. Keep in mind that assuming goodwill should not take the place of important conversations; it simply sets the tone for important conversations. Assuming goodwill should never be used to excuse disrespectful behaviors or rationalize hurtful comments. It's not a free pass for a person to say and do whatever they want because they "didn't mean it that way." Your conversations should still focus mainly on the impact of people's words and actions rather than the intent. But assuming that the person didn't mean to be hurtful will set a kind and respectful tone that is more likely to open their ears to new ideas and concepts.

This approach is very personal to me. I became an active ally in 2003 knowing almost nothing about the LGBTQ+ communities. I used the wrong terms. I asked inappropriate questions. I messed up spectacularly. My twenty years of professional work as an ally to the LGBTQ+ communities would never have happened if people had not assumed that I had good intentions and that I just didn't know any better.

For an entertaining and impactful video about assuming goodwill, check out Ash Beckham's TED talk *We're All Hiding Something. Let's Find the Courage to Open Up.*[3]

Avoid Labelling the Comment or Behavior

Many social justice educators agree that labelling people (e.g., "You're transphobic") is not an effective way to get people to listen or change their behavior. The popular solution seems to be to label the behavior instead (e.g., "What you just said was transphobic"). I'm going to go one step further and suggest that we don't label anything at all.

Let's imagine you and I are having lunch and I say, "That's so gay!" Unless I am talking about the upcoming Pride parade, that comment is not cool. If you now say to me, "That comment was homophobic," most likely I'll get super defensive and the conversation will veer off on a tangent about why the comment was or wasn't homophobic rather than focusing on the real issue at hand, which is that the comment made you feel yucky.

HELPFUL HINT

If you just said to yourself, "Ugh. This woman is being way too sensitive. No one means 'That's so gay' in a hurtful way," I hope you will take a look at the five-and-a-half-minute video, also by Ash Beckham, called "I Am SO GAY."[4] If it does nothing else, it's sure to make you literally LOL.

Use "I" Statements

One of the ways you can focus the conversation on what's important—the impact the comment had on you—is to use "I" statements or other language that focuses on you and how the comment made you feel. A possible response to "That's so gay" is, "I would love it if you used a different word. I'm sure you didn't mean it in a hurtful way" (like how I squeezed in the "assume goodwill" tip?) "but it upsets me when people use the word *gay* in a negative way like that. Maybe you could say, 'That's so pathetic' instead."

HELPFUL HINT

"I think you're being an idiot" is, in fact, an "I" statement, but it's not really what I had in mind.

Start with a Connecting Statement

People are more likely to open their ears to conversations when there's no power dynamic present. If you're able to start the conversation in a way that feels like two people who are equals, problem solving together, you'll be more successful than if you present yourself as the expert with knowledge to impart. Starting conversations with connecting statements is a great way to get rid of the power dynamic.

If you've ever accidentally messed up someone's pronouns, been resistant to changing your language to more inclusive terms, or told a joke that, as it turned out, was hurtful instead of funny, this is a great time to bring it up. Sharing this information will put you and the person you're talking with on the same level. For example: "You know, I used to say, 'That's so gay' all the time, too. Then a friend said something to me that made me stop and think about what I was saying." Or "I accidentally used their old pronoun last week, too, and I felt terrible! Can I share some tips with you that have been helping me get it right?"

If you've never messed up in the same way, you can still find common ground with someone by acknowledging that it's hard to keep up with changes in language and terminology. For example, you might start a conversation with this connecting statement: "I know this stuff can be super confusing."

Educate with Examples, Not Definitions

Using concrete examples and personal stories are incredibly effective ways to help people grasp new concepts. Let's look at how we might explain the difference between equality and equity to someone. We can offer a dictionary definition of the two terms. For example, "Equality means everyone is getting the same things or being treated the same, but this will create fairness only if everyone has started in the same place and has the same needs. Equity is about giving individuals what they need to succeed or to live happily." Or, we can give an example of how the two concepts can play out in the world. For example, "Equality is handing every soldier a pair of size 10 boots."

"Equity is handing every soldier a pair of boots that fits their feet."

I've used examples and personal stories throughout this book to help explain concepts. In chapter 2, I could have simply written about why new terms and identity words are so important. Instead, I shared Dee's story about her finding her identity term and the enormous impact it had on her understanding of herself and her ability to live authentically. This was the story that really made the light bulb go off for me as I was trying to understand this concept. Our instinct may be to share dictionary definitions of concepts, but concrete examples and personal stories (our own or those of other people who have given us permission to share them) are often the most effective tools for education.

For an outstanding example of using a story to explain a concept, take a look at the three-minute YouTube video "Sometimes You're a Caterpillar" by

Francesca Ramsey (aka Chescaleigh). She explains the concept of "privilege" using snails, caterpillars, a rockin' bug party, and lots of humor.[5]

Try the "Switch It" Technique

Remember the "switch it" technique, the self-coaching tool that we learned about in chapters 3 and 6? Well, the "switch it" technique is also a great tool for helping to educate others. Imagine a friend is struggling with a workplace situation: an employee doesn't want to share an office with a gay colleague, and your friend doesn't know how to handle it. Try switching it to a situation with an identity where your friend *does* know how they would handle it. What if this employee said they didn't feel comfortable sharing an office with a Black colleague, or a Muslim colleague, or a Deaf colleague? If they know how they would handle that situation, you can assure them that they have the tools they need to handle the LGBTQ+ concern.

A few years ago, in an Upstate New York school district, a father met with a high school principal to demand that his son be removed from a class that was taught by a gay teacher. The principal picked up a piece of paper and a pen and said, "Let's see. What if the teacher is a person of color? Is that okay? What if the teacher is Jewish? Is that okay?" And then he crumpled up the piece of paper and said, "Nope. We're not doing this. Your son is in that class." This story has a beautiful ending: The gay teacher ended up being the boy's all-time favorite teacher and the father later returned to thank the principal for what he had done.

Listen for Those Myths and Stereotypes

We read about the impact of LGBTQ+ myths and stereotypes in chapter 7. Well, now is our opportunity to listen for them and address them. Hidden within people's concerns about LGBTQ+ people are often myths, stereotypes, and misinformation.

Let's look again at the situation where a father doesn't want his son being taught by a gay teacher. If this father brings his concern to you and you respond by saying, "Huh. I don't feel that way. I wouldn't have a problem with my son being taught by a gay teacher," that shows support for the LGBTQ+ communities but does not actually address the underlying concern.

A better approach is to create a judgment-free space where this father can share his concerns with you. A neat trick I learned while getting my master's degree in social work is that people get more defensive if you start a question with "Why" than they do if you start with any other question word. So rather than, "Why would you say that?" try, "What makes you say that?" Or you can simply say, "I'd love to hear a little more about your concerns."

If you're successful and you've created an environment where this father is willing to share his concerns, then you will probably hear that this man's lump of knowledge includes some—or many—myths and stereotypes about gay men. Perhaps he truly believes that gay men are prone to pedophilia, are bad role models for boys, are out to recruit boys into the gay "lifestyle," are extremely promiscuous, or a combination of all of these.

Now you have a choice. You can think to yourself, "Zowie! This guy is a flaming homophobe!" Or you can empathize and admit to yourself that this man is doing exactly what a parent should do: He's being protective of his child and trying to keep his child safe in what he perceives to be a potentially dangerous situation. Thinking of this man as a good and caring father who just has some misinformation—instead of as a homophobic bonehead—is the best way to ensure that your tone is respectful.

Utilizing the tips above, you can now move into a respectful, nonjudgmental conversation where you both exchange your thoughts and experiences. This father can share where he has gotten his information about gay men and you can share your own experiences and information. If you've had good experiences with gay teachers, share those personal experiences. If you've done your homework and you have some myth-busting data to whip out of your savvy ally goody bag, share that.

You won't have all of the facts available for every myth, stereotype, or misunderstanding you run up against, so don't feel like you have to before you can go out into the world and have conversations. We all learn as we go. Continue to educate yourself and become familiar with the facts, and don't be afraid to return to a conversation later when you feel better informed.

Be Aware of Your Hot Buttons

We are not robots. We are humans. We will have emotional reactions to comments and questions, and we need to be aware of this fact and forgive ourselves. Hot-button issues are those comments or questions that get us especially riled up, heated, angry, and tongue-tied. When our hot buttons are pressed, we're less likely to assume goodwill and more likely to respond with anger and sarcasm.

Knowing which questions and topics are personal hot buttons for you is an important step toward being an effective educator. Once you're aware of your hot buttons, you can practice appropriate responses when you're calm and in your own space. If you're not yet aware of your hot buttons and a comment or question arises that causes the steam to pour from your nose and ears, a good strategy is to buy yourself some time. You might say something like, "I need to ponder that for a bit. I'll get back to you," or, "Ooooh! Pizza! Hold that thought. I'll be back in a few!"

I've been known to come back to conversations weeks later, with statements like, "Hey—remember that conversation we had a few weeks ago where you were asking me why there isn't a Straight Pride parade? Well, I've been pondering that, and I came up with a few thoughts." (Not sure how *you* would respond to this question? See chapter 9 for more on addressing common questions.)

I also firmly believe that there are no expiration dates on apologies. I've come back months later to conversations that are weighing heavily on my mind so that I could offer apologies where I may have messed up or responded too heatedly. I can't think of a single time when one of my belated apologies didn't end in a wonderful conversation and a stronger relationship.

A NIGHT OUT WITH LOU THE LUNCHROOM AIDE

Several years ago, I was facilitating a workshop for a group of school lunchroom aides. It was a mandatory training for them, so I went into it knowing that I wouldn't necessarily be preaching to the choir. Partway through the presentation, a man—whom I'll call Lou—raised his hand and asked a question. His manner was so quiet and calm that it took me a moment to realize that he was an unhappy camper. Essentially his question to me was, "You've just come into my space to share your agenda and your beliefs. Now may I come into your space at the LGBTQ+ center to share my agenda and beliefs as a Christian man?"

How did I respond to Lou, my respectful but unhappy camper?

1. I took a deep breath. I dislike conflict, and taking a deep breath always helps me relax.
2. I thanked him. I told him that I appreciated his honesty, and I said that he probably wasn't the only person in the room who felt that way or who had those concerns.
3. I reassured him that I wasn't there to try to force anyone to change their beliefs. We all come together at school or work from very different backgrounds and with different beliefs, and we must all work together in a respectful way.

POP QUIZ

Select all statements that are true.

A. Christians are anti-LGBTQ+.
B. All religions and faith communities are anti-LGBTQ+.
C. Many religions and faith communities welcome and support LGBTQ+ individuals.
D. You cannot be LGBTQ+ and also be religious.

Answer: C

It's a harmful myth that all religions and faith communities are anti-LGBTQ+. Many religions and faith communities, including Christians, have created wonderfully welcoming and affirming spaces for LGBTQ+ individuals and their families. One thing that really surprised me when I first began my work as an ally was how many LGBTQ+ people were people of faith and were very active in their faith communities. It's true that some religions have anti-LGBTQ+ beliefs, but not all do, and many are becoming more inclusive with time.

4. I clarified what my agenda was: that I was working toward making our schools safe and welcoming for everyone. This meant that schools must be safe and welcoming for the kid who has two moms *and* for the kid whose parents are teaching them that being gay is a sin. Lunchroom aides, other school staff, teachers, and administrators need to create a space where both of those children feel safe and respected, and they need the tools to do that. That was my agenda.

My response did what I hoped it would do. Lou and I continued to talk about this topic for a few minutes, modelling a respectful and professional exchange. Although Lou and I felt very differently about LGBTQ+ people, through our conversation we were able to find some common ground. We agreed that we both wanted schools to be safe places for all children.

When the workshop was over, I did something I'd never done before: I invited a participant (Lou) out to dinner. I was impressed that Lou had sat through my workshop feeling uncomfortable and annoyed that he was being forced to attend and yet had been so incredibly respectful in his response to me. He didn't yell or show anger in any way. This was someone I wanted to spend more time with. I rarely get a chance to talk with people who are opposed to the work that I do and who are willing to share their reasons in a calm and respectful way. I suspected that Lou and I could manage to have a pretty cool conversation, given the chance.

Lou was uncomfortable with the idea of dinner with me, he confessed to me later, so he went to his priest for advice about whether to accept the invitation or not. His priest told him he saw no harm in it, so a few weeks later Lou and I met at the Cheesecake Factory for dinner and a chat. This evening stands out as one of the most memorable moments of my career in LGBTQ+ education.

Here are the tips for having respectful and useful conversations that I utilized during our dinner:

Set Your Listen/Share Dial to At Least 50/50: Heading into the conversation I set my listen/share dial at about 70/30. I was not there to "educate" Lou. I had already had my opportunity to do that during the workshop. I was there to listen and learn.

Assume Goodwill: This one was easy to do. Lou had already demonstrated respectful behavior in the workshop, had shared his interest in keeping children safe, and had accepted my dinner invitation, which meant that he was interested in having a meaningful conversation. It was clear to me he was a decent fellow who wanted good things for the world.

Avoid Labelling the Comment or Behavior: This also was not a problem to accomplish. Imagine how poorly this conversation would have gone had I told Lou that he and/or his comments were homophobic and transphobic?

Use "I" Statements: "I" statements were used well by both of us. Neither one made sweeping generalizations about what the LGBTQ+ communities or all Christians have to say about this topic. We kept things personal by sharing our own thoughts and beliefs.

Start with a Connecting Statement: I was surprised by how often during our conversation I was honestly able to say things like, "I feel that way too." Lou and I had a shocking amount in common.

Listen for Those Myths and Stereotypes: Lou had brought with him the myth that LGBTQ+ people (and apparently even straight cisgender allies) have an "agenda" that involves recruiting and indoctrinating children. He believed that my objective was to talk with elementary school children about sex. (The confusion over orientation and intimate behaviors rears its ugly head again.) He came right out and stated these concerns, so it was easy to address them.

I succeeded in my goal of listening about 70 percent of the time and talking only 30 percent. Once he got warmed up, Lou did most of the talking that evening and I learned quite a bit from him. Here are some key things that I took away from this educational opportunity:

- I needed to be more careful with my language and clarify my goals with audiences, especially when attendance was required and I knew there would be people in the room who did not want to be there.
- I could have made a bigger effort to welcome everyone at the beginning of the workshop, regardless of their backgrounds and beliefs, and acknowledge that some folks might be uncomfortable with the topic.
- Although I did state that all questions were welcome throughout my presentation, I may have been able to create an even more effective workshop had I specifically said, "regardless of your opinions and beliefs."

Lou told me that he also got quite a bit out of the dinner conversation and that he left feeling more comfortable with the work that our agency was doing in the local schools. And I was right—neither of us raised our voices or got angry. In fact, it was such an enjoyable dinner that, as we hugged good-bye, Lou said he would welcome another opportunity to get together and talk.

Probably the biggest takeaway for me was that we had so much in common! We both wanted many of the same things for our children and for our world; we were just coming at it from different places. And rest assured that no lumps of knowledge were harmed during this dinner. I'm pretty sure that neither of us budged an inch on our core beliefs—we are resistant learners, after all—but we both left with some major respect for the other person and a much better understanding of where the other person was coming from. And who knows what potential seeds of change we planted in each other?

AN ALLY'S GIFT

If done well, with patience and an "assume goodwill" attitude, allies can offer the gift of good talks to others. We can provide a nonjudgmental space where people can share ideas, ask foolish questions, use outdated words, and mess up royally without feeling like jerks. Our small, under-$10 gift is imparting information that we have that someone else might not, but our big, full-paycheck gift is creating a space where we can listen and share without anyone feeling shamed or judged—something we need a whole lot more of in this world.

NOTES

1. Scott Fearing, personal correspondence, November 1, 2022.

2. Many of these tips originally came from Scott Fearing's work at OutFront Minnesota and his *Successful GLBT Education: A Manual* (Minneapolis: OutFront Minnesota, 1996).

3. Ash Beckham, "We're All Hiding Something. Let's Find the Courage to Open Up," TED, February 21, 2014, https://www.youtube.com/watch?v=uq83lU6nuS8&ab_channel=TED.

4. Ash Beckham, "Ash Beckham at Ignite Boulder 20," filmed March 2, 2013, at Ignite Conference, Boulder, CO, YouTube, https://www.youtube.com/watch?v=Gxs78C3XGok.

5. Chescaleigh, "Sometimes You're a Caterpillar," YouTube, March 24, 2015, https://www.youtube.com/watch?v=hRiWgx4sHGg&ab_channel=chescaleigh.

Part III

TAKING ACTION TO CREATE MORE INCLUSIVE SPACES

9

STRAIGHT PRIDE PARADES AND SPECIAL SNOWFLAKES

Addressing Common Questions

Instead of wondering why there isn't a straight Pride, be grateful you have never needed one. Celebrate with us.[1]

—Anthony Venn-Brown

During my twenty years as an LGBTQ+ educator, some questions that participants have asked me have taken me by surprise, such as:

Do you think that homosexuality is caused by aluminum cans?

Does your husband know you're a lesbian?

One of my favorites was from a participant at a diversity conference who wandered into my Power of the Ally training and asked:

Aren't we going to be talking about military strategies?

Other questions are extremely common and seem to come up again and again. As allies, we should be familiar with these common questions and be prepared with appropriate responses. Following are ten very common questions that are well worth your savvy ally time to become familiar with, as well as some suggested responses.

I JUST TREAT EVERYONE THE SAME; WHAT'S WRONG WITH THAT?

Lots of folks think that if they're treating everyone the same then they're putting in enough work toward creating an inclusive world. They feel that they don't need to learn about different groups of people in order to be fair and just. This comment is similar to, "I don't see color." Both are hot-button comments for many people within marginalized communities. What a great opportunity for an ally! We are in a prime position to step in, assume goodwill, meet people where they are, share what we know, and offer them a safe place to figure it all out.

An excellent place for an ally to begin when we hear this question is to take a deep breath and remember that it's coming from a kind place. The people I've talked with who have asked this question are folks who think that treating everyone the same is the best way to fix an unfair and biased world. Our job is to thank them for their kindness and their commitment to making the world a better place, and then to help them learn an even better way.

Explaining the difference between equality and equity can be a useful next step. You might want to use the concrete example of the soldiers and the boots that I used in chapter 8. What these big-hearted folks are doing by "treating everyone the same" is like handing every soldier a pair of size 10 boots.

Once the concept of equality versus equity is understood, I typically offer an example of "treating everyone the same" within an LGBTQ+ context, like this one. When I go into a medical office, I get handed a form to fill out, just like everyone else (equality). As a straight, cisgender, married, monogamous woman, I typically breeze through that form without any issues. Basically, I'm the soldier with the size 10 feet. If I were a lesbian trans woman in a polyamorous relationship, that form may not fit for me. If the form requires me to check an *M* or *F* box, I wouldn't know how to respond. I would wonder if the medical provider was asking for my biological sex or my gender. Either way this medical provider wouldn't be getting a complete picture of who I am. If the form requires me to circle my relationship status, and the options are the typical *married*, *single*, *divorced*, *widowed*, or *separated*, I wouldn't see my relationship status represented. This medical facility is treating everyone the same by handing them the same form, but the form doesn't actually fit for lots of people. When we look hard at what "treating everyone the same" means, we often discover that it means that we're treating everyone as if they're white, straight, cisgender, monogamous, hearing, non-disabled, and middle to upper class.

The second way an ally can approach this topic with someone who feels good about treating everyone the same is to help the person understand that individuals have different identities, beliefs, abilities, experiences, and needs, and they don't necessarily *want* to be treated the same as everyone else. The way I make this concept personal is to offer examples of how I treat my friends when they come over for dinner. When Mike comes over, I make sure there are nut-free food options, since he has a nut allergy. When Todd comes over, I try to keep the number of guests small, because he's Deaf and it's very hard for him to follow the conversation in large groups. When Owen and Sara come over with their little boys, I put out toys. And when Pam comes over, I make darn sure the whiskey bottle is full. I *never* treat my friends the same. Different behaviors on my part make their time at my house much more enjoyable.

WHY DO LGBTQ+ PEOPLE HAVE TO FLAUNT THEIR SEXUALITY AND GET IN MY FACE WITH IT?

My approach to answering this question typically starts by assessing what the asker means by the word *flaunt* and in what ways the alleged flaunter is being offensive. *Flaunting* is typically defined as parading or displaying something ostentatiously. I can think of several reasons why someone might actually flaunt or be falsely accused of flaunting their LGBTQ+ identity, and my reply will depend on the asker's response.

The Falsely Accused Flaunter

Sometimes it may seem as if a person is "flaunting" or "in your face" with their identity, but in fact they are doing no such thing. The offended person may simply have a double standard. My friend and mentor Scott (to whom I have dedicated this book) tells a story about when he moved from rural Minnesota to northern New Jersey. Suddenly everyone seemed to be "in his face" with their Jewish faith. He says that his "ears were bent out of shape" because he was hearing all these new words (like gefilte fish) and new holidays (like Rosh Hashanah), and it felt like people were inappropriately flaunting their faith and beliefs. With time, he realized that these folks were doing nothing different from what the folks back in his hometown did when they talked about Christmas, Easter, and potlucks at their local church. His ears were simply not used to hearing these new terms. The same can be true for some folks when they first hear men referring to their boyfriends or husbands and women referring to their girlfriends or wives.

Let's say a coworker asks a colleague what she did over the weekend, and she responds, "My girlfriend and I went to a *Star Trek* convention." The coworker may be thinking, "Yeesh! All I did was try to make polite conversation and she has to go and throw her sexual orientation in my face." However, if the colleague had said, "My boyfriend and I went to a *Star Trek* convention," this coworker would very likely have moved past this comment and onto bigger and better things, like offering up the Vulcan salute. This woman isn't flaunting her sexuality by answering the question the way she did. She's simply being authentic in the workplace and refusing to lie or switch pronouns for a coworker's comfort. She is a falsely accused flaunter.

The Temporary Flaunter

If the person is newly out and is actually full-on flaunting their identity (e.g., decorating their cubicle with rainbow streamers and talking incessantly about being LGBTQ+), it's possible they're in the identity pride stage, discussed in chapter 3. Remember how in that stage, the LGBTQ+ individual is finally out and authentic and it feels *so* frickin' good? This is the stage where a person might actually be a bit "in your face" with their LGBTQ+ identity—and, in my humble opinion, they deserve it! They've had to hide who they are for so long and it feels fantastic to be out. A little parading and ostentatious displaying are warranted, and a bit of patience on everyone else's part is ideal.

The savvy ally can help others understand why this individual might be super enthusiastic about their LGBTQ+ identity and excited about announcing it to the world. Personal examples are great. You might say something like, "I can't even imagine what it would be like to have to hide who I was or feel shame about my identity. What would that even be like, to have to constantly lie about who you live with and what you did over the weekend? It would be difficult to believe that there was nothing wrong with me. If and when I finally had the courage to break free from all of that and live authentically, holy cow! I'd be throwing rainbow confetti in *everyone's* faces! Let's just be happy for [fill in name of flaunty friend] and let them celebrate."

The Full-Time Flaunter

Hallelujah for full-time flaunters! What badass people they are. What I really want to do for the person who is bothered by the full-time flaunter is hand them the book *Covering: The Hidden Assault on our Civil Rights*, by Kenji Yoshino.[2] It's brilliant. Please read it. I especially like this quote from Yoshino's book. It's a mother's response to her trip to Fire Island with her gay son. She observed that gay men "must feel really suppressed in straight culture to need to flaunt so much when they were free of it."[3]

Covering is a strategy that people use to downplay a disfavored trait or identity in order to fit in or be better accepted into society. Some great questions to ask and possibly even ponder ourselves are: Is our full-time flaunty friend actually flaunting or are they simply refusing to cover? When we talk about wanting to live in a world where everyone can be authentic in all aspects of their lives, do we really mean it? How authentic is too authentic? Are we placing more value on lesbians, gay men, and bisexual/pansexual individuals who are more mainstream or "straight acting" than we are on those who are more exuberant, flamboyant, or obvious? Are we placing more value on trans folks who fit into society's gender binary than we are on trans folks who are nonbinary and/or androgynous in their gender expression?

Full-time flaunters are brave pioneers paving the way toward a healthier and more accepting world. Support them and help others understand and recognize them as the extraordinary people that they are.

HELPFUL HINT

How can you distinguish between the temporary flaunter and the full-time flaunter? You probably can't. Err on the side of the person being a full-time flaunter and revere them for being an audacious badass.

I *KNOW* MY FRIEND IS GAY—HOW CAN I GET HIM TO COME OUT TO ME?

You can't. No one can or should drag anyone kicking and screaming out of the closet. Remember the snail in the shell? The snail is only hiding because the outside world feels hostile and unsafe. What you *can* do is create safe and inclusive spaces with your language and your actions that make it clear to your friend that if they do come out you will support them 100 percent. Here are some ways that you can do that:

- Always use inclusive language when speaking and writing, for example, "Are you seeing anyone special?" rather than "Do you have a girlfriend?"

- Get "caught" watching or reading something that's so gay (in that real way)! Subscribe to an LGBTQ+ magazine or publication and leave it on your coffee table. Read books with LGBTQ+ themes and keep them on your bookshelf in a highly visible area. Suggest a movie with LGBTQ+ themes the next time you go out. Strategically place *The Savvy Ally*, with its glorious rainbow stripes, on your desk at work.
- Express your opinion when LGBTQ+ topics come up. This can be as simple as saying something like, "I really feel like we need to do a better job making this country safe and inclusive for LGBTQ+ people. There's still a lot of work to be done."
- Wear a pin or T-shirt with a big, fat rainbow on it!

All four of these tips are wonderful ways for us to stay up to date on LGBTQ+ culture and language and/or show the world that we're welcoming and inclusive, so do them all the time. Don't implement them only when your one particular friend who you think might be gay is around. And keep in mind that you may be wrong about your friend. Remember, gaydar is unreliable. But you're an ally! Go ahead and flaunt it! Maybe your "gay" friend—who, as it turns out, isn't really gay—will become an active ally too.

AREN'T WE IN A GOOD PLACE NOW WITH LGBTQ+ RIGHTS AND INCLUSION? WHAT'S LEFT TO DO?

Sadly, this question, which was common at the time *The Savvy Ally* was first published in 2020, is now much less common. With the recent wave of anti-LGBTQ+ legislation in the United States seeking to deny transgender youth of health care and restrict conversations about LGBTQ+ people and families in the classroom, most folks currently understand that there's a lot left to do. If, however, you want to share some horrific facts with folks who are interested in knowing about the current state of LGBTQ+ rights in the United States and globally, here you go:

- LGBTQ+ individuals don't have legal protections in place on a federal level in the United States. Only about half of the states specifically prohibit discrimination based on sexual orientation and gender in housing and public accommodations.[4]

- In 35 percent of the states, it's legal to refuse service or deny entry to LG-BTQ+ people in such public places as stores, restaurants, parks, hotels, doctors' offices, and banks.[5]
- As of April 2022, a record-breaking number of anti-LGBTQ+ bills (325) have been proposed in the United States.[6]
- Out of the nearly 200 countries that make up our world, same-sex intercourse, unions, and expression are illegal in 69 of them, and same-sex marriage is legal in fewer than 30.
- In some countries being LGBTQ+ is a crime punishable by arrest or in some cases even death.[7]

Be familiar with the legal rights and protections in your state or country. *Wikipedia* has a very useful page called "LGBT Rights by Country or Territory" that will help you find the most updated information.[8] To stay abreast of current anti-LGBTQ+ legislation in the United States, check out the American Civil Liberties Union's frequently updated webpage called "Legislation Affecting LGBTQ Rights across the Country."[9]

Sharing information about current rights for LGBTQ+ people is what I call a "big picture" response. A personal response can also work well to answer this question. The way I offer a personal response is by sharing some examples of stuff I can do and things that I don't have to worry about as a straight cisgender person that aren't true for my LGBTQ+ friends. A few examples are:

- I can find a restroom to pee in safely and conveniently anywhere that restroom facilities are provided.
- My husband and I can hold hands and walk almost anywhere in the world without fearing for our safety because of this display of affection.
- In an emergency medical situation, I know I won't have to hide who I am, worry about being treated disrespectfully, or worry about not being treated at all because of my sexual orientation, gender identity, or gender expression.
- When I was growing up, I saw straight cisgender people like me represented constantly in the school curriculum, in books, and in movies.

Another way to offer a personal response is to share LGBTQ+ people's experiences, either ones that are public or that you have permission to share. Here is a LinkedIn post from Inclusivity Expert Nate (Spierer) Shalev, talking about photographs they've posted of their vacation with their wife.

What you see: my wife and I having a really great time on a road trip.

What you don't see: the hours of research that went into each stop to prepare to travel as a queer and trans couple. We had a checklist to answer questions like:

- Does this state have protections against LGBTQ discrimination?
- Is this hotel LGBTQ friendly?
- Is it safe for me to go to the bathroom at this rest stop?
- If I get hurt here, will they treat me at the local hospital?[10]

These are the smaller daily realities that help people understand the work that still needs to happen to create a world that is safer and more inclusive for LGBTQ+ people. A good ally exercise is to move through your day and ask yourself, How would this situation be different if I were [fill in the blank: a trans woman of color, a Blind gay man, a sixteen-year-old asexual boy, etc.]? Use those examples to highlight things you can do with ease that others can't.

WHY ISN'T THERE A STRAIGHT PRIDE PARADE?

This topic is so very important for allies to understand and know how to address. It can present itself in a variety of ways. People have asked:

Why are LGBTQ+ people such special snowflakes?
Why should LGBTQ+ people get special rights?
Where's *my* special safe space?

The sentiment behind all of these questions is pretty much the same. Why are we focusing on one group of overly sensitive people? What makes them more important than the rest of us?

Here are just a few of the many realities of living life as an LGBTQ+ person. These reality checks may help people understand why the LGBTQ+ population has a greater need than the general public for identified safe spaces or a loud and proud Pride parade.

Reality Check #1

"Straight Pride" happens every day. What I mean by that is straight cisgender people see themselves represented constantly. I've never doubted that straight cisgender people have invented cool stuff, created awesome art, built tall buildings, and won Pulitzer Prizes. The average child working their way through a typical K–12 school system might get the impression that no LGBTQ+ person has ever done anything of consequence or contributed anything to our society. LGBTQ+ people in general don't see themselves represented in our school curricula. It's still difficult to find good, positive representations of LGBTQ+ individuals in mainstream media, films, news, or books. There's no White History Month or Non-Disabled Pride for the same reason. Once a year, at Pride—for those lucky enough to live in a city where it's celebrated—LGBTQ+ individuals get to see people like themselves being out and proud and celebrating their existence. Cheers to that!

Reality Check #2

I received my master's degree in social work in 1992. I found it interesting that in my diversity course, LGBTQ+ individuals were never discussed. But hey—that was 1992. Well, guess what? In 2016, I was facilitating a workshop in California and I had a young woman in my session who had just finished her master's degree in social work, and she told me that the same had been true for her! Diversity in her 2016 social work master's program had meant race, ethnicity, ability, class, and religion, but not LGBTQ+ identities. Even in diversity and inclusion conversations, LGBTQ+ people are often left out. Therefore, general statements like, "We do not discriminate," or, "Everyone is welcome here," might actually come with the unwritten subtext: "except for LGBTQ+ people." When LGBTQ+ individuals walk into a health clinic, counseling center, school, shop, or place of worship, they look for more than general diversity statements. They look for safe zone or safe space stickers, LGBTQ+ images on the walls, LGBTQ+ magazines in the waiting area, and visible nondiscrimination statements and policies that specifically mention LGBTQ+ people. They can't otherwise be certain that general promises to value diversity really apply to them.

Reality Check #3

LGBTQ+ people are not seeking special rights; they're seeking human rights that others already have. Discrimination is very real, and unfortunately it's still legal in many states and in many countries. Fighting for legal protections people don't have doesn't make them "special snowflakes." It also doesn't make someone like me, with my legal rights fully in place, less important—and it doesn't threaten my rights.

Reality Check #4

When a child or teenager is bullied at school for being different, in most cases they can seek comfort and support at home. If the bullying is about race, religion, or ethnicity, their parents may have experienced the same kind of bullying when they were in school, and they may have some helpful suggestions for their child on how to deal with it. But with LGBTQ+ children and teens, parents can sometimes be the main source of the stress and harm. LGBTQ+ children and teens are often in a unique situation where they truly feel like they have no one to turn to. As I mentioned earlier, the suicide and attempted suicide rates for LGBTQ+ individuals, especially for transgender people, are significantly higher than those for straight cisgender people. Having identified safe people and places for LGBTQ+ people literally saves lives.

APPARENTLY, I'M *CISGENDER*. HOW CAN I BE SOMETHING THAT I'VE NEVER HEARD OF? DO I HAVE TO GO AROUND TELLING PEOPLE I'M *CISGENDER* NOW?

Besides writing and offering workshops on LGBTQ+ inclusion and effective allyship, I also create fun, short videos with savvy ally tips and post them on YouTube. (Please subscribe to my website at www.savvyallyaction.com if you'd like to receive them once a month in your inbox.) In December of 2021, under my video called *What's Up with* Cisgender? I found this comment: "Before 2013 I was considered a WOMAN. I'm not cis. I don't care what Latin or the dictionary has to say. I am a WOMAN. What other people call themselves is none of my business." When people feel as if they're being labelled or defined by others, they can get pretty annoyed. And I completely understand that.

I remember the first time I heard the word *neurotypical*. *Neurotypical*, for those who aren't familiar with this term, describes people with typical neurological developmental or functioning. It's also defined as people who aren't *neurodiverse* (i.e., who aren't on the autism spectrum and who don't have any other developmental differences). I'm neurotypical and I was even before there was a word for being this way. But, when I first heard this word, I thought to myself, "Really? Now this? Do I have to use this term now to identify myself?" So, I completely understand why some people balk at the term *cisgender* and are resistant to the idea of using it.

As I look closely at my initial reaction to the word *neurotypical*, I can break it down into three areas of concern that arose for me and some coinciding emotions.

1. How can I be something that I don't even know about and why does someone else get to define me? (Confused/Irritated)
2. Is this new word really "a thing" or will it be gone next month? (Skeptical)
3. My list of identity terms seems to be constantly growing. Which ones do I have to share in order to be respectful? (Overwhelmed)

Let's examine these questions and emotional reactions individually and look at ways to get past these barriers. This may help you personally, if you've found yourself having similar reactions to new norm-busting terms that apply to you. It should also give you some strategies for ways to help other potential allies embrace new terms that give a name to the majority population.

How Can I Be Something That I Don't Even Know about and Why Does Someone Else Get to Define Me? (Confused/Irritated)

Rest assured that no one gets to define you. No one can force you to identify in a specific way. You get to choose which identity terms you use for yourself and in what contexts it makes sense to use them. (More on this below.) However, it's important to keep in mind that the folks who make statements like, "I'm just human" or "I don't believe in labels" tend to be the folks who fit into the expected societal norms (i.e., straight, cisgender, white, non-disabled, hearing, etc.). Typically, these folks don't need identity terms for others to make the correct assumptions about them. For example, I never need to educate others about the fact that I'm a hearing person. Strangers talk to me all the time in line at the grocery store or they lean out of their car window and ask me for directions. They assume I can hear and they're correct. There's no need for me to walk around sharing that I'm hearing. *I* can "just be human."

It's much more difficult to move through the world without using any identity terms when the world is set up in ways that make false assumptions about you or excludes you. Identity terms are necessary for folks who aren't in the majority (i.e., Deaf folks, LGBTQ+ folks, neurodiverse folks) in order for them to be included, get their needs met, and gain access to spaces and events.

But why do folks who are in the majority need new identity terms? Norm-busting words like *cisgender* and *neurotypical* help us move away from thinking about people as either "normal" or "different," or worse, thinking about people as either "normal" or "deviant." Norm-busting words help us understand that transgender, cisgender, neurodiverse, and neurotypical are just different ways to be.

Is This New Word Really "a Thing" or Will It Be Gone Next Month? (Skeptical)

There are so many words being created that it's not surprising people are skeptical when they hear new ones for the first time. I know when I've been confronted with new identity terms that apply to me, I'm often skeptical that the new term won't stick around long enough to take hold, making me hesitant to use it for fear of looking foolish or pretentious. I've also worried that if I use the new term, others won't know it and I'll be forced to explain what it means.

The best strategy I've found to reduce my own skepticism when confronted with a new term that applies to me is to do my research. I search online to find out who coined the term, why it came into being, and how long it's been around. I was surprised to learn that the term *neurotypical* has been around since the 1990s. Personally, I think more than three decades of use makes it an official "thing." Researching why the term came into being gives me the information I need to explain to others what it means and why it was needed.

If you're worried that people will think you're being pretentious, consider using a connecting statement when you share the information you've learned about the term. For example, "Yeah. I had no idea what the word *cisgender* meant either. I had to look it up."

Do I Have to Embrace This New Term? My List of Identity Terms Seems to Be Constantly Growing. Which Ones Do I Have to Share in Order to Be Respectful? (Overwhelmed)

It would be hypocritical of me to tell people who are not transgender that they must embrace the identity term *cisgender*. Earlier in this book I talked about how we should respect everyone's right to self-identify and we should mirror the terms that people use to describe themselves. Those rules shouldn't and don't apply only to LGBTQ+ folks. If someone who's not transgender doesn't like the word *cisgender* or doesn't feel like the word fits for them, you will never catch me telling them that they must embrace it. All I will do is talk about why I embrace the word *cisgender* for myself and why I believe norm-busting words are important.

For those of us who do understand and appreciate the need for norm-busting terms, we will find, as we continue to educate ourselves, that our list of identity terms continues to grow. I recently learned, for example, that I'm *allosexual* (i.e., not asexual) and in a *mixed-gender marriage*. When we're out and about in the world, should we share all our norm-busting terms? Should I constantly state that I'm a straight, cisgender, white, hearing, non-disabled, neurotypical, allosexual woman in a mixed-gender marriage? Of course not. It's rare if ever helpful to share all of our identity terms. But there are times and places where sharing certain ones is respectful and useful. For example, I would use the word *cisgender* in a sentence like this one. "As a straight cisgender woman, I felt very welcomed and included at the Pride parade."

As we engage in our "good talks" with people who are having difficulty understanding or are angered by the word *cisgender*, begin by asking them to tell you more about what's confusing or upsetting them. It's likely to be one or several of the issues mentioned above. Feel free to share the examples I've offered of my own initial struggle with the word *neurotypical* or, better yet, give examples of your own.

WHY ARE LGBTQ+ PEOPLE SO ANGRY?

LGBTQ+ people are often accused of being angry and aggressive. Invariably, my tactic for educating on this topic involves helping the person who asks this question to conceptualize what it's like to be in an LGBTQ+ person's shoes. Understanding the situation or incident that prompted this question gives me a concrete example to work with. A few examples I have heard are:

> "I accidentally used the wrong pronoun for my coworker and she went apeshit on me!"
> "I always try and help my single coworker find a nice girl. Today, when I tried to set him up with my neighbor, he yelled at me, 'I'm gay! Okay?'"
> "I met a really awesome woman at a bar last night. She told me that she was bisexual. I told her I thought that was super hot. She told me I was an asshole."

Using the wrong pronoun for a coworker, and these other scenarios, are all examples of microaggressions. The term *microaggression* was coined in the 1970s by Harvard University professor Chester M. Pierce.[11] Microaggressions are commonplace comments or behaviors that are hurtful, insulting, or demeaning. They may be intentional or unintentional. In the situations I've just shared, none took place with the intention of being demeaning or hurtful. In fact, the second situation, trying to set up a coworker with a date, is clearly meant very kindly. When this is the case, it makes it even harder for people to understand when they receive an angry response. As allies, we can acknowledge people's kind intent and then help them understand the impact of their words.

My friend Maur once shared with me that repeated microaggressions are like having someone flick you in the arm over and over.

Flick-Flick-Flick. The first few times you're all, "Whatever. I'm sure they didn't mean it."
Flick-Flick-Flick. Then you start to get a bit irritated.
Flick-Flick-Flick. Eventually, you get snippy with the flicker.
Flick-Flick-Flick. Finally, you can't stand it anymore and you explode.

Let's say a trans man has just had a long day at work, where he was repeatedly called "she" and "her." On his way home he stops for some milk at the grocery store and the cashier says, "Have a nice day, Ma'am." That cashier may have just administered that final "flick." The trans man explodes and the cashier is left thinking, "Wow! What the hell did I do?" or, if the trans man stuck around long enough to explain why he was so annoyed, the cashier may be left thinking, "Golly! Transgender people are *so* angry!"

LGBTQ+ individuals have a right to be angry when they're repeatedly marginalized by others, and angry people make terrible educators. Allies are often in a better position to step in with patience and kindness and handle the emotional labor of helping people understand the impact of their words and behaviors. The "switch it" technique is a useful tool for helping people to conceptualize what it's like to be an LGBTQ+ person. Ask the person who is struggling to understand this anger to think about how they might feel if their coworkers constantly called them by the wrong name and pronoun or repeatedly tried to fix them up with a nice guy (if they're a straight man) or nice gal (if they're a straight woman).

A final note on "angry" and "aggressive" LGBTQ+ people relates to the topic of intersectionality. In our society, the people who are perceived as or accused of being angry and aggressive are *much* more likely to be women and people of color.[12] Therefore, there's often a heightened sensitivity around this accusation in these populations—and rightfully so. White, straight, cisgender men are allowed, and in many ways encouraged, to experience and show anger and aggression. Women and people of color are not. As allies, we need to be aware of these double standards and stereotypes and work to combat them.

MY LESBIAN FRIENDS CALL EACH OTHER DYKES. WHY IS IT OKAY FOR THEM TO DO THAT BUT NOT ME?

Within marginalized communities, it's not uncommon for people to reclaim or joke around with words that have been or still are being used against them. It's a way to disarm the people who are using derogatory terms and to take back control of an ugly situation. We've seen this with the word *queer*, which I discussed in chapter 2. However, unlike the word *queer*, which has become fairly mainstream, there are some hurtful words that are truly off limits for folks not in the community.

My friends Gloria and Susan, a lesbian couple, told me a funny story once. One day they were sitting in Boston traffic, and they noticed two women in the car next to them. Gloria said to Susan, "I bet that's a couple of dykes on their way to Provincetown." They got a closer look and realized that it was their friends. Gloria then exclaimed, "Hey! It *is* a couple of dykes on their way to Provincetown!"

Because they told me this story, I might think that it's okay for me to use the word *dyke* to refer to my friends Gloria and Susan, because they used it. It's not. I might also think that because they shared this story with me, I am "in the club," so to speak, so that definitely makes it okay for me to use the term. It doesn't.

I have never had the word *dyke* used against me, so it's not my word to reclaim or neutralize. Rather than feel hurt that I am not allowed to use reclaimed terms, I should feel honored when my LGBTQ+ friends feel comfortable and safe enough around me to use them in my presence and trust me not to misuse them. Using a reclaimed derogatory term will not prove to anyone that I am "in the club"; it will just piss people off.

If you're not sure what's okay and what's off limits, simply ask: "Hey, I heard you use the term _____ earlier tonight. I want to make sure that I am being respectful. Is that an okay term for me to use, too, or should I avoid it?"

I THOUGHT PEOPLE WERE "BORN THAT WAY"; NOW YOU'RE TELLING ME THAT BEING LGBTQ+ CAN BE A LIFELONG JOURNEY OF CHANGING IDENTITIES? WTF?

People cannot choose their gender identity or control whom they are attracted to. If we could, then conversion therapy (i.e., "counseling away the gay") would actually work, which it doesn't. Conversion therapy has occasionally shamed or frightened people into temporarily altering their behaviors, but it's never been able to change people's orientations.[13]

So, if we can't control our gender identity or our orientation, what's up with folks who were straight for twenty-five years, then gay for ten years, and are now bisexual? (This totally happens.) Or, what about people who were cisgender lesbians and are now straight transgender men? (This also totally happens.)

We can't control our gender identity or whom we are attracted to, but our understanding and our acceptance of who we are can take lots of different twists, turns, and paths and can be an extremely long adventure for many people. Some people, like my friend Dee, whom I talked about in chapter 2, struggle to find their identity word and may initially use words that don't quite fit.

If people live in geographical areas where they're not exposed to the individuals or the communities that can help them find accurate terms for themselves, they're likely to latch onto the only terms they have. Over time, as people move through the world, meet new people, and hear new terms (Hurray for new terms!), they may have an "aha!" moment—or several "aha!" moments—with new identity terms that work better for them. My friend Jason, editor in chief at *FTM Magazine*, told me that finding his identity words, *straight trans* man, felt like slipping his feet into his girlfriend's soft, fuzzy UGGs.

Other folks may suppress or reject their identities for long periods of time, fearful of the consequences of living as their authentic selves. I know many individuals who consciously waited until their parents died before coming out and living authentically because they didn't want to deal with the trauma and shame they suspected would have been their reality if their parents knew their true identity.

A few years ago, I fielded a call from staff members at a senior-living facility. They described a resident in her early eighties who "suddenly become transgender—so weird!" But the reality is that this resident had been struggling her entire life with her identity as a transgender woman. When she saw Laverne Cox and Caitlyn Jenner on television and in magazines, she finally said to herself, "What the heck am I waiting for?"

It's also important to be aware that many people who are confused by other people's changing identities may actually be confusing attraction and behavior, as discussed in chapter 4. If this is the case, the question may sound something like this: "My niece came out as bisexual three years ago. Now she just announced that she's getting married to a guy. Did she turn straight?" Clearly the asker is confusing the niece's attraction/orientation with her behaviors/relationship choices. Try the "switch it" technique to help this person understand the difference: for example, if a straight woman gets a divorce from her husband and is currently not in a relationship with anyone, does that mean she's not straight anymore? The answer is: Of course not.

And finally, let's not forget about our gender-fluid and sexually fluid friends. These folks find that their gender and/or attraction to others fluctuate regularly.

FOOD FOR THOUGHT

Why do you think it's easier for humans to accept LGBTQ+ folks when they believe that they're "born that way?" Why do humans require an identity to be completely outside of a person's control before they can learn to respect it?

I FEEL LIKE I CAN'T SAY ANYTHING ANYMORE WITHOUT OFFENDING SOMEONE. DON'T YOU THINK WE'VE GONE TOO FAR WITH ALL OF THIS PC LANGUAGE?

I remember the first time a workshop participant suggested that I remove the word *preferred* from my question when I asked people if they would like to share their preferred pronouns. Did I immediately take that new piece of information, stick it into my lump of knowledge, and change my behavior? Nope. I thought about it for a moment and then dismissed it with a "nah."

As an educator, I think back to that moment often, not because I am proud of it—obviously I'm not—but because it's truly fascinating to me. There I was, facilitating a workshop focused on being mindful of language and making respectful word choices, and suddenly—*bam!*—I'm the learner, and a resistant one at that.

As you know, I now encourage people to remove the word *preferred* when they talk about people's pronouns. So, what happened? What made me change my mind? What was the process I had to go through before I added this new piece of information to my lump of knowledge? Well, first I began to hear a few other folks also recommend this language tweak. (Yes. I think that sometimes numbers *do* matter. I've had individuals from historically marginalized communities suggest that I change my language, only to find out later that this was their personal choice—one that the majority of the other members from that community didn't agree with. In these cases, I do my best to remember that language tweak when I am speaking with the individual, but I don't make that change in my workshops or daily life.) Then I did a little research into whether or not this was becoming "a thing." (That may sound odd, but some new trends take hold and become "things" while others disappear within months.) Finally, I applied the "switch it" technique. This helped me realize that we *don't* refer to cisgender people's pronouns as *preferred*, we just refer to them as their pronouns. Ultimately, I realized that removing the word *preferred* when I talked about people's pronouns was clearly a logical request. So, I changed my language.

The beauty of realizing that I'm fully capable of experiencing that "Really? Now I'm being asked to change this too?" reaction is that when someone asks me this question about PC language, I understand where they're coming from. I can relate. We have common ground. This is great for two reasons. First, it helps me be empathetic and understanding. Second, it allows me to use a connecting statement like, "I get it. I've felt that way too." A connecting statement like this helps to create those wonderful, judgment-free, ally-to-ally spaces for people to talk through their frustration with language.

If you can't find common ground with the person because you've never felt this way yourself, you can still use a connecting statement. You might try, "Language is constantly changing. I know it can be difficult to keep up."

I also recommend letting this person, who's frustrated by all the "PC" language, know that you think it's unfortunate that they feel they can no longer have conversations with people. People *should* be having conversations. So, commiserate, connect if you can, allow people to share their annoyance, and then offer pointers.

Here are three major stumbling blocks that can prevent people from changing their language and some tips for helping folks get over them:

- *Not Fully Understanding the Point:* As I discussed in chapter 2, when people already have their identity words, whether they're part of the LGBTQ+ communities or not, it's more difficult for them to understand the need for new ones. Use a personal example, if you have one, of the positive impact of someone using correct and respectful language. If you don't have an example at hand, consider sharing the story about Dee finding her identity word. You can also share the article by Alex Myers (referenced in chapter 2) about why we need more LGBTQ identity words, not fewer. Finally, if applicable, try the "switch it" technique. It helped me see the logic behind changing my language with *preferred* pronouns.
- *Disliking Being Told What to Do:* No one likes being told what to do. If people are feeling pressured or forced into changing something by the "PC police"—especially if the change doesn't make sense to them—they're very likely to feel frustration, anger, and resistance. One way to help

is to ask them to change what PC stands for in their heads. Instead of "politically correct," ask them to think about PC as standing for "please consider." *They* get to choose whether or not they change their language. Tell them to stop worrying about the "PC police" slapping them with a ticket and instead put their energy into thinking about *why* they're being asked to change their language. If it makes sense to them, then they should make the change. If it doesn't, they shouldn't. But do encourage them to make an informed decision and be open to altering their choice with time. Ask them to think about some words they used as a child that they now consider offensive. This should help them see that they've been being intentional with their word choices and their language has been evolving their entire lives.

- *Feeling Overwhelmed:* Even *I* sometimes get overwhelmed with all the language changes and updates that take place within the LGBTQ+ communities, and I run workshops on LGBTQ+ inclusion! It's no surprise that people who don't have a strong connection to the LGBTQ+ communities also feel overwhelmed. Trying to learn all the newest terms and remembering to use them to replace ones we've been using our whole lives can feel like a daunting task. One of my tips for combatting that overwhelmed feeling comes from my experience learning how to play racquetball. Having never played the game before, I started playing weekly with a friend who knew the game well. Each week I got my ass thoroughly kicked. I was completely overwhelmed by how many things there were to think about during the game, and I did none of them well. After about six weeks of this nonsense, I'd had enough. I decided I'd focus on just one skill every time we played. I'd forgive myself for everything else I did poorly and just focus on doing that one thing well. It worked like a charm. My skills increased and my frustration dissipated rapidly. If people are feeling overwhelmed with all the language changes they're being asked to make, encourage them to focus on just one. Ask them to choose one word or language tweak that is important to them or that makes sense to them and just work on that until they have it down. Then they can move on to another.

It's difficult to change the language we're used to, but typically people are willing to put in the work if the concept makes sense to them, if they're not feeling forced, and if they can keep from feeling completely overwhelmed in the process. With a little savvy ally encouragement, you can help people enjoy the satisfaction of being intentional in their language as a way of supporting other people in living their lives authentically and proudly.

NOTES

1. Reprinted with permission from Anthony Venn-Brown, *A Life of Unlearning: A Preacher's Struggle with His Homosexuality, Church, and Faith*, 3rd ed. (Australia: Ambassadors & Bridge Builders International, 2015).

2. Kenji Yoshino, *Covering: The Hidden Assault on Our Civil Rights* (New York: Random House, 2006).

3. Yoshino, *Covering*, 82.

4. *Movement Advancement Project,* "Nondiscrimination Laws," https://www.lgbt map.org/equality-maps/non_discrimination_laws.

5. Ibid.

6. Kelsey Butler, "Anti-LGBTQ Proposals Are Flooding U.S. State Legislatures at a Record Pace," *Bloomberg*, April 8, 2022, https://www.bloomberg.com/news /articles/2022-04-08/mapping-the-anti-lgbtq-proposals-flooding-u-s-state-legislatures.

7. Reality Check team, "Homosexuality: The Countries Where It Is Illegal to Be Gay," BBC News, May 12, 2021, https://www.bbc.com/news/world-43822234.

8. *Wikipedia*, "LGBT Rights by Country or Territory," https://en.wikipedia.org /wiki/LGBT_rights_by_country_or_territory.

9. *ACLU*, "Legislation Affecting LGBTQ Rights across the Country," https:// www.aclu.org/legislation-affecting-lgbtq-rights-across-country.

10. *https://www.linkedin.com/in/nshalev/*.

11. *Wikipedia*, "Microaggression," https://en.wikipedia.org/wiki/Microaggression.

12. Soraya Chemaly, "How Women and Minorities Are Claiming Their Right to Rage," *The Guardian*, May 11, 2019, https://www.theguardian.com/lifeandstyle/2019 /may/11/women-and-minorities-claiming-right-to-rage.

13. "The Lies and Dangers of Efforts to Change Sexual Orientation or Gender Identity," Human Rights Campaign, accessed October 21, 2019, https://www.hrc.org /resources/the-lies-and-dangers-of-reparative-therapy.

10

DUCT TAPE PATCH-UP JOBS AND BIG FIXES

I write in "nope," [under "Father"] . . . And sometimes, if I'm in the mood to create a teachable moment, I write, "sperm donor."[1]

—Susan Goldberg, "School Forms: What Happens When Both Parents Are Mother," 2013

Let's imagine that my friend Shimona comes over to my house for dinner and on her way to my front door she trips on an uneven section of walkway. She falls, rips her pants, and gets a big gash on her knee. Ouch!

I, of course, feel terrible. I apologize, I get her what she needs to clean the wound, and we bandage her knee. I've just offered a "duct tape patch-up job" solution to the situation: in this case, a sincere apology, some antiseptic, and a bandage. A lesser response would have been exhibiting extremely rude behavior: "Oh bummer, Shimona. That knee is a bloody mess. Can you please bleed on the kitchen tile instead of the rug?"

But the problem remains. I still have an uneven walkway. If I don't also come up with a "big fix" solution by repairing my front walkway, then next week, when my friend Manuel comes over for dinner, he's likely to trip as well. Even worse, a few months later, Shimona may come back and trip on the very same spot again. How embarrassing! By offering Shimona an apology and some first aid I've offered temporary care, but I haven't fixed the problem. I must implement the immediate short-term duct tape patch-up job *and* the big-picture fix to create a truly safe and welcoming space for my visitors. We must do the same at our schools, agencies, businesses, and faith communities in order to create safe, welcoming, and inclusive spaces for LGBTQ+ people.

Imagine that a nonbinary person named Bo comes in for care at a mental health center. The form Bo is given has an "M" or "F" box option, most of the staff members are unfamiliar with nonbinary identities, and there are only "Men's" and "Women's" restrooms. This center has a client who doesn't fit into its current system or its space. The immediate duct tape patch-up job should include a sincere apology to Bo, extra privacy for sensitive conversations, and an "all-gender restroom" sign taped on any single-stall restrooms. This center is not an inclusive space yet, but some efforts have been made to help Bo feel welcome.

When Bo leaves, there's more work to be done. The staff should now think about the big fixes that need to happen. In this case, some long-term changes that need to take place are building renovations (including the creation of some all-gender restrooms), mandatory and ongoing staff trainings about LGBTQ+ identities, and updated database categories, policies, and forms.

What follows are five key ways that allies can create safer, more welcoming, and more inclusive spaces. These are: educating others, increasing LGBTQ+ visibility, revising forms, updating policies, and fixing gendered facilities. I've offered examples of both duct tape patch-up jobs and big-fix solutions for each of these areas. This isn't an exhaustive list of solutions; it really can't be. Each setting and situation are different. People need to be creative with their solutions and adapt them to their environments. However, the examples below will give you a great place to begin as you assess your schools, agencies, businesses, and faith communities and start to implement duct tape patch-up jobs and big-fix solutions to create more inclusive spaces.[2]

EDUCATING OTHERS

Much of this book is focused on taking advantage of educational opportunities when they arise. Speaking up when we hear something offensive and creating judgment-free spaces for having respectful conversations with people are huge parts of an ally's role. In earlier chapters, I offered some tools allies can use to do this effectively. In this section, we'll look at when and where those respectful conversations can be used for both duct tape patch-up jobs and big-fix solutions.

Duct tape patch-up job educational efforts are immediate reactions to comments or behaviors that are not okay. These educational opportunities can spring up with anyone: a coworker, a neighbor, our kids, a teammate, and so on. Big-fix educational efforts change the environment in our workplaces, neighborhoods, homes, schools, and faith communities, making them safer and more inclusive.

Duct Tape Patch-Up Jobs with Our Educational Opportunities

- Speak up when a teammate refers to an opponent with a derogatory term.
- Offer a workplace or school diversity training as a reaction to an LGBTQ+ related incident or concern.
- Respond truthfully to your child's question, "What does gay mean?"
- Send a student who is bullying another student to the principal's office, where the bullying student should be dealt with appropriately.

HELPFUL HINT

A common obstacle to interrupting offensive language is not knowing what to say. I recommend that you prepare one or two "hip pocket" responses that you can whip out in any situation. Some good ones are:

"We don't use put-downs here."

"That language is not okay."

"Can you explain why that's funny?"

"I don't agree with what you just said."

"Can you say more about what you mean by that?"

Big Fixes with Our Educational Opportunities

- Make ongoing, mandatory LGBTQ+ workshops a part of your workplace or school diversity and inclusion efforts.
- Incorporate LGBTQ+ awareness and inclusion training into new staff orientations.
- Make sure LGBTQ+ individuals and families are represented in everyday school curricula (e.g., math, English, history, and science), not just health class.
- Read books to your child, starting when they are very young, that have all kinds of people and families in them, and where all types of gender roles and expressions are represented.

INCREASING LGBTQ+ VISIBILITY

I mentioned in chapter 9 that LGBTQ+ people are typically looking for more than a general sign stating that an agency or shop does not discriminate. This means we have an opportunity as allies to help LGBTQ+ people feel safe and welcome with visible images of LGBTQ+ people and inclusive policies posted in high-traffic areas. What would an LGBTQ+ person who was looking for indications that they would be welcomed and safe see if they walked into your shop, agency, school, health center, office space, faith community, or home?

Several years ago, a young cisgender gay man at a workshop I offered in the Philadelphia area told the group a powerful story. As a college student in an area of the United States not known for its LGBTQ+ inclusion, he felt alone and unsupported, was just barely tolerating himself as a gay man, and was contemplating suicide. During his junior year, two rainbow safe space stickers popped up on office doors in one of the buildings where he attended classes. He told us that he would wait until it was late in the evening, when he knew that no one would be around, and then he would return to that hallway where the stickers were and walk up and down to "gather strength" from them. The fact that there were two professors on his campus who thought that being gay was okay gave him an incredible amount of hope. He said that those stickers kept him alive. To this day those two professors have no idea that they saved a man's life by visibly showing their support of the LGBTQ+ communities.

When we offer visible signs that LGBTQ+ people are welcome in our spaces, we'll be aware of the LGBTQ+ folks who come in and chat about their identities or thank us for our support. However, our LGBTQ+ welcoming signs will have the biggest impact on the people who can't walk through our door.

Duct Tape Patch-Up Jobs for Increasing LGBTQ+ Visibility

- Toss an issue of an LGBTQ+ magazine or newspaper on a table in your waiting area.
- Tape up a sign with a rainbow that says, "All families welcome here."
- Fly a rainbow flag outside your workplace, home, or place of worship.
- Wear or attach a rainbow pin, zipper pull, or bag tag.

Big Fixes for Increasing LGBTQ+ Visibility

- Subscribe to an LGBTQ+ magazine or newspaper for your waiting area.
- Create permanent images of LGBTQ+ people and statements of inclusion for your walls and website.

- Update promotional materials (e.g., posters and pamphlets) to include images of all different types of families.
- Recognize LGBT Pride Month in June every year by creating a Pride display.

A HELPFUL HINT ABOUT SAFE SPACES

Anyone can put up a sign with a rainbow image that says, "All families welcome here." However, safe space (sometimes called safe zone) stickers and signs imply more. Safe space stickers and signs are typically offered after a safe space workshop, and they indicate that the person displaying them has had some training about LGBTQ+ identities and inclusion. Safe space signage is well known within the LGBTQ+ communities and hugely impactful. The stickers and signs indicate to LGBTQ+ people where they can go if they need to talk with someone, need help finding resources, or just need to be in a space where they can be authentic. If you're interested in being safe space trained, check with the college campus or LGBTQ+ center nearest you to see if they offer these workshops.

REVISING FORMS

Unless you live under a rock, you're likely to often find yourself filling out paper and online forms. We encounter them in copious amounts from schools, insurance companies, healthcare facilities, and employers. We must fill them out when we purchase airline tickets, join an athletic club, and shop online. They're everywhere.

My identities and relationship are fully recognized by our society and on all forms. I can walk into a doctor's office and check off the "F" box for my sex and gender. (These two identities are often confused and combined on forms, but it doesn't matter for me, since my sex and gender align.) Then I check off "Married" under the heading "Relationship Status." If it's an OB/GYN office or breast care center, most likely the questions will all be written with the assumption that I was assigned female at birth, that I am a woman, that I have one sexual partner, and that my partner is a man. Before I worked for an LGBTQ+ center, I would fill out these forms and not think twice about them or even notice that the questions were extremely narrow and limiting.

What is this medical visit going to look like if I'm intersex? Bisexual? Polyamorous? Transgender? Possibly patients with these identities will be disconcerted by the form and the fact that their identities are not represented there. This may cause them to fear that the staff won't be respectful, educated, and open to their identities. Some may leave without ever seeing the doctor. Others will fudge their way through the form, leaving some things blank or creating new boxes, then mentally prepare themselves for what is likely to be several awkward conversations with the medical staff—like my friend Dee, a transgender woman, who had this awkward conversation in a not-so-private area at her doctor's office:

Medical Staff Member: When was your last menstrual period?

Dee: Um.

Medical Staff Member: Was it within the past six weeks?

Dee: Well . . .

Medical Staff Member: You don't remember?

Dee: Not really.

Medical Staff Member: Are you irregular?

Dee: Yes. I'm irregular.

One of the first things patients are asked to do upon entering a medical facility is fill out a form. What a wonderful opportunity to show immediately that your agency is welcoming and inclusive. Rather than cause stress, medical professionals can welcome patients with a form that acknowledges everyone and all types of relationships. Check out Sarah Prager's article "When the Forms Don't Fit Your Family"[3] to get a good sense of how much stress the typical form can cause. A bonus of having more inclusive forms is that they help prevent situations like the one Dee encountered. If the staff member takes the form from Dee and sees that Dee is a transgender woman, she's unlikely to ask openly, where other patients can hear her, when Dee's last menstrual period took place.

Noninclusive school forms can also be a source of frustration and anger for LGBTQ+ folks. In her article, "School forms: What happens when both parents are Mother," Susan Goldberg writes "Nobody tells you before you become a queer parent just how often you will encounter forms that ask for—as this one did—your child's 'Father's name' and 'Mother's name.'"[4] School forms that ask for "Mother's name" and "Father's name" are not just unwelcoming for families that have two fathers or two mothers, but also for families where there's a single parent or where the guardian is a grandparent, foster parent, or other relative. After posting an image of a noninclusive form on her social media page, Goldberg received many comments from friends of hers who were equally frustrated. Goldberg wrote:

Several of my friends who are single parents pointed out that they also find the standard "Mother/Father" forms off-putting, or at least tiresome. "I face the same problem all the time as a solo (straight) parent," wrote one friend, a single mom by choice. "I write in 'nope,' [under 'Father']" said another friend. "And sometimes, if I'm in the mood to create a teachable moment, I write, 'sperm donor.'" [5]

I view noninclusive forms as a perfect opportunity for savvy ally action! A family that's enrolling their child in a new school may wonder if they'll be safe in a school district that doesn't acknowledge LGBTQ+ families on their forms. Let's not expect these families to take the lead on making suggestions to the school about how to make more inclusive forms. An LGBTQ+ patient in a noninclusive health center is likely feeling stressed and vulnerable. Let's not also burden this patient with the task of navigating a conversation with their health provider about ways that their medical forms can be more inclusive. Those of us who see ourselves represented on forms and aren't worried about how we'll be treated as straight cisgender parents or patients are the perfect folks to step up to the plate and advocate for more inclusive forms.

Typically, what I do when I'm given a noninclusive form is offer some suggestions on the side of the page, like: "Please consider asking this question in a different way to be more LGBTQ+ inclusive. Feel free to contact me if you would like some suggestions." (Yup, I really do this.) Usually my "helpful" comment gets ignored, but it's possible that I've planted a seed. If a dozen clients comment similarly on their noninclusive form, the staff are likely to take action.

Every once in a while, good things happen, and I'm asked to offer assistance. Here is an example of a time when a good thing happened. Several years back, the intake form at my OB/GYN office had this section below:

Marital Status (Circle):
Single – Married – Separated – Divorced – Widowed

I made my usual offer to help and heard nothing back. But at my annual exam the next year, I noticed the form had been changed and the section now read:

Marital Status (Circle):
Single – Married – Separated – Divorced – Widowed – Female Partner

This duct tape patch-up job is what I call a "tack it on" solution. I see "tack it on" solutions on forms constantly, for example:

Thank you for registering for our conference. We would like to make sure that this experience is as welcoming and inclusive as possible. Please check all that are applicable.

_____ I need ASL interpretation
_____ I would like a vegetarian lunch

The "tack it on" solution involves identifying a need ("Hey! We should offer a vegetarian meal") and tacking on a new option. But what about folks who'll be attending this conference who are in wheelchairs? What about folks who have peanut allergies? Do we keep tacking on boxes as the needs occur to us, or do we create a system that works for everyone?

Here is an example of a system that works for everyone:

Thank you for registering for our conference. We would like to make sure that this experience is as welcoming and inclusive as possible. Please let us know if you have any dietary restrictions or accessibility needs below.

_____ I do have dietary restrictions and/or accessibility needs. Please contact me.

So, back to our tacked-on "female partner" option. Adding this option is better than assuming that every woman they see is straight, but only marginally. Here's why:

- It makes "male partner" the norm or default. In other words, if I am married to a woman, I circle "Married" and "Female Partner." If I am married to a man, I circle only "Married." "Male Partner" is assumed. This is very othering. Because there is no "Male Partner" option, it's pretty clear that if you circle "Female Partner" you are different from most. Also, if I don't circle "Female Partner" the staff is likely to assume my partner is male, which may be false. What if my partner is nonbinary?
- It lumps together relationships and intimate behaviors, which may be different. For example: What do I circle if I'm a woman who's married to a man but who also has a sexual partner who's a woman? If I circle "Married" and "Female Partner," then the assumption will be that I'm married to a woman.
- It only scratches the surface of the information this provider actually needs and should know about their patients. If I circle "Female Partner" the assumption is likely to be, "This patient is a lesbian, she has one partner, and her partner is a woman." The reality is that they have no information

about my orientation (I may be bisexual), my gender (I may be a trans man), or my relationship status (just because I have a female partner doesn't mean I'm in a relationship with that person or that I am in a relationship with only one person).

This time, I waited until I was in the private room with my doctor. I told him that I was very pleased to see the effort his office had made to create a more inclusive form. Then I told him that there were ways to make it even better and that I would be happy to help.

A few weeks later I received an email from my doctor, with the intake form attached, asking for my help. Hurrah! In the email back to my doctor I sent my suggestions for a completely revised form that fits *everyone*. Here were my suggestions for the section on "Relationship Status" (formerly "Marital Status"):

What is your current relationship(s) status? _____

What is your sexual orientation? _____

Fill-ins are always best, as they allow people to tell you exactly who they are. However, if multiple-choice options were mandated, which they often are in health care, I suggested something like this:

Relationship Status (Circle all that apply):
Single – Married – Separated – Divorced – Widowed – Partnered – Polyamorous – Monogamous – A relationship/partnership not listed here

Sexual Orientation (Circle all that apply):
Lesbian – Gay – Bisexual – Straight – Pansexual – Asexual – Queer – An orientation not listed here

If a patient circles "A relationship/partnership not listed here" or "An orientation not listed here," and the medical office is restricted by limited options on their computer's database, this should be explained to the patient in a private setting and the best option should be chosen with the patient's involvement. Although this is not ideal, it's significantly better and more respectful than stressing patients out with forms and options that don't fit at all. This would also be a great time to ask the patient for their suggestions for improved categories— categories you can advocate for in the future.

I also shared with my doctor that this new form would give him some basic information that could help him discuss, in private, a patient's sexual behaviors.

He should not make assumptions about what people are actually doing sexually based on their relationship status or their orientation.

If you'd like to advocate for more inclusive forms but don't think you're the right person to offer suggestions, you can simply refer folks to the National LGBT Health Education Center's online guide *Focus on Forms and Policy: Creating an Inclusive Environment for LGBT Patients.*[6] Although the eight-page guide focuses on medical forms, much of it can be used for general form "makeovers."

Duct Tape Patch-Up Jobs for Revising Forms and Paperwork

- Tack on new options to an existing form, like "Female Partner."
- Offer all clients the option of filling out the current form one-on-one, with a staff member, in a private area.
- Add a statement that apologizes for the limited form. Let your clients know that you're currently in the process of updating it and welcome them to write whatever fill-ins or explanations they need on the current form.
- Include an "A gender not listed here" or "An orientation not listed here" option if the form doesn't already have this. These options are typically received better than "other."

Big Fixes for Revising Forms and Paperwork

- Think long and hard about what you actually need to know. *Then* look at whether or not the questions on your forms are getting you there. Do you need to know someone's sex assigned at birth or do you really want to know their gender? Is it important to know someone's sexual orientation or just what they're doing sexually in order to offer appropriate care? Do you need to know if someone is a man, a woman, or a nonbinary person or do you really want to know how you should address them? Forms should be adapted to your organization's actual needs, and they should change and be updated over time.
- Survey your clients and ask them how your forms can be more inclusive and can represent their identities and their relationships if they don't already. Use these suggestions when you update your forms.
- Have "Name" at the top of the form, and "Legal Name, if different" later or lower on the form. This way the person's correct and current name will always be the one that's used. Most forms have "Name" or "Legal Name" at the top of the form, with "Nickname" or "Preferred Name" listed later.

Typically what happens in this case is that the wrong name is used first, which can cause embarrassment and a potentially unsafe situation.

- If you're restricted to limited multiple-choice options by the databases that you're using, contact the companies that create the databases and advocate for more inclusive categories. Advocacy is creating real change! An "X" gender marker, signifying a gender that's not exclusively *man* or *woman*, is now available as an option on US passports. United and American Airlines have added a nonbinary option to their gender selections for passengers and several other major airlines have indicated that they will soon be following suit. The Social Security Administration recently announced that people can now self-select their sex on their Social Security number record.

HELPFUL HINT

If you're asking questions on forms that may confuse people, give examples of the information you're seeking. For example: How may we refer to you? (For example: "Lee," "Dr. Rodriguez," "Ms. Jones"). Or what is your gender? (For example: "woman," "man," "nonbinary").

UPDATING POLICIES

My education team members and I always found it incredibly ironic (and icky) when we entered a facility where we'd previously offered LGBTQ+ workshops on creating inclusive spaces only to have my transgender cofacilitator be misgendered, told they had to sign in with their "real" name, and forced to wear an ID badge with their old name printed on it for all to see. Often, we find in schools, health facilities, corporations, and agencies that good work is being done by a small group of concerned people, but the big-picture stuff is not being touched, nor is it even on the radar.

Creating updated and inclusive policies is critical to protect people's rights and privacy and to create the foundation for your work toward more welcoming and inclusive spaces. That's step one. Step two is ensuring that employees, students, parents, clients, and members are aware of these policies. Participants in my trainings often have no idea what the policies are at their workplaces or schools. Once you do the work to bring your policies up to date, let people know what they are. Send an annual email with your policies included, hang your nondiscrimination policy in a high-traffic area for all to see, and include your policies in displays celebrating honorary months like Black History Month, LGBT Pride Month, and Disability Awareness Month.

Duct Tape Patch-Up Jobs for Updating Policies

- Train front desk staff about LGBTQ+ identities and respectful communication so that every effort can be made to help visitors navigate check-in procedures that are difficult for them. Ungendering welcomes, sincerely apologizing for the current system, lowering voices, and finding a private space for conversations will go a long way toward helping people who are made uncomfortable by your noninclusive check-in procedures.
- If a legal name must be represented on all badges and email addresses, allow people to attach a ribbon to the bottom of their badge that says, "Please call me _____" and add this message to their email signature. Allies can wear ribbons and add these messages to their email signature too! This helps to normalize the behavior so it's not just the transgender employees being singled out.
- Take a stand as a local chapter. In our area of Upstate New York, several local Boy Scout troops took a stand against the Boy Scouts of America's decision not to allow gay men to be leaders. They showed visible support for their LGBTQ+ leaders, parents, and scouts on their websites and in their literature.
- Offer optional pronoun stickers or pins as people enter your workplace, school, or faith community building. Wear one yourself! This is a great way for allies to help create a more welcoming and safe space—plus, you're bound to have some great conversations about why you're wearing your pronoun on your shirt.

Big Fixes for Updating Policies

- Ensure that equal opportunity employment statements, codes of conduct, antiharassment policies, benefits statements, and nondiscrimination policies include these three categories: Sexual Orientation, Gender Identity, and Gender Expression. Often you'll find the first one, sometimes the second, and rarely the third. Here is how these three categories protect us:

  Sexual Orientation: People cannot be discriminated against because of whom they are attracted to. This protects gay men, lesbians, bisexual people, pansexual people, asexual people, and more.

Gender Identity: People cannot be discriminated against for how they identify their gender. This mainly protects transgender individuals, including nonbinary folks.

Gender Expression: People cannot be discriminated against for how they express their gender. This protects people from being told they need to dress in a way that's more feminine or more masculine. This category protects everyone.

- Ungender dress codes and uniforms. Dress codes should place restrictions on clothing, not on who gets to wear the clothing. So, rather than stating, "Women may wear pants, skirts, or dresses to this event," state, "Employees may wear pants, skirts, or dresses to this event." Instead of stating, "Girls may not wear shirts that expose their bellies," state, "Students may not wear shirts that expose their bellies." If uniform options are pants or a skirt, these options should be offered to everyone, regardless of gender. When working with youth in schools, camps, or recreation centers, it's important to be aware that swimwear can be especially traumatizing for trans and gender-expansive youth, who may have intense feelings of distress about their bodies. Allow youth to wear any swim attire that makes them comfortable, including swim shirts.
- Ask everyone to share their pronouns and how they would like to be addressed if they feel comfortable doing so. Add these optional questions to your forms. Always have pronoun stickers or pins available as people enter your facility. Not everyone will want to participate, and that's fine, but it's incredibly welcoming for those who do.
- Create policies and guidelines for supporting transgender and transitioning employees/students. Employers, colleges, and K–12 schools should have these guidelines and policies in place *before* they have to use them, so the first transitioning person doesn't end up being a guinea pig. Policies should support all transgender people, including binary, nonbinary, transitioning, and nontransitioning individuals. One big area to address is name-change policies. When someone legally changes their name, how is this handled when it comes to name tags, email address, ID badges, directories, attendance lists, confidentiality, and communication? Are there also policies in place for someone who changes their name but has not gone through a legal name-change process? Both the Human Rights Campaign (HRC) and the Mozilla Workplace Transition Policy Guidelines are great resources for creating transitioning employee workplace guidelines.[7] For a wonderful resource to help with transgender-inclusive

policies in schools, check out "Schools in Transition: A Guide for Supporting Transgender Students in K–12 Schools."[8]

Whether or not you work for a corporation, I recommend taking a look at the HRC's *Corporate Equality Index* for a very thorough description of what inclusive LGBTQ+ policies and practices look like.[9]

FIXING GENDERED FACILITIES

FUN AND NOT-SO-FUN FACTS

- The bathrooms in your home are probably all-gender.
- In March 2016, North Carolina's House Bill 2 became the law. This bill stated that individuals may only use restrooms that correspond to the sex identified on their birth certificate. There was an enormous amount of backlash to this decision: musicians canceled rock concerts, the NCAA refused to allow North Carolina to host championship games, and large companies canceled their plans to build North Carolina–based facilities. It has been estimated that the state will lose more than $3.76 billion over the next dozen years as a result of this decision.[10] In March 2017 the bill was adapted, removing restroom restrictions for transgender people.[11]

> Some things are more important than a rock show and this fight against prejudice and bigotry—which is happening as I write—is one of them.
>
> —Bruce Springsteen, regarding his canceled concert in Greensboro, North Carolina

- More US politicians have been arrested for misconduct in public bathrooms than have trans people.[12]
- In March of 2017, California became the first state to require that all single-stall public restrooms be all-gender.[13]
- More Americans claim to have seen a ghost than claim they have met a trans person.[14] What does this have to do with restroom facilities? Nothing, really; I just thought it was a ridiculous fact. What it does indicate, however, is that we have all encountered transgender people and we have not necessarily known it. It's highly probable that you have already peed next to a transgender person. If you meet folks who feel that we should hire security guards to stand at restroom entrances and check driver's licenses, birth certificates, or genitals, direct them to the #WeJustNeedToPee campaign, initially started by Brae Carnes.[15] This campaign is a series of bathroom selfies taken and posted by transgender people to show how uncomfortable life would be if we forced people into restrooms according to the sex they were assigned at birth.

Single-stall, all-gender restrooms should be made available whenever possible. Access to gendered restrooms and locker rooms should be based on an individual's gender identity, not the sex they were assigned at birth, the sex printed on their birth certificate, or their assumed biological sex. No one should ever be told which facility they must use.

POP QUIZ

Who should use an all-gender restroom?

    A. Transgender individuals
    B. Transgender, nonbinary, and transitioning individuals
    C. Anyone

Answer: C

Many people think of all-gender restrooms as "transgender bathrooms." Some transgender individuals will use all-gender restrooms, but others won't. All-gender restrooms are there for anyone to use. What this means is, if my coworker is transitioning and I'm uncomfortable being in the same restroom with her, I can go and use the single-stall all-gender restroom and have my privacy. Ta-da! All-gender restrooms and changing facilities are incredibly helpful for people with a caregiver of a different gender, families with young children who don't want to be separated, and nonbinary, transitioning, and gender-expansive folks, who often experience harassment in gendered restrooms.

Helping cisgender people understand that everyone should have access to safe facilities and relieving people's fears with facts are great tasks for allies. Feel free to use the data I offered on facility use in chapter 7 or do your own research. The data will confirm that it's not cisgender people, but our transgender friends who are at risk in public facilities.

Duct Tape Patch-Up Jobs for Fixing Gendered Restrooms and Other Facilities

- If you have gendered single-stall restrooms at your school or workplace, tape "all-gender restroom" signs over the existing gendered signs.

- Create a map to help people find all-gender restrooms in your building or on your campus. If all-gender restrooms are few and far between at your workplace or campus, this will help folks find them. Add this map to the Diversity and Inclusion or Pride page on your organization's website.
- Allow students or employees who feel uncomfortable using the gendered restrooms access to special accommodations. For example, allow a student to use the private restroom in the nurse's office until better accommodations can be made.

Big Fixes for Fixing Gendered Restrooms and Other Facilities

- When renovating or designing new buildings, create at least one single-stall all-gender restroom on every floor.
- Create locker room facilities that have private changing areas and private showers. This is likely to make many students very happy! How many middle-school kids are comfortable putting their naked bodies on display for their peers? (That was a rhetorical question. I know the answer.)
- Offer only all-gender single-stall restrooms when feasible. Many restaurants now offer only a single all-gender restroom, a couple of all-gender restrooms, or a whole row of them. Ever see women waiting in a long line for the single-stall women's room, while the single-stall men's room sits unused? There are almost always a few rebels (myself included) who say, "This is so ridiculous," and just go ahead and use the men's room. Why are we gendering single-stall restrooms?

A Special Note about Signage

I field a lot of questions about the best sign to use for all-gender restrooms. (I've just given you a big hint.) "All-Gender Restroom" will do just fine. "Restroom" also works.

All-Gender Restroom Signage

 Sam Killermann, author of *A Guide to Gender* and creator of the website It's Pronounced Metrosexual[16] (both truly wonderful resources for all things gender), created a very simple all-gender restroom sign that looks like this.

TOILET TALK

I have now had enough conversations with cisgender women who are against all-gender restrooms based solely on the complaint that "men pee everywhere" that I felt it merited some candid toilet talk. Let me begin by stating that, generally, if my husband, Ed, is coming out of the men's room at a gas station or restaurant shaking his head and saying, "Gross," I'm coming out of the women's restroom doing the same thing. However, for argument's sake, let's say that all-gender restrooms are generally less clean than women's restrooms. What we're now weighing is inconveniencing cisgender women against keeping transgender people safe. I'll take the messy restroom any day. Perhaps our work as allies should include advocating for cleaner restrooms so everyone can pee and peace out safely and without sticky shoes.

On a more positive note, I've been to many restaurants that offer a row of clean, private, all-gender restrooms, and I think they're much better than the large, gendered rooms with stalls. If you're pee-shy, you can pee (or take care of other stuff) comfortably, without angst over who is listening. You get your own personal sink. And you don't have to worry about how silly you look checking your teeth for green stuff.

Ideally, your single-stall, all-gender restroom will also be accessible for people in wheelchairs. If so, you can use this sign.

Here are a few signs to avoid and the reasons why.

Woman and Man Images

This implies that there are only two genders. It's very binary. Are nonbinary folks welcome to use that facility? What about women who aren't wearing dresses? What about people with necks? (Too far?)

Family Restroom

The implication here is that folks using this restroom should have a child or children in tow. A single person exiting a "Family" restroom is at risk for getting the stink eye.

Half-and-Half Person

 Please avoid the image of the person who has pants on one side of their body and a dress on the other side. The only time I ever saw a person look like this was Halloween 1984, when my friend Billy showed up at a party as half man and half woman. He did the half beard thing and everything. It was very creative. However, giving people the impression that transgender individuals are "half men and half women" is not accurate and not cool.

Aliens

 Really? This bathroom issue confuses lots of people already. Let's keep it human.

Whatever, Just Wash Your Hands

 Okay, I'll admit it. I definitely chuckled the first time I saw this sign. However, upon consideration I realized that it is a bit dismissive of this very important topic.

NOTES

1. Reprinted from Susan Goldberg, "School Forms: What Happens When Both Parents Are Mother," Today's Parent, St. Joseph Communications, December 31, 2013, https://www.todaysparent.com/family/what-happens-when-both-parents-are-mother/.

2. Some of the information offered in this section comes from the Joint Commission, *Advancing Effective Communication, Cultural Competence, and Patient- and Family-Centered Care for the Lesbian, Gay, Bisexual, and Transgender (LGBT) Community: A Field Guide* (Oak Brook, IL: Joint Commission, 2011), https://www.joint commission.org/assets/1/18/LGBTFieldGuide.pdf.

3. Sarah Prager, "When the Forms Don't Fit Your Family," *New York Times*, September 1, 2020, https://www.nytimes.com/2020/09/01/parenting/lgbtq-family -paperwork.html.

4. Susan Goldberg, "School forms: What happens when both parents are Mother," *Today's Parent*, October 31, 2013, https://www.todaysparent.com/family/what-happens-when-both-parents-are-mother/.

5. Ibid.

6. National LGBT Health Education Center, *Focus on Forms and Policy: Creating an Inclusive Environment for LGBT Patients*, https://www.lgbthealtheducation.org/wp-content/uploads/2017/08/Forms-and-Policy-Brief.pdf.

7. Human Rights Campaign, "Workplace Gender Transition Guidelines," https://www.hrc.org/resources/workplace-gender-transition-guidelines and Mozilla, "Mozilla Workplace Transition Policy Guidelines," https://blog.mozilla.org/careers/mozilla-workplace-transition-policy-guidelines/.

8. Asaf Orr and Joel Baum, "Schools in Transition: A Guide for Supporting Transgender Students in K–12 Schools," https://hrc-prod-requests.s3-us-west-2.amazonaws.com/files/assets/resources/Schools-In-Transition.pdf.

9. Human Rights Campaign, *Corporate Equality Index 2019*, last updated April 4, 2019, https://assets2.hrc.org/files/assets/resources/CEI-2019-FullReport.pdf?_ga=2.72494480.2003376306.1571331256-1109047636.1571331256.

10. CNBC, "'Bathroom Bill' to Cost North Carolina $3.76 Billion," March, 27, 2017, https://www.cnbc.com/2017/03/27/bathroom-bill-to-cost-north-carolina-376-billion.html.

11. Jason Hanna, Madison Park, and Elliott C. McLaughlin, "North Carolina Repeals 'Bathroom Bill,'" CNN Politics, March 30, 2017, https://www.cnn.com/2017/03/30politics/north-carolina-hb2-agreement/index.html.

12. Amanda Wicks, "More Republican Legislators Arrested for Bathroom Misconduct than Trans People," Complex, March 2016, https://www.complex.com/life/2016/03/republican-legislators-arrested-for-bathroom-misconduct.

13. Transgender Law Center, "CA Governor Signs 'All-Gender' Restroom Bill," September 29, 2016, https://transgenderlawcenter.org/archives/13317.

14. Noah Michelson, "More Americans Claim to Have Seen a Ghost than Have Met a Trans Person," HuffPost, December, 21, 2015, https://www.huffpost.com/entry/more-americans-claim-to-have-seen-a-ghost-than-have-met-a-trans-person_n_5677fee5e4b014efe0d5ed62.

15. Mitch Kellaway, "Trans Folks Respond to 'Bathroom Bills' with #WeJustNeedToPee Selfies," *Advocate*, March 14, 2015, https://www.advocate.com/politics/transgender/2015/03/14/trans-folks-respond-bathroom-bills-wejustneedtopee-selfies.

16. Sam Killermann, *A Guide to Gender: The Social Justice Advocate's Handbook*, rev. and updated ed. (Austin, TX: Impetus Books, 2017) and Sam Killermann, It's Pronounced Metrosexual, https://www.itspronouncedmetrosexual.com.

11

CREATING LGBTQ+ INCLUSIVE SPACES IN DIFFERENT SETTINGS

He should have just ripped the label off so everybody could see that he's blue! He's happy drawing blue stuff.[1]

—Alastair (age 6) reacting to the book *Red: A Crayon's Story*

In addition to what I've already offered in this book regarding actions for creating LGBTQ+ inclusive spaces, there are some great pointers that apply to specific settings. In this chapter, we'll look at some additional tips for creating LGBTQ+ inclusive spaces in your home, in health and mental health settings, in the workplace, in faith communities, and in schools.

IN YOUR HOME

I'm starting with advice for parents, grandparents, foster parents, legal guardians, and other responsible adults and family members because, in most cases, you get the first crack at raising your children right. (No pressure. Haha!) Creating a safe and inclusive home environment, where your children know that you're there for them no matter what, is important whether your children are LGBTQ+ or not. If your child does discover that they're part of the LGBTQ+ communities, you've established a safe and supportive haven for them to help them thrive. If your child isn't LGBTQ+, what a powerful message you'll be giving them about acceptance and respect for all people.

I frequently get asked by parents, "At what age do you think it's appropriate to talk with children about LGBTQ+ people?" My answer? As soon as you can prop their chubby little bodies up against your belly and put a book in front of their faces. We should be introducing our children to books that represent all types of people and families as soon as we start reading to them.

Read your children picture books that represent people with a variety of skin tones, body sizes, abilities, and gender expressions. Read them books about boys who like to dress in colorful, flowing clothes, like *Julián Is a Mermaid* by Jessica Love. Read them books like *Red: A Crayon's Story* by Michael Hall, in which the moral of the story is that being yourself, even if it's difficult, is the right way to be. Read them books about all kinds of family structures. Two of my favorite children's picture books that represent different types of families are *Families, Families, Families* by Suzanne Lang and Max Lang and *A Tale of Two Mommies* by Vanita Oelschlager.

HELPFUL HINT

When you encounter books with stereotypical characters and gender roles, mess with the names, titles, and pronouns. Most of the animals in the picture books I read to my children when they were young, had names like, "Mr. Squirrel," "Mr. Rabbit," and "Mr. Hedgehog." Only if the character had babies would they be depicted as female, for example "Mrs. Mouse." As I read my children these books I intentionally messed with the animals' titles and pronouns to create more inclusive and progressive worlds—worlds where, for example, "Ms. Squirrel" oversaw the construction of the new school. I kept this up until my kids were able to say, "Mom! That doesn't say, 'Ms. Squirrel.' It says, 'Mr. Squirrel.'" I decided that once they were old enough to catch me at it, they were old enough to have a conversation about why I was doing it.

My children are now in their twenties. This took place two decades ago, at a time when I wasn't aware of nonbinary individuals. You may want to consider avoiding titles all together and simply refer to the characters as "Squirrel" and "Mouse." That way you can add a few characters who use the pronoun *they*, introducing the concept of nonbinary folks!

Here are a few more pointers for creating open and accepting homes.

1. Fight gender roles and gender expectations. Dress your child in all colors, not just blue for boys and pink for girls. When your child is old enough, let them choose what they want to wear. Accept and encourage

your child in all their interests and activities, even if your daughter loves climbing trees and your son loves playing with dolls.

2. *Lesbian, gay, bisexual,* and *transgender* are not naughty words. Use them in your house as easily and as naturally as you'd use words like *tall, green, silly,* and *kind*.

3. Use ungendered terms when gender isn't known. For example, if your child asks you if they can have a friend over, you might respond, "Of course. Do they want to stay for dinner?" If your teenager tells you they've been asked to the prom, you might respond, "So exciting! Who's your date?" Check out the wonderful short video on YouTube called "The One You Never Forget,"[2] which brings the importance of this concept to light.

4. When you talk with your children about sex and healthy relationships, make sure you're using language that implies that your children's crushes and potential partners could be anyone. If you discover that your child is LGBTQ+, don't shy away from conversations about sex and healthy relationships because you don't know what to say. Think about how you would talk with a straight cisgender child about these things: You might discuss what healthy and unhealthy relationships look like, dating safety, where to go for resources and health care, and how fun crushes are. Talk with your LGBTQ+ child about the same things. Keep in mind that you don't need to know all the answers. Let your child know, regardless of their gender and orientation, that you'll help them find the answers to their questions and the care they need.

5. If your child is LGBTQ+ avoid trying to figure out why. Your child is not LGBTQ+ because of that time you let them paint their fingernails or because you switched up the animals' genders in their picture books. No one knows why some people are LGBTQ+ and others aren't. Resist the temptation to blame anything or anyone for your child's LGBTQ+ identity. Not only is there no causal evidence, but blaming implies that your child is somehow defective.

6. Tell your child you love them over and over and over. It never gets old.

Four great resources for families wanting to create an LGBTQ+ inclusive home are:

- PFLAG: the first and largest organization specially for parents, family members, and friends of LGBTQ+ people

- Gender Spectrum: online LGBTQ+ information, resources, and support for family members of LGBTQ+ teens and children
- My Kid Is Gay: a website with resources to help families understand their LGBTQ+ kids
- Planned Parenthood: a nonprofit organization providing reproductive health care that offers great tips on how to talk with your children about LGBTQ+ people and families
- The Rainbow Book List: a resource, created by the American Library Association, with LGBTQ+ related book suggestions for children and teens.[3]

IN HEALTH AND MENTAL HEALTH SETTINGS

The long history of oppression, discrimination, and abuse toward LGBTQ+ patients in the health and mental health fields creates a unique set of challenges and barriers to receiving care. Previous negative experiences and current legal inequalities often result in LGBTQ+ people distrusting health and mental health care professionals and delaying seeking care. Providers and facilities that are explicitly LGBTQ+ welcoming and inclusive are critical for building trust and offering effective care to LGBTQ+ people.

Knowing that LGBTQ+ people may be resistant to even walking through the door of a health or mental health facility, it's important for you to think about what folks are seeing and learning about your facility from the outside. Before patients even schedule their first visit, what are they seeing on your website, in your brochures, and on your social media sites? Do they see indications that LGBTQ+ people are welcomed there? Is your nondiscrimination policy easy to find on your website and does it explicitly state that your staff doesn't discriminate on the basis of sexual orientation, gender identity, and gender expression? Does your brochure have images of LGBTQ+ people and families? What is your agency's reputation in the community? Is your agency known for hosting a table at Pride? Do you advertise in the local LGBTQ+ paper?

If you've "talked the talk" by getting the word out that your agency is LGBTQ+ welcoming and inclusive, make sure you're also "walking the walk." How disappointing to advertise to the LGBTQ+ communities that your agency is welcoming and inclusive, only to have a new transgender patient walk in and immediately get misgendered or a lesbian patient get asked about her husband. Here are some best-practice tips for welcoming LGBTQ+ patients once they're through your door.

Start by making a great first impression with inclusive forms on which everyone sees themselves represented, as discussed in chapter 10. A few great pointers to remember are to use fill-ins instead of multiple choice, whenever possible. When fill-ins aren't possible, make sure you have a multiple-choice option that says, "A gender [or sex, race, etc.] not listed here." Make sure that "Name" is at the top of the form, with "Legal name if different" lower down, so the correct name is always used. Add an optional section for patients to share their pronouns and how they would like to be addressed. Finally, rethink your "M" or "F" boxes. No matter how you slice it, these limited boxes aren't getting you the information you need. Do you need to know the patient's sex assigned at birth, their gender, and/or the gender listed on their insurance card? Think about what you need to know and ask the appropriate questions accordingly.

It's also imperative that agencies are asking the right questions on their forms regarding sexual orientation and behavior in order to get the answers they need to care for people. For example, if your health center focuses on sexual health and treating sexually transmitted infections, the questions on your forms should be about a person's sexual behaviors, *not* about their sexual orientation. Too often healthcare workers either ignore these questions altogether (assuming that everyone is straight) or they ask about a patient's orientation (e.g., "Do you identify as LGBT?"). The term *MSM*, which stands for "men who have sex with men" and is often used in communities of color, was created for this exact reason. Men who identified as straight but were having sex with other men were not getting the care they needed at health centers because the centers were not asking about their sexual behaviors. Healthcare providers should think about what information they need to treat the whole person and use this information to craft their intake forms.

Here are a few more suggestions for creating LGBTQ+ inclusive agencies.

1. Post a sign with a rainbow on it that says, "All families welcome here."
2. Subscribe to an LGBTQ+ magazine for your waiting room.
3. Create systems where you're ensuring that you're calling patients by their correct name or where you're not using names at all. Consider texting patients or using a pager system, like restaurants do, to call people from the waiting room when you're ready for them. This way no one ever has to do the walk of shame from their chair in the waiting room to the inner door because a staff member misgendered them with a dead name.
4. Meet privately with patients whenever you're discussing personal information.

5. Ask open-ended, ungendered questions like, "Who do you consider family?"
6. Wear a rainbow pin.
7. Display your pronouns on your name badge so patients know that it's safe for them to share theirs.
8. Ask all patients how they would like to be addressed.
9. If you uncover important information about how a patient wants to be addressed or how they refer to their loved ones and the patient is comfortable with you sharing the information, make a note in the chart for other staff members to see. For example, "Please refer to this patient as Georgette, even though this is not her legal name, and use *she*, *her*, and *hers* for her pronouns."
10. Advocate for single-stall, all-gender facilities and ongoing LGBTQ+ inclusion training for your staff.

Great resources for offering quality care to LGBTQ+ people are:

- The Joint Commission's "Advancing Effective Communication, Cultural Competence, and Patient- and Family-Centered Care for the Lesbian, Gay, Bisexual, and Transgender (LGBT) Community: A Field Guide"
- The National LGBTQIA+ Health Education Center's "Focus on Forms and Policy: Creating an Inclusive Environment for LGBT Patients."[4]

Caring for LGBTQ+ People of Color

Every research paper or article you ever read on health disparities among LGBTQ+ people will undoubtedly include a statement like this, "these disparities are exacerbated for LGBTQ+ people of color." The health disparities and barriers to care that exist for the general LGBTQ+ communities are, across the board, worse for LGBTQ+ people of color. This, of course, doesn't mean that LGBTQ+ people of color are innately sicker than their white counterparts. It means that our systems are set up in ways that discriminate against LGBTQ+ people of color, causing health disparities and barriers to care that lead to poorer health outcomes for this community of people.

LGBTQ+ people of color have higher rates of alcohol abuse, diabetes, and suicide than their white LGBTQ+ counterparts and they're less likely to have health insurance coverage.[5] In the 2016 article "NIH Recognizes LGBTQ Community as 'Health Disparity Population,'" Kellan Baker, a senior fellow for the LGBT Research and Communications Project at the Center for American Progress, says, "It goes back to a fundamental idea that populations facing disparities are diverse. Nobody's just gay, or transgender, or black, or Asian, or disabled—we're all living at the intersections of other identities. And folks living at intersections of multiple identities facing discrimination face a greater disparity."[6]

Best-practice ally actions to create systems that are more inclusive and that reduce barriers to care for LGBTQ+ people of color include advocating for more educational and awareness trainings on this topic for staff, better strategies for recruiting and retaining medical professionals from different communities and diverse backgrounds, regular auditing and oversight of current systems, and documentation of the disparate impact of current policies.

For more information about creating safer and more inclusive health and mental health facilities for LGBTQ+ patients of color, check out these articles:

- "Improving Care of LGBTQ People of Color" by Stephani Bi, Scott C. Cook, and Marshall H. Chin
- "Understanding and Addressing Racial Disparities in Health Care" by David R. Williams and Toni D. Rucker[7]

Caring for Transgender Individuals

For professionals providing health care to transgender individuals, it's important to be aware of the fact that some transgender people have intense feelings of distress about their bodies. This can cause discomfort and stress even during routine examinations. Best practices for reducing stress for your transgender patients include asking the patient the words they use to refer to their body parts and mirroring those terms, explaining exactly what the patient can expect during exams and procedures, and ensuring that the patient understands that they're in control of the exam and they can ask to pause, or even stop it, whenever they want.

Great resources for creating transgender welcoming and inclusive health and mental health facilities are:

- The Center of Excellence for Transgender Health
- Fenway Health's Trans Health Program and Gender-Affirming Care.[8]

Caring for Older LGBTQ+ Adults

The incredible increase in LGBTQ+ visibility and inclusion over the past few decades may make it difficult for some people to understand the fears and anxiety experienced by many older LGBTQ+ adults as they consider accessing health and mental health care. What's important to keep in mind is that older LGBTQ+ adults have survived an era when being open about their orientation and/or gender identity may have resulted in a diagnosis of a mental disorder, arrest for "sexual deviance," or involuntary electroshock therapy or castration.

Several studies have shown that, compared to older straight cisgender adults, older LGBTQ+ adults are at an increased risk for disability, mental distress, social isolation, and chronic conditions.[9] This, combined with the fact that older LGBTQ+ adults are also less likely to seek care, is heartbreaking. Those who do access care often hide who they are and whom they've spent their lives with. Too many LGBTQ+ adults, after living authentically for most of their lives, tragically return to a life of secrecy when they enter senior-living facilities in their final years. Don't make the mistake of thinking that the suggestions offered in this book for creating LGBTQ+ inclusive spaces are less important when you're working with older adults.

Great resources for additional information on creating welcoming and inclusive spaces for older LGBTQ+ adults are:

- Boulder County Area Agency on Aging's "Project Visibility"
- The National Resource Center on LGBT Aging
- SAGE: Advocacy & Services for LGBT Elders.[10]

IN THE WORKPLACE

Here's some extra motivation for creating LGBTQ+ inclusive workplaces: Research shows that LGBTQ+ employees who can bring their authentic selves to work are more productive at their jobs, feel more connected to their colleagues, have increased workplace satisfaction, and are more likely to remain at their jobs.[11] In addition, companies that have implemented policies specifically supporting LGBTQ+ employees have higher profitability and stock market value.[12] LGBTQ+ inclusion is good for business! Here's the bad news: Half of the LGBTQ+ employees in the United States hide who they are at work.[13]

One of the biggest stumbling blocks to LGBTQ+ inclusion in workplaces is confusion over what being "out" at work means. I often hear this comment from straight cisgender people, "No one should be out in the workplace. That's not appropriate." Actually, the vast majority of straight cisgender people are out in the workplace. They talk about the movie they saw over the weekend with their wife. They have a photo of their husband on their desk. They bring their girlfriend to the company's holiday party. This is what being out in the workplace looks like. Being out at work doesn't mean that someone is going to tell you about the great new sexual position they just discovered with their partner. An important role for allies is to help folks understand the difference between sexual orientation (which comes with us to work) and sexual behaviors (which do not).

Large companies should consider creating and supporting a Pride ERG (employee resource group). ERGs help to create a sense of belonging for employees who share a common identity, background, or culture. They offer education, resources, mentorship, and support for historically underrepresented groups. ERGs demonstrate a strong commitment by companies to ongoing diversity and inclusion excellence.

Here are a few more great tips for employers seeking to create more LGBTQ+ inclusive workplaces. Add diversity and inclusion efforts and actions to your employees' performance evaluation to encourage everyone to get involved in concrete ways. Actively recruit LGBTQ+ talent by advertising job opportunities in LGBTQ+ publications and on LGBTQ+ websites. Ensure that LGBTQ+ images are represented on your website and on your brochures.

As you work toward creating more LGBTQ+ inclusive spaces at your workplace, keep in mind that growing pains are common. Diversity and inclusion efforts are sure to make some employees uncomfortable. People who have never had to hide who they are at work may not understand why things can't remain the way they've always been. They may feel that these diversity efforts are violating *their* rights and beliefs. Having respectful conversations with employees about these diversity efforts and allowing people to share their fears and concerns are terrific tasks for allies. Listen ("Tell me more about how you're feeling"), connect ("I was confused by a lot of this stuff too"), reassure ("Please know that no one is asking you to change your beliefs"), and share ("These efforts are happening so everyone can feel safe and included at work").

Two great resources to check out for more information on creating LGBTQ+ inclusive workplaces are:

- Out and Equal Workplace Advocates: an organization focused on LGBTQ+ workplace equality
- The Human Rights Campaign (HRC): an LGBTQ+ advocacy and lobbying organizations with lots of workplace resources[14]

Some wonderful books for being active allies in the workplace are:

- *Better Allies: Everyday Actions to Create Inclusive, Engaging Workplaces* (Second Edition) by Karen Catlin
- *Brian McNaught's Guide to LGBTQ Issues in the Workplace* by Brian McNaught.[15]

IN FAITH COMMUNITIES

Like health and mental health facilities, many faith communities historically have poor track records when it comes to LGBTQ+ inclusion. Building trust with the LGBTQ+ communities is likely to take more than hanging an "All are welcome" sign on your door. Here are some suggestions for creating a welcoming and inclusive LGBTQ+ faith community.

- Ensure that your welcome statement specifically includes LGBTQ+ people and families or states that all are welcome regardless of sexual orientation, gender identity, or gender expression. Then read your welcome statement aloud at the beginning of weekly services.
- Share that your faith community is open and affirming by posting about it on your social media sites, in your newsletters, and in email messages.
- Hang a rainbow flag on your building.
- Advertise in the LGBTQ+ communities when you have job openings or volunteer opportunities.
- Offer workshops for your staff, volunteers, and members on LGBTQ+ inclusion.
- Place a basket of pronouns pins or stickers at the entrance of your building.
- Touch the hearts and minds of your congregants by offering LGBTQ+ panel discussions where LGBTQ+ community members share their stories, talk about what their faith means to them, and answer questions.
- Include LGBTQ+ people in your teachings on sexuality, marriage, love, and family.
- Observe Pride month with displays and banners.
- March in the local Pride parade.
- Host an LGBTQ+ themed film or documentary followed by a group discussion. Check out the documentary film *For They Know Not What They Do*, which explores the intersections of faith and being LGBTQ+ in America.[16]

Some great resources for faith communities are:

- The *Interfaith LGBTQ Toolkit* assembled by Randy A. Block, director and founder of the Michigan Unitarian Universalist Social Justice Network
- HRC's "Faith Resources"
- PFLAG's "Faith Resources for Interfaith/Non-Denominational Communities"
- Building an Inclusive Church: A Welcoming Toolkit 3.0 by Reconciling-Works[17]

IN SCHOOLS

My friend Matt grew up in an Upstate New York suburb and attended the public school there. From kindergarten until about tenth grade, he never heard the word *gay* spoken in a positive way by anyone—students, teachers, school staff, or administrators. As a young man figuring out his identity as a cisgender gay man, he didn't experience much name-calling or bullying at school; there was just this resounding silence when it came to anything LGBTQ+ related. It wasn't until tenth-grade health class that he finally heard the word *gay* spoken by a teacher—and guess what they were talking about: HIV and AIDS. The very first time Matt heard his identity spoken by a teacher, it had to do with disease and death. Matt said this made him want no part of being gay. He sat in that stage of identity tolerance for years and years instead of moving forward and being able to live authentically.

It's probable that the administrators and teachers at Matt's school thought their school was really inclusive because there was little to no bullying of LGBTQ+ students. This is typical of what is currently happening in most of the K–12 schools in the United States. Most schools believe that if they're either not seeing LGBTQ+ related bullying or they're dealing with the bullying, then they have created an inclusive environment. They haven't. They are simply snuffing out a negative behavior. The underlying issue is still there. In his book *Safe Is Not Enough: Better Schools for LGBTQ Students*, Michael Sadowski asks, "Is safety the only thing to which LGBTQ students are entitled at school?"[18] Let's hope not.

Matt shared with me that if one teacher in elementary school had added a word problem in math class that said: "Peter invited 12 kids to his birthday party. His two moms bought 3 pizzas with 8 slices each . . ." his mind would have been blown! He told me that seeing a gay couple normalized in this way in the school curriculum would have sent him down a much healthier path toward self-acceptance.

My children, along with most kids in the United States, have known how to stop, drop, and roll since kindergarten. They were taught and retaught this home fire safety technique throughout their K–12 school experience. I am truly thankful. However, I once investigated the likelihood of a child dying in a house fire in the United States: It's about 1 in 90,000. What are the chances that that child will discover at some point in their life that they're LGBTQ+? The estimates are about 1 in 20. Yet our schools remain mostly silent on the subject. In a 2021 survey of more than 22,000 students between the ages of thirteen and twenty-one from all fifty states, only 1 out of every 6 students reported having seen LGBTQ+ people and families represented in their school's curriculum in a positive way.[19] Without LGBTQ+ teachers as role models, LGBTQ+ historical figures included in the curriculum, and any positive LGBTQ+ characters in textbooks or literature, LGBTQ+ children are left to cope with understanding and accepting their identities completely on their own. Parents are left unsupported, not knowing how to react when their children come out to them or how to support them. Schools' silence about LGBTQ+ people sends a very loud and clear message. So, let's look at some big-fix solutions for creating LGBTQ+ inclusive schools.

You just read about how one little math problem would have changed my friend Matt's life, so let's begin this section on tips for teachers and school staff by looking at ways to include LGBTQ+ people and families in everyday school curriculum. Don't make the mistake of thinking that conversations about LGBTQ+ people are only for health class. Normalizing LGBTQ+ people and families in all subjects puts an end to the silence that creates an environment where bullying thrives and instead creates a truly inclusive school. Here are some suggestions for including LGBTQ+ people in the curriculum for different subject areas, if you live in a state or a country where you're legally allowed to do this.

Language Arts: Assign books that challenge ideas about traditional families and gender roles or that deal with bullying. Give students the opportunity to talk about whether or not they see themselves and their families reflected in the books they read. Have students write about families different from their own.

Social Studies: Include famous LGBTQ+ people such as civil-rights activists Harvey Milk, Bayard Rustin, and Marsha P. Johnson in your history lesson. Discuss LGBTQ+ discrimination and successes in history (e.g., the Stonewall Riots). Have students bring in articles about LGBTQ+ issues in the news. Talk about the importance of allies in past civil-rights movements.

Math: Highlight famous LGBTQ+ mathematicians like Alan Turing. Use your word problems to reflect all kinds of families (e.g., "Kendra's two dads bought five pizzas . . ."). Have students use data and statistics to illuminate social justice issues that they're interested in. Google "social justice mathematics" for some great resources.

Science: Highlight famous LGBTQ+ scientists like Sir Francis Bacon, Sonya Kovalesvsky, and Florence Nightingale. Discuss natural biological variation in biology to bring attention to and to normalize intersex people.

Music, Theater, and Art: Talk about LGBTQ+ artists and musicians as well as famous people who don't follow traditional gender roles. Watch for those teachable moments if students tease about boys who dance, sing, or paint. Allow students to try out for any part in the school play, regardless of gender.

Physical Education: Promote mixed-gender Physical Education, allowing all students to participate in all the sports and activities together. Ask anyone who's feeling strong to help move equipment, not just the boys. Prepare responses ahead of time so you are ready to challenge comments like, "You throw like a girl."

Health: Offer information about all types of relationships. Use ungendered terms like *partners* and *dates* instead of gendered terms like *boyfriends* and *girlfriends*. Use a diagram that highlights the components of sex, gender, and sexuality, like the ones I used in chapter 4, to educate students about identities like nonbinary, pansexual, intersex, asexual, and more.

Library: Work to ensure your school library has a large selection of books that include protagonists with a variety of genders, orientations, cultures, races, body types, and abilities. Create a display of LGBTQ+ books for LGBTQ+ history month (October) or Pride month (June).

HELPFUL HINT

Are you worried that if you read the picture book *King and King*, about two princes falling in love, to your elementary school class, some precocious little scamp will ask what two men do in the bedroom? Keep cool and use the "switch it" technique! How would you respond if you were reading a book about a prince and a princess falling in love and some precocious little scamp asked you what the prince and princess do in the bedroom? I'll bet somewhere in that goody bag of magical teacher tricks you've already got a way to wiggle out of that question with an age-appropriate response. So, use the same method to wiggle out of the question about the two princes.

Before I move on from this topic of including LGBTQ+ people and families in everyday school curriculum, I have to acknowledge that this is much easier (and safer) for some than for others in the United States. We live in a time when some states currently mandate the inclusion of LGBTQ+ people and families in their K–12 curricula and others forbid it. At the time of this book's publication, California, Oregon, Nevada, Colorado, New Jersey, Connecticut, and Illinois public school teachers have curricular standards that include affirming visibility of LGBTQ+ people and families. In Louisiana, Mississippi, Oklahoma, and Texas, anti-LGBTQ+ curriculum laws, also known as No Promo Homo Laws (no, I'm not kidding), are in place. (Check GLSEN's policy maps for the most updated information.[20]) In Indiana, Nevada, and Utah, teachers have been banned from displaying Pride flags, Black Lives Matter symbols, or both.[21] So, when teachers tell me that they're worried about parent pushback and/or repercussions from their school's administrators if they include LGBTQ+ people and families in their curriculum, I get it. What I've shared here are best practices for creating LGBTQ+ inclusive schools. They may not be things that you can safely and legally implement at your school. Someday, I believe it will change for the better. For now, if you live in a state that is restricting your ability to represent LGBTQ+ people in a positive way, see if you can find more subtle ways to indicate to your students that you support LGBTQ+ people. Tell students that you believe all people are perfect the way they are, combat gender policing when you see it, make special connections with colleagues who you suspect may be hiding who they are, advocate for more inclusive policies, and stay safe!

My second tip for teachers and school staff is one you've already learned about in chapter 6: Ungender your language. Let's dive a little deeper into this concept as it relates to educators and creating more inclusive schools. We'll

A CALL TO ACTION

We are living through unprecedented times regarding anti-LGBTQ+ legislation. In 2022 in the United States, nearly two hundred anti-LGBTQ+ bills were filed seeking to erode protections for LGBTQ+ youth and create severe restrictions on classroom discussions, curriculum, and books that mention LGBTQ+ people and families. Allies, please vote against politicians who back these bills! Please call your state lawmakers, rally, and lobby to rescind these hateful laws. (More on how to do this coming up in chapter 12.)

look at an eye-opening school-based study, and I'll offer some suggestions for ungendering language, activities, and expectations in a school setting.

Let's imagine an elementary school classroom where the teacher has just asked the students to line up by boys and girls, something that, unfortunately, is still quite common. As an LGBTQ+ educator, my first reaction is, "Ugh! What is a nonbinary student supposed to do in this situation? They literally won't know which line to stand in." However, I recently became aware of a study that shows that when teachers highlight gender, even by simply referring to *boys and girls* instead of *students*, the children in these classrooms are more likely to reinforce gender stereotypes and even discriminate by gender when deciding which children to play with.[22] The study shows that "merely calling attention to the fact of gender caused children to agree more with stereotypes, such as the idea that only girls should play with baby dolls or become dancers, and that only boys should use tools and become firefighters."[23] Gendered language negatively affects all of our kids by limiting their understanding of who they are and who they can be.

The "switch it" technique may help us explain the importance of ungendering our language to others. Pennsylvania State University development psychologist Lynn Liben, one of the people who conducted this study, says, "You would never say 'good morning black children and white children,' or have white and black kids line up separately."[24] Most people understand how segregating by race in this way would be at best uncomfortable for the children and at worst damaging. The same is true for gender. So, instead of separating groups by boys and girls, get creative! Try separating or creating groups by who's wearing a belt and who's not wearing a belt, the number of letters in the student's name, the number of vowels in their name, the number of family members they have, how many pets they have, the type of pets they have, their birth month, their birthday, the color of their socks, who's wearing lace-up shoes and who's wearing slip on or Velcro. The possibilities are endless. And your students are likely to love your fun, new, innovative shift from the old routine.

Here are a few final tips for ungendering your language in schools before we move on. If you like to use endearments with the students, like *love* or *sweetheart*, make sure you're using the same ones for all students, regardless of gender. When you're teaching about feminine and masculine forms of words, include the gender-neutral forms as well. For example, woman/man/person, mother/father/parent, and sister/brother/sibling. Talk about how these gender-neutral terms should be used when gender is unknown or when someone doesn't use gendered terms to refer to themselves. Avoid unconscious gender bias in the classroom by pulling names from a hat to decide which student will lead the next activity or answer the next question. Implement anonymous grading by enabling this option in your web-based classroom management system or by using codes. Advocate for single-stall, all-gender facilities.

Check out the video "Gender Neutral Education: Can Our Kids Go Gender Free," which documents an effort to ungender an elementary school classroom. Although the focus and language in the video is quite binary, using the terms *boys* and *girls* throughout, it's well worth watching. There are some fantastic takeaways for teachers.[25]

My final tip for teachers and school staff has to do with sharing, gathering, and using pronouns. Once students are old enough to know what a pronoun is, they're old enough to be offered the opportunity to share theirs, if they want to. An excellent place to do this is on the "Getting to Know You" questionnaires that teachers often distribute to their students at the start of each semester. Two reasons why this type of questionnaire is such a great medium for gathering pronouns are that it's private and it utilizes a system that works for everyone, avoiding having to single someone out. As suggested previously in chapter 5, offer your pronouns first on the form and make sure the students know that sharing their pronouns is optional. Also, consider including a question like this one: "Is there any information you'd like to share regarding when and where you'd like me to use these pronouns?"

I can't remember a workshop that I've offered teachers and school staff in the past four years when a question like this one hasn't come up: "I have a student who is asking me to use a new name and pronoun in school, but they can't use them at home because their parents aren't supportive. What should I do and how should I navigate this situation?" This is a tricky situation indeed. (Can I just say that we *really* don't pay teachers enough?) Here are some of my thoughts on navigating it.

1. Check out your state guidelines. Where I live, in New York, there are specific guidelines from the State Education Department that require teachers and school staff to use the name and pronouns that students are asking them to use. Teachers and school staff are also required to keep these new names and pronouns confidential if the student is asking them to do so. These guidelines are called "Guidance to School Districts for Creating a Safe and Supportive School Environment for Transgender and Gender Nonconforming Students." See if there's something similar in your state. There's lots of great information on the American Civil Liberty Union's "Know Your Rights: Students' Rights" webpage.[26]

2. If you're working with a student who's asking you to use a new name and/or new pronouns and they don't have support at home, talk with them about the support services offered at your school. Your school's mental health professionals may be able to offer the student additional support and help them navigate conversations with their family.

3. Don't get ahead of yourself by assuming that names and pronouns reflect specific identities. Keep things in perspective. If a student asks you to use a new name and/or pronouns, all they're doing is giving you information on how you can respectfully refer to them. If a student's parent insists that their child be called "William," but the child hates this name and asks that you call him "Billy," are you going to refuse the child's request and continue to call him "William?" When a student asks you to use a new name and/or new pronouns, it may mean that they're changing how they identify and/or how they define their gender, but it may not. Try not to jump to the conclusion that the student is transgender or is going to be transitioning.

   This is such an important point for teachers, administrators, and school staff to understand. I often hear this pushback against allowing students to share their pronouns: "It's not appropriate to ask students how they identify." I agree. It's not. Asking students if they'd like to share their pronouns *isn't* asking them how they identify. It's asking them how people can respectfully refer to them. It's similar to asking what title someone uses, for example, *Ms., Mrs., Miss, Mr., Dr.,* or *Mx.* We can't tell by looking at someone what title they use. We also can't tell by looking at someone what pronoun they use.

4. Understand the impact you're having. I mentioned in chapter 3 that in my previous role as education director at our local LGBTQ+ center, I had the privilege of hearing hundreds of coming-out stories. LGBTQ+ folks frequently told stories about how they were only able to get by in school or were literally kept alive by one teacher or one school counselor who supported them and welcomed them to be their authentic selves. Some LGBTQ+ folks talked about a teacher who let them eat lunch in their classroom so they could avoid being bullied in the cafeteria. Others talked about how once a week for fifteen minutes they were able to hear their correct name and pronouns used by a school counselor. Even if your hands are tied by restrictive policies, make no mistake, your small efforts to validate and affirm students' correct names and pronouns can have a huge positive impact.

Here are some of my favorite resources for creating LGBTQ+ inclusive schools:

- HRC's Welcoming Schools: offers LGBTQ+ resources, lesson plans, booklists, and films, including their award-winning short film called *What Do You Know? Kids Talk about LGBTQ+ Topics*
- Learning for Justice (formerly Teaching Tolerance): offers lesson plans for educators and provides social justice resources, including their "Speak Up at School: How to Respond to Everyday Prejudice, Bias and Stereotypes" guide
- GLSEN: offers resources to ensure that LGBTQ+ students are free from bullying and harassment, inclusive lesson plans, curriculum suggestions for educators, and GSA (i.e., Gay-Straight Alliance or Gender and Sexuality Alliance) resources and support.
- Gender Spectrum: offers online LGBTQ+ information and resources for teachers dedicated to creating more LGBTQ+ inclusive schools.[27]

NOTES

1. Alastair, personal correspondence, November 9, 2022.

2. Morgan Jon Fox, "The One You Never Forget," YouTube, August 25, 2020, https://www.youtube.com/watch?v=1aa9SttW0zk&ab_channel=MorganJonFox.

3. PFLAG, www.pflag.org; Gender Spectrum, https://www.genderspectrum.org/; My Kid Is Gay, https://www.mykidisgay.com/; Planned Parenthood, https://www.plannedparenthood.org/learn/parents/identity; and Rainbow Book List, https://glbtrt.ala.org/rainbowbooks.

4. Joint Commission, "Advancing Effective Communication, Cultural Competence, and Patient- and Family-Centered Care for the Lesbian, Gay, Bisexual, and Transgender (LGBT) Community: A Field Guide," October 2011, http://www.jointcommission.org/lgbt; and National LGBTQIA+ Health Education Center, "Focus on Forms and Policy: Creating an Inclusive Environment for LGBT Patients," August 7, 2017, www.lgbthealtheducation.org/publication/focus-forms-policy-creating-inclusive-environment-lgbt-patients.

5. American Progress, "Health Disparities in LGBT Communities of Color," January 15, 2010, https://www.americanprogress.org/article/health-disparities-in-lgbt-communities-of-color/ and Human Rights Campaign, QTBIPOC Mental Health and Well-Being, https://www.hrc.org/resources/qtbipoc-mental-health-and-well-being.

6. Noel Gutierrez-Morfin, "NIH Recognizes LGBTQ Community as 'Health Disparity Population,'" NBC News, October 7, 2016, https://www.nbcnews.com/feature /nbc-out/nih-recognizes-lgbtq-community-health-disparity-population-n661161.

7. Stephani Bi, Scott C. Cook, and Marshall H. Chin, "Improving Care of LGBTQ People of Color," *AFT Health Care*, Fall 2021, https://www.aft.org/hc /fall2021/bi_cook_chin and David R. Williams and Toni D. Rucker, "Understanding and Addressing Racial Disparities in Health Care," *Health Care Financing Review*, Volume 21 (4), Summer 2000: 75–90, https://www.ncbi.nlm.nih.gov/pmc/articles /PMC4194634/.

8. Center of Excellence for Transgender Health, https://prevention.ucsf.edu /transhealth and Fenway Health's Trans Health Program and Gender-Affirming Care, https://fenwayhealth.org/care/medical/transgender-health/.

9. Movement Advancement Project and SAGE, *Improving the Lives of LGBT Older Adults*," March 2010, https://www.lgbtmap.org/improving-the-lives-of-lgbt -older-adults and Soon Kyu Choi and Ilan H. Meyer, *LGBT Aging: A Review of Research Findings, Needs, and Policy Implications* (Los Angeles: The Williams Institute, 2016), file:///C:/Users/jgain/Documents/Savvy%20Ally%20Action/Resources/Older%20 Adults/LGBT-Aging-A-Review%202016.pdf.

10. Boulder County Area Agency on Aging, "Project Visibility," https://www.boul dercounty.org/families/seniors/services/project-visibility/; National Resource Center on LGBT Aging, www.lgbtagingcenter.org; and SAGE: Advocacy & Services for LGBT Elders, www.sageusa.org.

11. "The Cost of the Closet and the Rewards of Inclusion: Why the Workplace Environment for LGBT People Matters to Employers," Human Rights Campaign, https:// assets2.hrc.org/files/assets/resources/Cost_of_the_Closet_May2014.pdf.

12. Josie Cox, "Pride Pays: LGBT-Friendly Businesses Are More Profitable, Research Shows," *Forbes*, May 24, 2021, https://www.forbes.com/sites/josiecox/2021/05/24 /pride-pays-lgbt-friendly-businesses-are-more-profitable-research-shows/.

13. "The Cost of the Closet and the Rewards of Inclusion: Why the Workplace Environment for LGBT People Matters to Employers," Human Rights Campaign, https:// assets2.hrc.org/files/assets/resources/Cost_of_the_Closet_May2014.pdf.

14. Out and Equal, https://outandequal.org/ and Human Rights Campaign, https:// www.hrc.org/.

15. Karen Catlin, *Better Allies: Everyday Actions to Create Inclusive, Engaging Workplaces* (Second Edition) (Better Allies Press, January 2021) and Brian McNaught, *Brian McNaught's Guide to LGBTQ Issues in the Workplace* (independently published, November 2017).

16. Daniel G. Karslake (director), *For They Know Not What They Do* (DK Works, April 25, 2019).

17. "Interfaith LGBTQ Toolkit," http://www.uujustice.org//wp-content/up loads/2019/04/LGBTQ_Toolkit_Final-1.pdf; "Faith Resources," Human Rights Campaign, https://www.hrc.org/resources/faith-resources; "Faith Resources for Interfaith/

Non-Denominational Communities," PFLAG, https://pflag.org/nondenominational; and "Building an Inclusive Church: A Welcoming Toolkit 3.0," *Reconciling Works*, 2017, https://www.reconcilingworks.org/wp-content/uploads/2018/10/BIC-Toolkit .pdf.

18. Michael Sadowski, *Safe Is Not Enough: Better Schools for LGBTQ Students* (Cambridge, MA: Harvard Education Press, 2016), 11.

19. Joseph G. Kosciw, Caitlin M. Clark, and Leesh Menard, "The 2021 National School Climate Survey," GLSEN, https://www.glsen.org/sites/default/files/2022-10 /NSCS-2021-Full-Report.pdf.

20. GLSEN, Policy Maps, https://maps.glsen.org/.

21. Eesha Pendharkar, "Pride Flags and Black Lives Matter Signs in the Classroom: Supportive Symbols or Propaganda?" *Education Week*, January 25, 2022, https:// www.edweek.org/leadership/pride-flags-and-black-live-matters-signs-in-the-classroom -supportive-symbols-or-propaganda/2022/01.

22. Clara Moskowitz, "When Teachers Highlight Gender, Kids Pick Up Stereotypes," *Live Science*, November 16, 2010, https://www.livescience.com/8966-teachers -highlight-gender-kids-pick-stereotypes.html.

23. Ibid.

24. Ibid.

25. Real Families, "Gender Neutral Education: Can Our Kids Go Gender Free," YouTube, https://www.youtube.com/watch?v=3Y4lgKnmWSk&ab_channel =RealFamilies.

26. American Civil Liberty Union, "Know Your Rights: Students' Rights," https:// www.aclu.org/know-your-rights/students-rights/.

27. Welcoming Schools, https://welcomingschools.org/, *What Do You Know? Kids Talk about LGBTQ+ Topics*, https://welcomingschools.org/resources/what-do-you -know-lgbtq-video; Learning for Justice, https://www.learningforjustice.org/, Brian Willoughby, "Speak Up at School: How to Respond to Everyday Prejudice, Bias and Stereotypes," Teaching Tolerance, 2018, https://www.learningforjustice.org/sites /default/files/2019-04/TT-Speak-Up-Guide.pdf; GLSEN, https://www.glsen.org/; and Gender Spectrum, https://www.genderspectrum.org/.

TAKING IT
TO THE STREETS

There are risks and costs to a program of action. But they are far less than the long range risks and costs of comfortable inaction.[1]

—John F. Kennedy, a written message to the 14th Annual Convention of Americans for Democratic Action, May 11, 1961

Much of what I've shared in this book involves ways we can be respectful in our language, effectively educate others, and advocate for change within our workplaces, schools, faith communities, and social circles. This chapter focuses on moving outside of these smaller circles with community efforts that create political change, offer financial support to LGBTQ+ organizations, and support events that celebrate the LGBTQ+ communities in big and visible ways.

RALLIES, MARCHES, PROTESTS, AND LOBBYING

Being with like-minded and active people at peaceful rallies, marches, protests, and lobbying events can be powerful and energizing. After a violent incident here in Rochester, New York, I participated in a rally to support transgender people of color. We gathered on a busy city intersection, held signs, and walked to a different corner every time the light changed. It was a beautiful and simple way to draw attention to the cause.

I've also attended large, loud events like national marches, which have an entirely different vibe. I find it exciting to be a part of something so big. If you've never attended a rally or march, try one out and see if it's your thing, but do your homework ahead of time and be prepared. Find out who's organizing the event and what the expectations are for participants. Amnesty International has a helpful document on protests and marches, including what to do, what to bring, what to wear, and what your rights are as a protester.[2]

Lobby or advocacy days are organized with the purpose of visiting the state capitol and bringing awareness and concerns to state politicians. Lobby days provide an opportunity for LGBTQ+ community members and allies to voice their opinions to politicians and share the personal impact that polices have on them and their families. Often there's a focus for the day, like transgender rights or safe schools. Many times, organizing agencies offer workshops on how to lobby effectively and provide bus transportation to and from the event. This is a great way to meet other activists, stay informed about political issues relating to LGBTQ+ lives, and practice your "talking with politicians" skills.

TALKING WITH POLITICIANS

"Wait—what? I have to talk to politicians?" No, you don't have to, but according to the organization 5 Calls (which offers a great online resource for connecting with your local politicians with ease and impact) calling is the most effective way to communicate your thoughts and concerns. When you make your call, you'll simply state why you're calling in a sentence or two, probably either to an aide or a machine. You won't be expected to debate anyone. Check out 5 Calls' two-minute YouTube video "How to Call Your Representative with 5calls.org,"[3] which will walk you through the calling process. PFLAG's "Advocacy One-Pagers" are also excellent resources for advocacy and lobbying.[4]

Still scared? I feel your pain. This is not my forte. That's why I contacted my go-to guy Noah for some words of advice. "People are fine going to restaurants because they *know* the expected script," he says. "Table for four, follow host, figure out what to drink, figure out appetizers, figure out meal, eat, ask for refills, ask for bill, pay, tip, leave. Politics is just like that, except we haven't gotten a chance to practice it before (or not nearly the thousands of times we've done the restaurant script)."

Noah suggests that you write out what you want to say before you call. For example: "Hi. My name is [fill in your name], and I'm a constituent from [fill in your town name and/or zip code]. I'm calling because students deserve sex education in their schools that's medically accurate and inclusive of LGBTQ+ people. Can I count on [fill in politician's name] to support this issue?"

It's as simple as ordering a pizza, only instead of a warm pie you'll get a warm glow of pride from a job well done. And if this was really out-of-your-comfort-zone scary, consider rewarding yourself with the pizza. Self-care, baby!

FUNDRAISING

I've never met anyone who likes fundraising. Most people hate asking family members and friends for money and would rather have a root canal. If you are one of these folks, *please* don't move on to the next chapter until you've read about my metamorphosis from a miserable and reluctant fundraiser to the coordinator of our LGBTQ+ center's most successful fundraising event.

Many years ago, two friends of mine (both straight and cisgender) decided that they needed an excuse to bike and drink beer. They proposed a bike ride fundraiser that raised money for the nonprofit LGBTQ+ agency where I was employed. That first year, all I did was pedal in their bike ride and sheepishly ask my friends and family to support me. The ride took place in September 2010. We had eighteen riders. We rode one hundred kilometers. We raised $4,000. I lost track of the number of beers we consumed.

The next year my two friends didn't want to coordinate the ride again, so I decided to try my hand at it. I ended up coordinating the ride for the next eight years. This little bike ride fundraiser became my passion, pride, and joy. It grew and grew until our biggest year, when we had seventy-five riders, who brought in $63,000 for our center.

Toward the end of my tenure as the ride coordinator, I had consistently become the top-earning rider, typically bringing in between 8 and 10 percent of the total donations for the ride. Inevitably, I became a fundraising coach for others who didn't want to "make the ask." Here are some things I learned along the way:

- People are most inspired to donate by heartfelt asks that talk about what the money will be used for and what the cause means to you.
- Fundraising far and wide connected me to tons of allies I never knew existed.

- Lots of folks were truly grateful to have an opportunity to make a difference and ended up thanking *me* for giving them the opportunity to support a great cause. Asking is intertwined with giving, grace, vulnerability, hope, and love. I learned this from singer, songwriter, and author Amanda Palmer. If you're not convinced, consider watching her TED Talk "The Art of Asking." Even better, read her book by the same title, which opens with the sentences, "Who's got a tampon? I just got my period."[5]
- Having a hook or a gimmick can put the "fun" in fundraising. One of my more creative gimmicks was writing on my body, in permanent marker, the name of every person who sponsored me with a donation so they could come along with me on the ride. For a donation of $50 or more my donors got to pick their body part. Ooh-la-la!

Fundraisers are an excellent way for allies to connect with other allies and to offer support for LGBTQ+ organizations and school clubs. Don't shy away from fundraising. Have some fun! Deliver homemade cookies to the door of your top donor. Dye your hair blue if you make your fundraising goal. What are *you* willing to do for a donation?

PRIDE

I am not typically a fan of loud, crowded festivals and parades, but Pride truly energizes me. In a country where half of all LGBTQ+ people hide who they are at work,[6] being able to be out, loud, proud, covered head to toe in rainbows, and surrounded by supportive people for a few days out of the year can be truly liberating. I love to be a part of it.

For allies who live in or near a city that runs Pride events, volunteering to help make them as wonderful and as safe as possible for our LGBTQ+ friends is a kind gift that you can offer. This gives LGBTQ+ community members time to rest and enjoy their own celebration. You are also welcome, of course, to simply rainbow up, flaunt your pride, and enjoy the event. I've never experienced a Pride festival or parade that wasn't ally friendly and welcoming.

Pride celebrations are a tribute to the past, a way to honor the warriors who paved the way for a better world, a jubilant celebration of sexual and gender diversity, and an unapologetic display of self-love that offers hope to those who cannot yet live and love authentically. So, unfurl your most fabulous rainbow outfit, get involved, and celebrate diversity!

HELPFUL HINT

In addition to the LGBTQ+ etiquette tips and common bloopers I've already shared in this book, here are a few Pride-specific tips for allies that will help to ensure that you're being as respectful as possible during Pride events.

1. Don't yuck anyone's yum. At Pride events you're likely to see people expressing themselves in all kinds of ways. You may see bare-chested people wearing chaps, people in rainbow pasties and thongs, and people in leather masks with ball gags. Embrace it all. Be respectful to everyone, whether they're plain vanilla or triple berry with mint.
2. Don't attempt to label anyone. At Pride of all places, give people the space to just be fabulous without attempting to figure out their identities. When you're heading out the door to a Pride event, leave your "gaydar" at home. Better yet, chuck it out. As I mentioned in chapter 7, it's a useless item.
3. When you pass people at Pride events and you want to acknowledge them, the appropriate greeting is "Happy Pride!"

NOTES

1. Reprinted with permission from JFK Library Textual Archives, President John F. Kennedy's written message to the 14th Annual Convention of Americans for Democratic Action, May 11, 1961, https://www.jfklibrary.org/asset-viewer/archives/JFKWHCF CHRON/002/JFKWHCFCHRON-002-008?image_identifier=JFKWHCFCHRON -002-008-p0069.

2. Amnesty International, "Safety during Protest" [flyer], https://www.amnestyusa .org/pdfs/SafeyDuringProtest_F.pdf.

3. 5 Calls, "How to Call Your Representative with 5calls.org," YouTube, April 13, 2017, https://www.youtube.com/watch?v=N62ViRRn61I&ab_channel=5Calls.

4. PFLAG, "Advocacy One-Pagers," https://pflag.org/resource/advocacy-one-pagers.

5. Amanda Palmer, "The Art of Asking," speech given at TED2013 in February 2013, https://www.ted.com/talks/amanda_palmer_the_art_of_asking?language=en; *The Art of Asking: Or How I Learned to Stop Worrying and Let People Help* (New York: Grand Central, 2014).

6. Human Rights Campaign, *A Workplace Divided: Understanding the Climate for LGBTQ Workers Nationwide*, https://www.hrc.org/resources/a-workplace-divided -understanding-the-climate-for-lgbtq-workers-nationwide.

13

NOW WHAT?

Questions from Allies in the Real World

Why is gender something that we have all decided we get to call out and guess for other human beings?[1]

—Glennon Doyle, "Playing Our Roles: How Does Culture's Invention of Gender Typecast Every Last One of Us?" 2021

I love getting questions from allies out in the world doing great ally stuff. After I facilitate workshops, I always invite participants to keep in touch with me and email any questions they may have about allyship and LGBTQ+ inclusion. The questions I receive are wonderful. Many of them inspire me to research new LGBTQ+ related topics and areas of pushback. I extend this invitation to my readers as well. Keep the questions coming, folks! Go to my website at www .savvyallyaction.com and message me. Your questions and thoughts help make me a savvier ally.

Below are some of the many questions I've fielded over the past few years as well as my responses to them.

QUESTIONS ABOUT TERMS AND IDENTITIES

Is there a difference between biological sex and sex assigned at birth?

Not for everyone, but yes, they can be different. Biological sex has to do with a person's chromosomes, hormones, genitalia, and reproductive organs. Biological sex is never entirely certain at birth because medical professionals don't routinely run genetic testing and ultrasounds on newborns. All medical professionals routinely do is look between a newborn's legs and assign a sex based on the appearance of the baby's genitalia. Most of the time, the sex they assign aligns with the person's biological sex, but not always. Here's an example of biological sex and sex assigned at birth not aligning. I know of a young woman whose genitalia appeared typical for a baby girl when she was born. She was assigned *female* at birth. At age sixteen, her parents took her to her doctor to have her assessed because she had not yet menstruated. What they found was that she had undescended testicles instead of ovaries. Even though her sex assigned at birth was *female*, her biological sex was *intersex*.

Is it important to make the distinction about someone being a trans man versus just calling him a man? On the one hand, I don't want to diminish his identity, but I also don't want to draw any unwanted attention to it.

Most binary trans folks that I know move through the world simply as *men* and *women*. I only know one person, whose lifework is being a transgender activist, who actually does move through the world announcing that he's a *trans man*. So, in most cases we would simply refer to transgender men as *men* and transgender women as *women*. However, there are situations where the adjective *transgender* may be useful. A few examples are: in a medical setting, in a setting with an intimate partner, and if you're writing a book about how to be an ally to the LGBTQ+ communities. It would have been extremely difficult to write this book without referring to trans men, trans women, and the trans communities.

I really appreciate this comment about not wanting to diminish a trans person's identity. One way that you can make sure you're not doing this is on the forms in your workplace. If you're asking questions about gender on a form, it's important to avoid listing options like this, "man, woman, trans man, trans woman, nonbinary." These options *do* diminish a trans person's identity by implying that a trans man is not a man. Better options for your forms, depending of course on what you actually need to know, are below.

Sex Assigned at Birth: (Fill-ins are best, but if you must
use multiple choice, try these.)
Female – Male – Intersex – A sex not listed here

Gender: (Fill-ins are best here too,
but if you must use multiple choice, try these.)
Woman – Man – Nonbinary – Agender – A gender not listed here

I grew up in the South and I was taught that using *Sir* and *Ma'am* are signs of respect. This was hammered into my head by my parents. Now I'm being told that I may be hurting people by using these terms. How do I navigate this? Additionally, *Sir* and *Ma'am* are so ingrained, it will be really hard to change. What are you thoughts?

What I find fascinating about this issue is that what we have here is a clash of two cultures both trying to implement respectful language choices that are in direct opposition to each other. We've got American Southerners (in general), especially older adults, telling us that using *Sir* and *Ma'am* is a sign of respect. And we've got folks in the LGBTQ+ communities and allies (in general) telling us that *Sir* and *Ma'am* are antiquated words that assume gender and are hurtful.

I feel the same way about *Sir* and *Ma'am* as I do about gendered titles and pronouns. I hope that eventually we'll live in a world where it's generally accepted and considered respectful to refer to everyone using gender-neutral pronouns like *they* and gender-neutral titles like *Mx*, rather than guessing at gender, but we're not there yet. Plus, we don't even *have* a gender-neutral option yet to use instead of *Sir* and *Ma'am*. I don't think *Sma'am* is going to take off any time soon. We currently live in a world where I believe we'll offend more people by using *they* and *Mx* for everyone than we will by making educated guesses about people's pronouns and titles, when we're forced to. Along these same lines, we also have to make educated guesses about whether or not we should use the terms *Sir* or *Ma'am*.

So, when you're in Alabama waiting in line at the Piggly Wiggly, it's probably safe to say, "Excuse me, Ma'am, I think you dropped your keys." When you're in line for the New York City Pride festival, you should definitely remove the *ma'am* and simply say, "Excuse me, I think you dropped your keys." How do we navigate the rest of the situations we find ourselves in? We make our best guess at how to be respectful and we apologize and adjust our language when we mess up. It's an imperfect solution for the incredibly imperfect, binary world that we live in.

SOMETHING TO PONDER

Glennon Doyle, in her podcast *We Can Do Hard Things*, questions why as a society we've decided that using gendered forms of address is okay, but not other forms. We don't use language that guesses at people's orientation, race, or ethnicity. An airline employee who takes our boarding pass, for example, would never say, "Thank you, lesbian, white, Irish woman."[2]

I do believe that the terms *Sir* and *Ma'am* are antiquated and are eventually going to die out, even in the South. If you're motivated to eliminate these words from your vocabulary, remember that it will be difficult at first. Review my tips in chapter 6 regarding changing the language you've used your whole life and being kind to yourself while you're under construction. We *can* do hard things!

I'll end this section by sharing the poem "Coffeeshop" by Penny Sterling,[3] an award-winning storyteller who's a transgender woman.

I'm in this coffeeshop, see?
And I'm supposed to be writing the story of my life
Because that's what I want my life to be
I want my life to be the story of my life
Written and rewritten and spoken and applause
Reaching people who wonder why or
Think they know or want to know or just like jokes and tears
Because that's the story of my life
But I'm not.
I'm staring at her. I'm peering over my mac staring at her
Peering at her mac
She seems nice
She sits with friends or coworkers or both
Eyes on the screen
Fingers absently twitching
Mugs of coffee cooling
And I want to walk up to her and say
Excuse me, but why?
I was at that table a while ago
There was a man there
And we were talking
About art and toasters and pencils and creation
Of art about toasters using pencils and it was
Engaging and exciting
Creativity discussed giving me the energy
To go back to my mac and
Write more about the story of my life
But you came through between me and him
With your mac and your coffee and your friends
Excuse me sir
Is all you said

CHAPTER 13

To the person with the coffee
And the lipstick
And the earrings
And blood red nails
And serviceable tits
In the boots and leggings and tunic in the greys and maroons
Of the modern woman
And I was so enthused
About pencils and toasters
And art and the story of my life
That it didn't hit me until I sat down
Excuse me sir
Wow
The man gave you his table
Because he was one and you were many
Wandering around this coffeeshop, see?
Looking for a table
And he left
He seemed nice
But you stayed
And instead of writing about the story of my life
I tap tap tap and erase and tap
I peer at you over my mac
And want to ask you
WHY
What is it about me
That makes you think I want
To be called sir
But I don't
And that's the story of my life

QUESTIONS FROM FAMILY MEMBERS

My sister's child just came out as nonbinary. How do I now refer to them? Is there a gender-neutral word for the child of your sibling?

There are several gender-neutral words for the child of your sibling. But before I share them, my advice to you is to ask your sister's child how they would like you to refer to them. Using a gender-neutral word for your sister's child will draw attention to their identity. If they haven't told many people that they're nonbinary, they may not be ready for you to start using a gender-neutral term to refer to them. They may simply want you to refer to them as "my sister's child." So, checking in with them is an important first step. If your sister's child lets you know that they're comfortable with everyone knowing they're nonbinary and they like the idea of you using a gender-neutral word to refer to them, a few options that they can consider are *nibling*, *chibling*, and *sibkid*.

For more gender-neutral terms, check out the list created by YourDictionary .com called "42 Everyday Gender-Neutral Terms to Use."[4]

When is my child old enough to be told that she has an aunt who's in a lesbian relationship?

Now. We should talk to our children about our LGBTQ+ relatives and their relationships in the same way that we talk about our straight cisgender relatives and their relationships. If talking about your child's lesbian aunt requires a special, well-timed, age-appropriate conversation, you're setting up a situation where your child is likely to think about that aunt as abnormal and deviant. You're also creating a situation where your child will no doubt think of her lesbian aunt's relationship as being based mainly on sex; otherwise, why would it require them having to be "old enough" before you brought it up?

We typically don't explain an aunt's and uncle's relationship to our children, we just refer to them as Aunt so-and-so and Uncle so-and-so from the day our children are born. Normalize your LGBTQ+ relatives and their relationships in the same way by referring to them as Aunt so-and-so and Aunt so-and-so without any explanation or "special talk."

I have a ten-year-old transgender daughter. She has insisted that she's a girl since she was three years old. It's very clear to my husband and me that she *is* a girl and that she's on the right path. The recent anti-trans legislation attempting to limit healthcare options for trans youth and criminalize parents for supporting their trans children has been so troubling. Do you have any statistics or talking points to help me educate others on the importance of supporting our trans youth on their journeys?

We are living through such difficult times for transgender youth and their parents. The current onslaught of bills in the United States targeting transgender youth and their families that, among other things, seek to criminalize health care for trans youth, is horrifying. Here are some telling statistics from reputable sources to help you educate others on the realities of transgender well-being and gender-affirming care.

Cornell University's What We Know Project conducted a systematic literature review of every study published in English between 1991 and June of 2017 that assessed the effect of gender transition on transgender well-being. There were fifty-five such studies. Here are the project's findings: fifty-one studies (93 percent) found that gender transition improves the overall well-being of transgender people, four studies (7 percent) reported mixed or null findings, and zero studies concluded that gender transition causes overall harm. In conclusion, the authors of the What We Know Project wrote,

> This search found a robust international consensus in the peer-reviewed literature that gender transition, including medical treatments such as hormone therapy and surgeries, improves the overall well-being of transgender individuals. The literature also indicates that greater availability of medical and social support for gender transition contributes to better quality of life for those who identify as transgender.[5]

A study by Harvard Medical School psychiatrist Dr. Jack Turban surveying more than twenty thousand transgender people found that puberty blockers are linked to lower rates of suicidal thoughts in transgender people.[6] Puberty blockers are medications that temporarily halt the puberty process. If these medications are stopped, puberty resumes.

Puberty-blocking medications have been used for decades in cisgender girls who begin puberty too early. They're currently also being used with some trans youth, typically around age fourteen, to delay puberty that doesn't align with the youth's gender identity. Puberty blockers give trans youth more time to figure out if hormonal therapies and/or surgeries are the right choice for them and can reduce the need for expensive and extensive gender-affirming operations in adulthood. As an example, a trans girl who pauses and eventually avoids going through male puberty won't have a need later in life to go through a tracheal shave to reduce the size of her Adam's apple, because she won't develop a prominent one.

Although many doctors and gender specialists agree that more research needs to be done to understand the long-term effects of these medications, most agree that the benefits currently outweigh the risks.[7]

I'll end this section with these facts. The post-surgery regret rate after knee replacement surgery is approximately 20 percent.[8] The post-surgery regret rate after cosmetic surgery is approximately 65 percent.[9] The post-surgery regret rate after gender-affirming surgery for transgender people is approximately 1 percent.[10]

HELPFUL HINT

Maybe don't rush into that facelift.

QUESTIONS FROM THE WORKPLACE

So basically, we're working toward a workplace where LBG people can comfortably and safely share their identities and where T people can keep their identities confidential and private. Is that right?

A simpler and more accurate way to think about this is that we're working toward creating workplaces where everyone can comfortably and safely share their identities if they want to, talk about their loved ones if they want to, and put a family photo on their desk if they want to. If an employee chooses not to do these things, then their colleagues should not make assumptions about who they are and whom they love. This should be the case whether an employee is part of the LGBTQ+ communities or not. The information we *should* focus on gathering about employees in the workplace is how we can respectfully refer to them (i.e., titles, names, and pronouns) if they feel comfortable sharing that information with us.

I was in a work meeting the other day and someone misgendered my coworker. Should I have said something right then and there?

There's no right answer to this question about whether to say something in a staff meeting after a coworker is misgendered. This falls into that gray area of allyship where you need to make a judgment call depending on several factors. You'll need to consider things like how well you know the coworker who was misgendered, whether you think the person will appreciate the support or be made uncomfortable by having attention drawn to the mistake, and how past efforts to support this coworker have been received. You'll also need to think about who else is at the table during the meeting. Is it all folks that everyone

POP QUIZ

You're at a dinner party at a colleague's house. You should . . . (Choose all that apply.)

A. Help carry the dirty dishes to the kitchen after dinner.
B. Load the dishwasher.
C. Scrub the host's toilet if it looks dirty.

Answer: ???

Most folks agree that we should help carry the dirty dishes to the kitchen but we shouldn't scrub our host's toilet. But loading our host's dishwasher is kind of a gray area. Our decision is likely to depend on how well we know the host and social cues we're picking up from the environment.

The same is true with allyship. Some actions are clearly good choices. An example is suggesting that agencies update their forms when you see the limited "M" or "F" boxes. And some actions are clearly bad choices. An example is speaking over the community members you're trying to support. And then there are gray areas.

knows and trusts or are there new people at the table? If the latter, safety and confidentiality may be at risk if you speak up.

Whether you choose to say something or not, a great ally action is to check in later, privately, with the person who was misgendered. You can say something like, "I wasn't sure how to respond when you were misgendered in the meeting today. If that happens again, how can I best support you?" Communication is key. The next time this situation occurs with this coworker, you'll know exactly how to respond. If you chose not to say anything in the meeting, you may also want to ask if there's a role you can play in speaking with the person who messed up. That way you can be proactive in preventing the mistake from occurring again.

I never know how to respond to someone in an email when I don't know how to refer to themselves. Responding with "Dear _____ (whatever their first name is)" seems too informal for a work email, but I don't want to guess at a title, like Mr. or Ms. What do you suggest?

In the same way that it would make referring to everyone correctly so much easier if we all shared our pronouns, it would also make referring to everyone correctly so much easier if we all shared information on our titles or how people should address us.

Here's how my email signature currently reads:

Jeannie Gainsburg, MSS
Savvy Ally Action|Founder
https://www.savvyallyaction.com
Please refer to me as "Jeannie" (pronounced G-knee) when you respond.
My pronouns are she/her/hers *(Why did I share this?)*

(Note: "Why did I share this?" is hyperlinked to my YouTube video called "Why Share Pronouns?" for folks who are confused about why I've included pronouns in my signature. Feel free to hyperlink this video to the pronouns in your email signature too!)[12]

My sister, Julie, is a university department chair. When she read my suggestion to include "Please refer to me as . . ." in her email signature, she brought up this concern:

This seems to work great if you want to be referred to by your first name, but it seems stuck up if you want to be referred to as Mrs. Smith or Dr. Gainsburg. This is a struggle for me. I wish students knew they should always start with Dr. Gainsburg, especially when they've never met me, but I feel silly saying "Please call me Dr. Gainsburg." It also matters who's responding to my email. I don't need my colleagues to refer to me as "Dr. Gainsburg."

This is a good point. My suggestion for folks who are in this situation is to add your title to your email signature as a hint that this is the way folks should address you. Hopefully students will take the hint. If a few colleagues reply with "Dear Dr. Gainsburg," you can respond with "Please call me Julie."

HELPFUL HINT

In her book *Better Allies*, Karen Catlin talks about the importance of pronouncing people's names correctly as an important step toward making colleagues feel welcome, supported, and part of the team. She suggests using the website www.pronouncenames.com to learn appropriate name pronunciations.[11] So, while we're sharing our pronouns and information on how people can refer to us (i.e., using our first name or a title and our last name), let's help them out by also adding information on how to pronounce our names!

To help create a world where everyone shares information on how people can respectfully refer to them and no one has to guess anymore, I recommend that you model this behavior by putting this book down and taking a moment to update your email signature. I'll wait.

Nice! Okay, so back to your question. We're in a situation where someone we don't know has emailed us and offered no information on how to refer to them. The first thing I do in this situation is I scroll down and see how they signed their email. If they've signed it "Tanisha," then I feel comfortable responding with "Good morning, Tanisha." I personally don't use "Dear"—it seems a bit intimate—but that's just me. If they've signed their email "Dr. Miller," then I'll respond by using that name and title.

Often, however, people either don't sign their email at all or they sign with their full name. In these cases, I look at how they've addressed me. If they've used "Jeannie," I feel comfortable responding using their first name. If they've used my full name, guessed at my title, or not addressed the email at all, I look at their email signature. If they have "PhD" after their name, I respond by using the title "Dr." If they don't have a "PhD" by their name and I have the time and the energy to do a bit of sleuthing, I'll see if I can find information about the person online. Bios can be helpful for both titles and pronouns. If I don't have the time to investigate or I've found nothing online, I simply respond with "Good morning" or "Good afternoon." In these situations, I also think it's fine to respond with the person's full name, for example, "Good morning, Tanisha Miller" or "Dear Tanisha Miller."

I work with someone who continually gets a colleague's pronouns wrong. Is it my place to say something? If so, how should I approach this?

If safety and confidentiality are not a concern, which it sounds like they aren't in this situation, then my answer is yes, this is a good place for an ally to jump in and help out. Most LGBTQ+ individuals I've talked to appreciate it when allies take on the task of helping others get their pronouns correct.

I approach this type of conversation with different levels of intervention. I start by modelling the correct pronoun around the person who's been misgendering my colleague. This is a kind and subtle first step to indicate to someone that they're using the wrong pronoun. Sometimes folks catch on with this simple nudge. Others require step two.

Step two involves pulling the person aside in a private place for a brief discussion. Don't forget to use some of the tips I shared in chapter 8 to increase your likelihood of having a good talk without the person becoming defensive.

A few tips that will work well in this situation are to assume goodwill, find common ground with a connecting statement, and avoid labelling the behavior. You might try something like, "Hey, I just wanted to remind you that Avery's pronoun is *he*. You may not have even realized it, but you've been referring to him as *she*. I know it's not always easy to remember people's pronouns when they've changed. Is there anything I can do to help remind you?"

A great scenario would be if the person responds with, "Oh my gosh! I'm so embarrassed! I didn't even realize I was doing that. Would you be willing to shoot me a text or a message whenever you hear me messing up? I think that will help." A poor scenario would be if the person responds with, "Whatever. This pronouns stuff is such crap. We're born boys or girls and that's all there is to it. I'm not going to play that pronoun game." Continually and intentionally misgendering someone without attempting to correct the error is abuse. This latter response will require step three.

Step three involves connecting with the colleague who is being misgendered and asking if they would like support or help in reporting the incident or incidents to a supervisor or to someone in human resources. If they answer, "Yes," work with them to plan a strategy so you can ensure that you're offering help and support that's wanted. If they answer "No," please respect that. It's possible that your colleague doesn't want that much attention drawn to their gender or they fear retaliation. Ask if you can support them in any other way.

QUESTIONS FROM TEACHERS AND SCHOOL STAFF

We have a few parents in our school district who have been complaining that they don't want their children exposed to anything related to LGBTQ+ identities. They say it goes against their beliefs. Do you have any tips for how I can respond in a respectful and effective way?

People who benefit from the status quo are less likely to understand why things can't remain the way they have always been, because it has always worked for them. They may feel that diversity and inclusion efforts violate *their* rights and beliefs. I would begin this conversation by assuring these parents that no one is asking them to change their personal beliefs. Everyone comes to school from different households with different backgrounds, beliefs, and values. Once at school, all students and family members are welcomed, included, and respected regardless of their race, ethnicity, religion, ability, body size, sexual orientation, gender identity, or gender expression. Having conversations in class that include different families and different kinds of people will help to ensure that all students feel safe and included and is essential for a healthy learning environment. Some students are being raised by a single parent, a grandparent, foster parents, divorced parents, two moms, or two dads. All of these children should see their families included in the school curriculum.

Next, I would clarify that this concept of respecting all students applies to everyone. In other words, if a student is being picked on because of their religious beliefs, even those that are widely practiced in the United States, that's not okay and won't be tolerated. Students are never forced to agree with one another, but they are required to be respectful to one another.

A few other tips and thoughts that may help you craft an effective response are below.

1. Practice a few statements in your head beforehand, like, "We value diversity at this school. All children and families are welcome here."
2. Clarify that classroom inclusion of LGBTQ+ people and families *doesn't* mean that anyone will be talking about sex. Conversations will be about different kinds of families and whom people love.
3. You may have the tools you need to have this conversation already. How would you respond to a parent who complained about their children being exposed to people of color, Jewish families, or students whose parents are divorced? Applying the "switch it" technique can help guide you in crafting an appropriate response to LGBTQ+ related pushback and concerns.
4. Reach out to your school's administration for support. If your school district supports LGBTQ+ inclusion, then clear messaging on their commitment to diversity and inclusion should be documented and communicated to all parents. This messaging should help to reduce parent pushback on this issue and offer you definitive talking points about district policy when you're engaged in these conversations.

Be on the right side of history. Think back to the intense battle for desegregated schools in the United States in the 1950s and 1960s. Many white parents fought fiercely to keep schools segregated by race. And yet, desegregating schools was clearly the right choice for working toward equality in education. Recognize that normalizing LGBTQ+ people and families in your classroom is creating safer and more inclusive schools.

What are your thoughts on fairness in sports regarding gender? Should a transgender girl, for example, be allowed to play on a high school girls' volleyball team?

Growing up, I was a lanky, shy, and unpopular girl. Playing volleyball in high school completely turned things around for me. Learning a valued skill, working hard physically, becoming a part of a team, discovering how to be a good team-mate, figuring out how to win and lose with grace, and eventually thinking of myself as an athlete changed my life. Being able to participate on a varsity team in high school turned me into a much more confident, resilient, and adventurous young woman.

I'm not alone in experiencing positive outcomes from playing on a sports team. Students who participate in sports are known to have better grade point averages, higher self-esteem, and bigger educational and occupational aspirations than students who aren't involved in sports.[13] These are life-altering benefits that we deny transgender students when we refuse to let them play or make the environment so hostile that they decide not to play on sports teams.

As I mentioned in chapter 4, the Olympic Committee has their work cut out for them on this issue. The natural biological variability that exists in humans makes it impossible to separate everyone on the planet into *males* and *females*. So, unfortunately, there are no easy answers for Olympic-level or professional athletics. However, I believe that middle school, high school, and (dare I say it?) even college-level athletics are different and should be treated differently when it comes to decisions around inclusion for transgender athletes.

Consider what we're teaching youth when we refuse to allow a transgender girl to participate on the girls' volleyball team: Competition and winning are more important than inclusion, diversity, equity, and acceptance. Dr. Deanna Adkins, associate professor of Pediatrics at Duke University School of Medicine, states, "When a school or athletic organization denies transgender students the ability to participate in sports, it condones, reinforces and affirms their social status as outsiders or misfits who deserve the hostility they experience from peers."[14]

Let's take a look at the most common argument against allowing trans students to participate in middle and high school sports. The argument is that transgender girls will have a huge physical advantage over cisgender girls. But at the middle and high school level, we're just not seeing that play out. Adolescents exhibit a huge range of physical characteristics because they grow and develop differently and at different rates. This fact alone should help people realize that the rules governing collegiate sports should not be applied to high schools, a time when bodies are still growing and developing. Additionally, an increasing number of transgender youths are being prescribed hormone blockers to protect them from the unwanted physical changes that can result from puberty. These medications pause puberty until the youth is old enough to make mature and informed medical decisions about transitioning. A transgender girl taking hormone blockers has removed all possible advantages that she might have received as the result of a male puberty.[15]

At the collegiate level, transgender inclusion in athletics is still important. The NCAA (National Collegiate Athletic Association) has created policies for transgender inclusion in sports that include very specific guidelines to even the playing field. For example, the NCAA has ruled that transgender women may not participate on women's collegiate sports teams unless they've been on hormone treatments for at least one year. They also must meet testosterone thresholds set specifically for their sport. Hormone treatments for transgender women greatly reduce muscle mass and strength. After one year of treatment, many experts believe that transgender women have no competitive advantage over cisgender women. You can see all of the collegiate recommendations in the *NCAA Inclusion of Transgender Student-Athletes Handbook*.[16]

We're simply not seeing transgender girls and women dominating high school and college sports. In a *New York Times* article covering the collegiate swimmer Lia Thomas, Billy Witz wrote, "While there have been an increasing number of transgender athletes who have transitioned while in college, the ones who generate the most attention (and criticism) are transgender women who compete in women's events—and who win. Those have been exceedingly rare."[17]

Guess what else we're not seeing? High school boys pretending to be girls in order to play on girls' sports teams or access girls' locker rooms. There have been no reported incidents of this in the United States. The fear-inducing propaganda that we're seeing around this issue of transgender inclusion in sports is reminiscent of the fear-inducing propaganda that we've seen around the bathroom bills and attempts to exclude trans folks from public restrooms that align with their gender identity. Let them pee. Let them play.

I'm a high school French teacher. As I'm sure you know, in French, pronouns, nouns, and adjectives are all gendered. Gender-neutral doesn't exist in French. Do you have any suggestions for how I can create a safe and supportive environment for my transgender and nonbinary French students?

I field this question from lots of frustrated educators who teach languages that use masculine-feminine noun classification, like French, Spanish, and Italian. You need to teach the language in its traditional form so your students can become proficient and pass their standardized tests, but you also want to teach acceptance and inclusion for all students. You're put in a difficult position, for sure.

In chapter 10, I talked about duct tape patch-up jobs and big fixes. You can certainly get involved in the movement to change the language itself (the big fix), but that's likely to take a while. What you need right now are some immediate duct tape patch-up job solutions to create an inclusive and supportive classroom for your students. Here are a few suggestions.

1. Teach the traditional form of the language but share your frustrations about the lack of gender-neutral word options with your classes. Have a frank discussion with your students about the limitations of the language and how it's noninclusive of nonbinary people. If you find it problematic that the masculine always dominates over the feminine in these languages (e.g., if you have a group of a dozen women and one man, you refer to the entire group as masculine), talk about this too.

2. The movement to make languages that don't have a gender-neutral form more inclusive has been raging for decades. Encourage students to share their opinions on the evolution of languages. Ask your students if they think that language shapes culture and society or culture and society shape language, or whether both occur. Does a language that doesn't have gender-neutral options create and maintain a society that doesn't acknowledge and respect nonbinary individuals? Does a language where the masculine always dominates over the feminine create and maintain a society that values men over women?

3. Educate students on the progress that has been made to add gender-neutral words to these languages. *Elle* is an emerging gender-neutral Spanish pronoun and *loro* (a literal translation of English *they*) is an Italian gender-neutral pronoun option. In November of 2021, the gender-neutral pronoun *iel* was added to the French dictionary. Announce that any student who would like to use one of these gender-neutral pronoun options for themselves is welcome to do so.

Check out these two articles for more information or to spark discussions on this topic with your students: "The Push to Make French Gender-Neutral" from *The Atlantic* and "A Guide to How Gender-Neutral Language Is Developing around the World" from the *Washington Post*.[18]

We have a group of students in our high school (9th grade mostly) who are asking to be called names like Coma and Stench and for us to use pronouns like *sin* to refer to them. These students changed their names and pronouns frequently last year. We want to be supportive of students who are questioning or transitioning. We also struggle to support teachers with these ever-changing name/pronoun requests. Do you have any advice or practical tips for us? Can we say "no" to a name or pronoun request if it's too out there?

Oh, my goodness! These youngsters! Always pushing the limits. I kind of respect it and hate it at the same time. (Did I mention that teachers don't get paid enough?)

The regulations regarding the use of students' chosen names and pronouns by teachers and school staff vary from state to state. Even in states where teachers and school staff are required to use the students' chosen names and pronouns, the details of how these rules should be implemented and enforced are often murky. My guess would be that teachers and school staff do have the right to say "No" to a student's chosen name or pronoun if they have good reason, for example, if the name or pronoun is obscene or disrespectful to others.

Let's look at your situation with Coma, Stench, and the student who would like you to use *sin* as their pronoun. I believe there are three possible reasons these students are asking for these changes.

1. The students are truly questioning their identities and trying out names that might work for them.
2. The students are trying out new names and pronouns because they can, and they see other students doing it.
3. The students are seeking attention, clowning around, and/or seeing how far they can push things because that's what some teens do.

In the interest of protecting and creating safe spaces for students in the first two categories and honoring their odyssey, it's best to try to work with the names and pronouns that students are asking you to use, unless they're obscene or disrespectful. This strategy ensures that you're supporting the students who are truly questioning and exploring, but it has the added advantage of removing the teacher from the role of judge, having to decide which names are okay and which are too much.

If you work in a state where you're not allowed to inform the student's parents about their request if the student doesn't want you to, then here are some things to consider. Does your school have a standardized name/pronoun change support plan in place for students who are asking for new names and pronouns to be used? Support plans are great because they guide teachers and school staff in the correct procedure for using new names and pronouns, ensure student safety, and establish uniformity of implementation. If a student, for example, shares a new name and/or pronoun on a teacher's "getting to know you" form at the beginning of the semester, what should the teacher do with that information? Without a support plan, the teacher might just start using the new name and pronoun in class, which may or may not be the best action for this student. Your school's support plan might include, for example, guidelines for the teachers to set up a private conversation with the student about where they feel safe using their new name and/or pronoun, who else knows about this change, what type of support they have at home, and what their plan is for rolling out this new information to the broader school community. During this conversation it may become evident that the student could benefit from talking with a school counselor for additional support. The document "Schools in Transition: A Guide for Supporting Transgender Students in K–12 Schools" is a great resource that includes a support plan template.[19]

If your school creates a name/pronoun change support plan, then Coma, Stench, and the student who would like you to use *sin* as their pronoun would need to go through the standard procedures listed in the plan just like all the other students who are asking to have new names and pronouns used. If Coma, Stench, and the student who would like you to use *sin* are serious about their new name and pronoun choices, then this process should be very helpful for them. If they're just clowning around and seeing how far they can push things, this will probably call their bluff. They're likely to drop their request when they realize they need to meet one-on-one with a teacher to answer questions about the level of support in their homes and their plan for informing others of their new names and pronouns.

If you work in a state where schools are required to inform parents of their children's requests to change their names or pronouns, you're going to have the parents involved in the decision. Although I personally think this requirement is problematic and unsafe for many students, it does have the advantage of opening the door to a partnership with parents on this sensitive issue.

To assist and support your teachers and school staff with the ever-changing names and pronoun requests, here are few other things your school could consider.

1. Allow students to place name and pronouns cards on their desks to help the teacher refer to them respectfully. These should, of course, be optional.

2. Limit how often students can change their names per semester. Explaining, of course, that this is not intended to limit or be disrespectful to anyone, but to realistically help the teachers manage all the changes in the system.

3. Keep in mind that the frequent changing of pronouns may be a different situation from the frequent changing of names. Students who are gender-fluid may have pronouns that change daily. In these situations, it's best if the teacher and student have a private chat about ways that the student can indicate to the teacher which pronoun to use on any given day.

I'm continually in awe of the kindness, patience, and dedication that teachers and school staff pour into their work in an effort to care for and support our children. Y'all rock!

NOTES

1. Reprinted from Glennon Doyle, "Playing Our Roles: How Does Culture's Invention of Gender Typecast Every Last One of Us?" Momastery, August 24, 2021, https://momastery.com/blog/episode-20/.

2. Glennon Doyle, "Playing Our Roles: How Does Culture's Invention of Gender Typecast Every Last One of Us?" We Can Do Hard Things with Glennon Doyle, August 24, 2021, https://podcasts.google.com/search/Playing%20Our%20Roles%3A%20How%20does%20Culture%E2%80%99s%20Invention%20of%20Gender%20Typecast%20Every%20Last%20One%20of%20Us.

3. Penny Sterling, "Coffeeshop," Penny Sterling blog, February 9, 2018, https://www.penny-sterling.com/post/im-in-this-coffeeshop-see.

4. Michele Meleen, "42 Everyday Gender-Neutral Terms to Use," YourDictionary.com, https://grammar.yourdictionary.com/style-and-usage/30-everyday-gender-neutral-terms-to-use.html.

5. What We Know Project, Cornell University, "What Does the Scholarly Research Say about the Effect of Gender Transition on Transgender Well-Being?" (online literature review), 2018, https://whatweknow.inequality.cornell.edu/topics/lgbt-equality/what-does-the-scholarly-research-say-about-the-well-being-of-transgender-people/.

6. Tim Fitzsimons, "Puberty Blockers Linked to Lower Suicide Risk for Transgender People," CBS News, January 24, 2020, https://www.nbcnews.com/feature/nbc-out/puberty-blockers-linked-lower-suicide-risk-transgender-people-n1122101.

7. Lena Wilson, "What Are Puberty Blockers?" *New York Times*, May 11, 2021, https://www.nytimes.com/2021/05/11/well/family/what-are-puberty-blockers.html #:~:text=Puberty%20blockers%20are%20medications%20that,align%20with%20 their%20gender%20identities.

8. C. E. Scott, C. R. Howie, and D. MacDonald et al., "Predicting Dissatisfaction Following Total Knee Replacement: A Prospective Study of 1217 Patients," *Journal of Bone & Joint Surgery*, September 2010, 92(9):1253–58, https://pubmed.ncbi.nlm.nih .gov/20798443/.

9. Medical Accident Group, "Do You Regret Having Cosmetic Surgery?" https:// www.medicalaccidentgroup.co.uk/news/do-you-regret-having-cosmetic-surgery /#:~:text=Many%20people%20regret%20having%20had,very%20happy%20with%20 its%20results.

10. Valeria P. Bustos, Samyd S. Bustos, and Andres Mascaro et al., "Regret after Gender-Affirmation Surgery: A Systematic Review and Meta-Analysis of Prevalence," *Plastic and Reconstructive Surgery Global Open*, 9(3): e3477 March 19, 2021, https://www.ncbi.nlm.nih.gov/pmc/articles/PMC8099405/.

11. Karen Catlin, Better Allies: Everyday Actions to Create Inclusive, Engaging Workplaces (Second Edition) (Better Allies Press, January 2021), 124–25.

12. Savvy Ally Action, "Why Share Pronouns?" YouTube, https://youtu.be/h0a2sd BKRpU.

13. GLSEN, "Transgender Inclusion in High School Athletics," July 2019, https:// www.glsen.org/sites/default/files/2019-10/GLSEN-Transgender-Inclusion-High -School-Athletics.pdf.

14. ACLU, "Four Myths about Trans Athletes, Debunked," April 30, 2020, https:// www.aclu.org/news/lgbtq-rights/four-myths-about-trans-athletes-debunked/.

15. Pat Griffin and Helen J. Carroll, "On the Team: Equal Opportunity for Transgender Student Athletes," October 4, 2010, https://www.nclrights.org/wp-content /uploads/2013/07/TransgenderStudentAthleteReport.pdf.

16. NCAA, *NCAA Inclusion of Transgender Student-Athletes Handbook*, August 2010, https://ncaaorg.s3.amazonaws.com/inclusion/lgbtq/INC_TransgenderHand book.pdf.

17. Billy Witz, "As Lia Thomas Swims, Debate about Transgender Athletes Swirls," *New York Times*, January 24, 2022, https://www.nytimes.com/2022/01/24/sports/lia -thomas-transgender-swimmer.html.

18. Annabelle Timsit, "The Push to Make French Gender-Neutral," *The Atlantic*, November 24, 2017, https://www.theatlantic.com/international/archive/2017/11 /inclusive-writing-france-feminism/545048/ and Miriam Berger, "A Guide to How Gender-Neutral Language Is Developing around the World," *Washington Post*, December 15, 2019, https://www.washingtonpost.com/world/2019/12/15/guide-how-gender -neutral-language-is-developing-around-world/.

19. Asaf Orr and Joel Baum, "Schools in Transition: A Guide for Supporting Transgender Students in K–12 Schools," https://www.aclu.org/sites/default/files/field_docu ment/schools.in_.transition.2015.pdf.

PART IV

ALLYING RESPONSIBLY

14

MESSING UP PROPERLY

I want a bunch of people who are interested in becoming allies to me to get it wrong. Because I promise, you will get it wrong, likely more than once. But please get it wrong, for me. Be wrong on my behalf. Try stuff, learn stuff, make attempts, and fail. Embrace the discomfort of not knowing, of not being certain, of not understanding, and then be motivated enough to learn and get better.[1]

—Megan Carpenter, "Get it Wrong for Me:
What I Need from Allies," 2020

If a lot of this stuff is new to you, you may be feeling a bit overwhelmed by all the information in this book and worried that you're surely going to mess up. You will. We all do. The trick is not to put unrealistic pressure on yourself never to mess up. Here's the game plan. Try hard not to mess up. When you do, forgive yourself, make an appropriate apology to the person you messed up with, and put in the work to get it right the next time. Then, repeat the process. Being an ally is an ongoing journey of messing up. Get comfortable with it.

In this chapter, I'll walk through the process of messing up properly using two common types of mess-ups: accidentally misgendering someone and making an offensive or hurtful comment. Knowing how to recover gracefully from these mess-ups and improve in the future are key for being a great ally.

ACCIDENTALLY MISGENDERING SOMEONE

Accidentally misgendering someone by using the wrong name or pronoun is a common blunder. It's awkward and embarrassing and it happens to everyone, me included. Let's look closely at each of the three steps that should occur after you've misgendered someone.

Offer an Apology or a Thank-You

A simple apology is a great response to misgendering someone if it's a situation where you've caught yourself using the wrong name or pronoun. For example, you just said *she*, and as the word was exiting your mouth you suddenly remembered that the person you're referring to uses the pronoun *they*. The best way to apologize in this situation is to imagine that you just bumped into the person whom you misgendered on the street. If you accidentally bumped into someone on the street, you probably wouldn't walk on without saying anything, because that's rude. But you also probably wouldn't make a huge deal out of it, begging them for forgiveness, telling them over and over how sorry you are, and sobbing on their shoes. You would simply say something like, "Excuse me" or "I'm sorry." Your apology when you misgender someone should be done in this same way. You can simply say something like, "Excuse me, I meant *they*."

Since you're reading this book, you're clearly invested in making the world a safer and more inclusive place for LGBTQ+ people, so it's likely that when you accidentally misgender someone you're going to feel *terrible*, and your instinct may be to apologize profusely. Here's the problem with that. Even though apologizing profusely may make *you* feel better, it's likely to make the person you messed up with feel worse. It will draw a lot of attention to the person you messed up with, attention they probably don't want. It can also pull the focus of the conversation on to you and how badly you feel. If you manage to make a really impressive fuss, you may even end up in a situation where the person you misgendered is now trying to make *you* feel better. Awkward! So, a quick, "Excuse me," is the way to go.

When you're in a situation where the person you've misgendered or someone else who's participating in the conversation lets you know that you messed up, a simple thank-you is best. For example, "Yes. Thank you for reminding me." The beauty of the thank-you, as opposed to the apology, in this scenario is that you don't end up forcing the person you misgendered into a situation where they feel like they have to say, "It's okay."

Forgive Yourself

Oh, it sounds so easy, doesn't it? I find that I can beat myself up for weeks over my mess-ups, but I'm truly working on the self-forgiveness thing. What I try to do when I mess up is remind myself of three things:

1. I'm human. Years ago, someone said to me, "Allow yourself to be raggedy." I absolutely love this sentiment. I do try to accept raggediness in myself. I hope you'll accept it in yourself too.
2. Mistakes force me to think about issues, make me more aware of my language, and help me become a better ally.
3. My mess-ups help me connect with others when they mess up in the same way. As I mentioned in chapter 8, acknowledging that you've messed up in the same way as someone else is a wonderfully kind and effective way to connect with them when you're helping them change their language.

Get It Right the Next Time

Here's the big moment that separates the eagles from the slugs! (How's *that* for getting creative with ungendered language?) You can either forget all about this incident and write it off as no big deal or you can do the work to get it right the next time. Occasional and accidental misgenderings are embarrassing, but we all commit them. Repeated or intentional misgendering, without caring or doing the work to correct the error, is abuse.

Here are a few tips that have helped me to fly like an eagle and get it right the next time after I've misgendered someone.

Try Again Right Away

If I'm still in a conversation with the person I messed up with, I make a point of using their correct name or pronoun right away. This helps to cement it in my brain. It also shows the person I messed up with that I'm actively working to get it right.

Practice in Your Head

Running what I'm about to say through my head before it comes out of my mouth has proven a very successful strategy for fixing my errors.

Write It Down

I'm a visual person. When I write things down, I'm more likely to remember them. For example, I might write "Jo (they/them)" somewhere I'll see it often. I still use a paper daily planner. I look at it constantly throughout the day. This is my favorite spot for writing down names and pronouns that I want to see often so I can remember them. I use this same technique when I have trouble remembering how to pronounce someone's name. I'll write their name on my calendar phonetically so I can practice it throughout the day.

Add Pronouns to Your Phone Contacts

If you're struggling to remember the correct pronouns for a friend or family member, add their pronouns after their name in your phone contacts. This way every time the person calls or texts you, their pronouns will be displayed, providing a great visual reminder.

Practice on Your Pet

If you're struggling with nonbinary pronouns, like singular *they* or *ze*, you're not alone. Lots of folks find these newer pronouns difficult to master. If you don't have a close friend, family member, or colleague who uses gender-neutral pronouns, it's difficult to get good at using them because you don't get many chances to practice them. When I was struggling with the use of singular *they*, my friend Kayden suggested I use it when referring to my cat Carlos, to increase

HELPFUL HINT

I've chosen to use the word *misgender* in this section to refer to using the wrong name or pronoun for someone because it's currently the most common word being used to describe this error. However, it's not a very accurate term. As I mentioned in chapter 5, pronouns don't necessarily imply gender. For example, just because someone uses the pronoun "she," it doesn't necessarily mean she's a woman. And just because someone uses "they," it doesn't necessarily mean that they're nonbinary. It would be more accurate to say that we *misnamed* or *mispronouned* someone. I didn't think *mispronoun* was an actual word, but I just googled it and there are a few examples where folks have used it! So, using these two more accurate words may be becoming "a thing." Don't you just love word evolution?

the frequency of its use. It worked like a charm! And Carlos didn't seem to care what pronoun I used to refer to him as long as I remembered to feed him on time and occasionally scratch his head. Excuse me—scratch *their* head.

Imagine a Mouse

Here's a tip from my friend Eridan, whose pronoun is *they*. They told me to imagine that they have a mouse in their pocket. Eridan + Mouse = They. "They're coming to dinner. Get out the mini cheese tray!"

MAKING AN OFFENSIVE OR HURTFUL COMMENT

Another common blunder is unintentionally making an offensive or hurtful comment. Some examples are using an outdated term that is now considered derogatory (examples of outdated and derogatory LGBTQ+ terms were shared in chapter 6), perpetuating stereotypes about LGBTQ+ people (as discussed in chapter 7), and using a term that is only acceptable if it's used by community members (as discussed in chapter 9). Apologizing and recovering gracefully from these mess-ups are a bit more complicated and typically more challenging than recovering gracefully from misgendering someone. Let's look closely at each of the three steps that should occur after you've accidentally made an offensive or hurtful comment.

Offer a Thank-You and an Apology

When someone lets us know that we said or did something offensive we should offer *both* a thank-you *and* an apology. Start by thanking the person for taking the time to speak with you and having the courage to let you know that you made a mistake. Few people enjoy telling others that they messed up. If someone is letting you know that you made an error, it probably means that they value your relationship, have faith that you're interested in learning, and believe that you're capable of listening and changing your behavior. Accept this intervention for the compliment that it is and thank the person for committing to an action that's no fun for anyone. For example, "Thank you so much for bringing this to my attention."

Next, apologize. You can make a simple apology like this, "I apologize for my error." Or, you can add a statement of intent like this, "I apologize for my error. I'm going to do better."

HELPFUL HINT

"I'm sorry that you were offended" is an example of a perfectly awful apology because it puts the blame on the other person for being overly sensitive and doesn't acknowledge that you did anything wrong. Accept the fact that what you said was offensive and offer a sincere, high-quality apology. (This tip comes from Franchesca Ramsey [aka Chescaleigh]. Check out her video *Getting Called Out: How to Apologize*[2] for more pointers on how to apologize well.)

Remember in chapter 8 when I talked about how, when we're in the role of educator, it's kind to allow people the opportunity to say, "Oh my gosh! I didn't mean to offend anyone!" Even though the focus of the conversation should be on the impact of the offensive language or behavior, allowing people some space to share that they didn't mean to offend anyone is simple human decency. Well, here we are in a situation where *you're* the learner. So, go ahead and say that you didn't mean to offend anyone if that feels right for you, but do keep it brief and make sure that your intent isn't the focus of the conversation. Also, make sure that your "I didn't mean to offend" comment doesn't smack of defensiveness. For example, steer away from comments like, "Are you implying that I'm homophobic?" or "I'm not a bad person."

Here, to make a great point and make us laugh a little, is a wonderful example of the "switch it" technique being used to teach us how *not* to respond when we've just hurt someone with our language or behavior. Presley Pizzo switches the situation by using the example of someone saying to you, "Ouch! You just stepped on my toes." If we accidentally step on someone's toes we would likely, and very naturally, say something like, "Oh my gosh! I'm so sorry." If we felt that it was necessary to throw in, "I didn't mean to," so be it. But, we're unlikely to get defensive and respond in any of these ways described by Pizzo:

- Centering yourself: "I can't believe you think I'm a toe-stepper! I'm a good person!"
- Denying that others' experiences are different from your own: "I don't mind when people step on *my* toes."
- Derailing: "Some people don't even have toes. Why aren't we talking about them instead?"
- Refusing to center the impacted: "All toes matter!"
- Tone policing: "I'd move my foot if you'd ask me more nicely."

- Denying that the problem is fixable: "Toes getting stepped on is a fact of life. You'll be better off when you accept that."
- Victim blaming: "You shouldn't have been walking around people with boots!"
- Withdrawing: "I thought you wanted my help, but I guess not. I'll just go home."[3]

So, don't be a defensive toe-stepper. Thank the person who's brought your mess-up to your attention, make a brief statement about your intent (if you need to), and offer a sincere apology.

Forgive Yourself

Seriously. See above.

Get It Right the Next Time

Sometimes I mess up, someone informs me that I messed up, and I find it easy to never mess up like that again. An example is, if I've told a joke that, as it turns out, wasn't so funny. I hurt people with that joke, I'm embarrassed by my behavior, and I'm not going to tell that joke again. Other mess-ups have been more difficult for me to change. For example, when I'm asked to change language that I've used my whole life.

I remember, many years back, being in a workshop focusing on creating more inclusive spaces for people with disabilities. I learned that the word *handicapped* was considered derogatory and that I should use the word *disabled* instead. My intention was, of course, to make this change immediately. However, having used the word *handicapped* my whole life (especially when referring to parking spaces and toilet stalls), I found it difficult to make that change. Here are a few tips that helped me change my language and may help you as well.

Do Your Homework

I was told in the workshop that *handicapped* was now considered a derogatory term, but I wasn't told why. When I investigated online, I found that the word *handicapped* was a term used in horse racing. Faster horses would be *handicapped* with weights to slow them down and make the race fairer. This led to the word *handicapped* being applied to people with disabilities, who were

HELPFUL HINT

I also recently discovered that the word *able-bodied*, which I used throughout the first edition of this book to refer to someone who doesn't have a disability, is now considered derogatory. (Thank you again, Karen Catlin!) The reasoning is that if we describe non-disabled people as *able-bodied*, it implies that all people with disabilities lack able bodies or the ability to use their bodies well. A better choice, which I've switched to in this second edition, is *non-disabled*.

considered at the time to have an impediment that needed to be overcome in order to succeed in life.[4] Ick!

I didn't investigate the origin of this word in order to be convinced that I shouldn't use it. When a group of folks from a community tell me that a word that describes their community is offensive, I believe them. But reading about the origin of the word *handicapped* helped me understand its negative connotation, which in turn helped me remember to replace it with *disabled*.

Use-It-or-Lose-It

German psychologist Hermann Ebbinghaus tested memory retention and found that when people first learn a new thing, memory retention is typically 100 percent. If we don't intentionally recall or practice that new thing, retention drops to 40 percent after only a few days and continues to decline rapidly after that.[5] Basically, if we don't use information we've learned, we lose it. Apparently, the first few days after learning something new are critical times to recall and practice this new thing if we really want to retain the information. So, immediately after you get new information about an updated word or a language tweak, practice it a few times. Then practice it again a few hours later. Then practice it the next day. Then practice it the next week. Eventually, it will become a natural part of your vocabulary.

Share What You've Learned with Someone Else

When you learn something new, share it with someone else who may be interested in learning it too. Teaching what we know and having conversations about it lead to much better memory retention and recall. This is known as the Protégé Effect.[6]

Remind Yourself That Catching Yourself Is the First Step to Success

As I mentioned in chapter 6, change takes time. People often get frustrated with themselves when a word they're trying to eliminate slips out. When this happens to me, I've found it helpful to remind myself that catching myself using the wrong term is step one in the process. It's a sign of progress. If you hear yourself using a term that you're trying to eliminate, even if you weren't fast enough to catch it before it slipped out of your mouth, that's good! Stop yourself when you realize your mistake, state that you're trying to eliminate that word, and replace it with your new and improved word. Like this: "Don't park there. That's a handicapped . . . Ugh!!! I mean that's a parking spot for folks who are disabled." Pretty soon you'll move onto step two: catching yourself before the word slips out of your mouth.

BLUNDERING AGAIN

Yup. It's going to happen. Get used to it. Mess up, apologize, learn, share, grow, repeat, and embrace the adventure!

NOTES

1. Reprinted from Megan Carpenter, "Get It Wrong for Me: What I Need from Allies," LinkedIn, May 28, 2020, https://www.linkedin.com/pulse/get-wrong-me-what-i-need-from-allies-megan-carpenter/.

2. Chescaleigh, "Getting Called Out: How to Apologize," YouTube, September 6, 2013, https://www.youtube.com/watch?v=C8xJXKYL8pU&ab_channel=chescaleigh.

3. Presley Pizzo, "Boots & Sandals: How to Handle Mistakes," Guide to Allyship, https://guidetoallyship.com/#THE-WORK-OF-ALLYSHIP.

4. Douglas Baynton, "Language Matters: Handicapping an Affliction," Disability History Museum, https://www.disabilitymuseum.org/dhm/edu/essay.html?id=30.

5. The Intrepid Guide, "10 Proven Memory Hacks: How to Remember New Vocabulary Faster," August 30, 2020, https://www.theintrepidguide.com/memory-hacks-how-to-memorize-vocabulary-faster/.

6. Ibid.

15

BACKLASH
AGAINST ALLIES

I will no longer use the term "ally" to describe anyone. Instead, I'll use the phrase "currently operating in solidarity with." Or something. I mean, yeah, it's clunky as hell. But it gets at something that the label of "ally" just doesn't.[1]

— Mia McKenzie, *Black Girl Dangerous: On Race, Queerness, Class and Gender*

If you're already out there doing good work as an ally, you're probably aware that there is such a thing as backlash against allies from within the LGBTQ+ communities. If you're new to the game, please don't get discouraged. There are good reasons why people from historically marginalized communities might be disenchanted with people who identify as allies. Bad allyship has caused frustration and anger. In this chapter, I'll discuss some of the most common reasons for backlash against allies. With any luck, you'll all pop out the other end feeling even more empowered to get involved and to do the job right!

ALLY IS A PRACTICE, NOT AN IDENTITY

In the essay "No More 'Allies'" from her book *Black Girl Dangerous*, Mia McKenzie writes, "*Ally* cannot be a label that someone stamps onto you—or, god forbid, that you stamp on to yourself—so you can then go around claiming it as some kind of identity. It's not an identity. It's a practice."[2]

I was chatting recently with a friend over lunch. They were upset because someone at work, who has been blocking their efforts to create a more inclusive space, kept saying, "Look, you know I'm an ally." My friend said it was as if this colleague was using his ally identity as a pass that allowed him to steamroll ahead with some pretty transphobic policies. In my friend's opinion, no one should ever identify as an ally; they should just do the work for change. If someone calls another person an ally, then that's a really nice compliment.

On a practical level, using "currently operating in solidarity with," as Mia McKenzie suggests, is challenging. It would have been extremely difficult to write this book, for example, without using the word *ally*. So, the reality is that I do use the term *ally* to describe people who are not a part of a particular marginalized group but who stand up and advocate for the rights of people in that group. But I think it's incredibly important for us to understand the pushback against the term. If we ever catch ourselves thinking, "It's okay for me to say that or do this because I'm an ally," we're doing allyship wrong.

You may have heard or read about new terms that have been developed to take the place of the word *ally* or describe different levels of action. Some of the ones I've seen are *accomplice*, *advocate*, and *co-conspirator*. I'm fascinated by this development. I've read lots of articles and blogs about these different terms, trying to understand what they all mean and how they should be applied, and I keep coming back to the same thought, which is that none of these new words would be needed if allyship were being done well. *Ally* is becoming a word with negative implications because allyship is being done poorly by so many. In my opinion, we don't need any more terms to describe allies or differentiate levels of commitment and action. We need to put our energy into educating folks on how to do allyship well.

Thinking of the word *ally* as an in-the-moment compliment, rather than who we are, helps us remember that being an ally is about action. It's not a static identity that we wear on a badge: "Tada! I made it! Pop the champagne! I'm an ally!" It's about doing stuff and constantly learning. Becoming an ally is a never-ending process. So, switch out that ally pin for a rainbow pin and carry on with your excellent work!

Here's the good news: Every time someone is pleased with your level of involvement and the work you're doing toward inclusion and they call you an ally, I give you my full blessing to pat yourself on the back and pop a soda or one of those mini champagnes to celebrate!

SHUT UP AND LISTEN

I've been to many social justice events, workshops, and rallies where allies were told to "shut up and listen." If you ever hear this, I hope you'll do these four things:

1. Be kind to yourself. In your head, remove the "shut up" from this statement and focus on the "listen."
2. Assume goodwill. Think about where this anger, frustration, and snarkiness are coming from. If a community of people feels the need to tell allies to "shut up and listen," it means that they've repeatedly been in situations where professed allies have used their voices to talk over people in the community. If we got involved in social justice work because we wanted to create change, then we need to make sure that we're letting the people within the marginalized communities lead the way and that they're the ones deciding what that change should look like.
3. Remember, it's not your story. Remind yourself that you will *never* fully understand what it's like to be a part of the marginalized group you're advocating for. You can and should read about, watch videos on, and listen to the experiences of people in those groups, but you will never have that lived experience.
4. Make your choices. *You* get to decide which groups you will advocate for and support. If you feel that you're being treated in a disrespectful way and because of this you cannot get on board with a specific group or movement, peace out. Find groups to work with whose mission statements and messaging feel right for you.

"A" IS FOR ASEXUAL

Sometimes you'll see the initialism written with an "A" included, like this *LGBTQA+* or this *LGBTQIA+*. Have you wondered whether the "A" stands for *asexual* or *ally*? The answer is that it depends on who wrote it and what year it was written. When I began working at the LGBTQ+ center in Upstate New York in 2003, the "A" almost always stood for *ally*. Now, two decades later, you should most definitely assume that the "A" stands for *asexual* or, more accurately, the entire asexual community.

Honestly, when I first heard someone say that *ally* should not be included in the initialism, I got my trousers in a twist and thought it was pretty darn anti-ally. But then I did some reading to understand various perspectives and found that not including *ally* in the LGBTQ+ initialism makes total sense. Sydney Lynn wrote in the article "The A Stands for Asexuality: Putting the A in the LGBTQA+ Community" that allies aren't "part of the community"; they are "part of the movement."[3] Can't argue with that. The definition of an ally is someone who is *not* a part of a particular marginalized group but who stands up for and advocates for the rights of people in that group.

Another thing to think about is that it must surely cause some discontent to have allies represented in the initialism when many people within the LGBTQ+ communities aren't represented. If LGBTQA+ stood for lesbian, gay, bisexual, transgender, queer, ally, plus so much more, and I'm intersex (part of that "so much more"), I can see how I would be a bit annoyed that *ally* got a letter and I didn't.

One final thought on this topic is that most people who are a part of a marginalized group know that sometimes getting together in your [fill in the blank]-only space is empowering, rejuvenating, and less exhausting than being in spaces where not everyone "gets it." If the "A" stands for *ally*, then how do we distinguish between the spaces where allies are welcome and the ones where we aren't?

Assume the "A" stands for *asexual* or the asexual communities. If there are multiple "As" in the initialism, assume they stand for *asexual, aromantic,* and *androgynous.* Remember, *ally* isn't an identity, it's all about action.

KEY ALLY TAKEAWAYS

Now that you've read about the most common causes of pushback against allies, I hope you're feeling empowered to be the best ally that you can be. In summary, here are some basic principles of good allyship:

- Think of the word *ally* as a compliment, something you earn with your actions, not an identity that gives you privileges.
- Be mindful of the fact that you're part of the movement, not part of the community.
- Respect spaces and events where people from marginalized groups gather and allies are asked not to attend.
- When you're invited into LGBTQ+ spaces, listen to the people in the communities and let them guide your support efforts.

- Support and advocate for groups and movements that feel right and are a good fit for you.
- Be kind to yourself. (See chapter 16 for some suggestions if you stink at this.)

PAY IT FORWARD

When I began working as an active straight cisgender ally to the LGBTQ+ communities, I was very fearful of pushback against me. Although there have been a few minor anti-ally incidents here and there, there have been many, many more situations where I've been welcomed with open arms into the LGBTQ+ rights movement. Early on my heart was in the right place, but I was ignorant of the correct terms and unaware of the issues. I needed a lot of hand-holding, and, thankfully, I got it. If LGBTQ+ community members had not thanked me for the efforts I was making, answered my silly questions, and offered me words of encouragement, I would not have become the education director at our local LGBTQ+ center and I would not have written this book.

What I like to do now, whenever I can, is pay that gift of kindness and patience forward. When I'm in a position as the educator, either as a more experienced ally educating a newbie, or as a woman educating a man who's learning how to be an ally to the women's rights movement, I can tell people to "shut up and listen," or I can take the opportunity to thank them for their efforts, kindly answer their questions, and offer a hand of support. I choose the latter. I hope you will too.

NOTES

1. Reprinted from Mia McKenzie, *Black Girl Dangerous: On Race, Queerness, Class and Gender* (Oakland, CA: BGD Press, 2014).

2. Ibid.

3. Sydney Lynn, "The A Stands for Asexuality: Putting the A in the LGBTQA+ Community," *Thought Catalog*, April 3, 2015, https://thoughtcatalog.com/sydney lynn/2015/04/the-a-stands-for-asexualityputtingthea-in-lgbtqa-community/.

16

SUSTAINABILITY

Caring for myself is not self-indulgence, it is self-preservation, and that is an act of political warfare.[1]

—Audre Lorde, *A Burst of Light: And Other Essays*

Being an LGBTQ+ person is not a choice, but being an ally is. One of the reasons I was motivated to write this book was to offer a practical, realistic, and useful guide for being an ally to the LGBTQ+ communities. Workshops and books for allies often tell you what you *must* do. Many feature a daunting list of expectations and imply that if you don't hold yourself accountable to every single one you're not a true ally. I find these workshops and books intimidating and unrealistic. Instead of motivating allies to be better and more involved, I believe they have the opposite effect, convincing people that they're never going to be "ally enough" and discouraging them from even trying.

I was fortunate to be able to turn being an ally into a full-time career, but the reality is that most people can't. Typically, there are jobs, family, homes, and pets that need our attention during the majority of our waking hours. With an unyielding list of ally expectations and an unforgiving attitude when people mess up, who would ever willingly choose to be an ally with all of these other things vying for our time? If we're going to add allyship to the long list of other life obligations and choices, then we must do it wisely, so that it fits into our lives in a way that is sustainable. This chapter offers some pointers for how to do that.

TAKE CARE OF YOURSELF

Caring for yourself is critical to your work as an effective ally. Below are some suggestions for how to care for yourself when ally life gets challenging.

Be on Your Own Team

Be aware of your needs and take them seriously. Here is an example of how I take care of myself after I facilitate a full-day workshop. At the end of these sessions, I am exhausted and vulnerable. I've been on my feet for more than ten hours, I've taken care of my participants' emotional and physical needs, I've worked to keep the energy in the room up, and I've put my heart and soul into the workshop. I know that a helpful tip written on a workshop evaluation about how I can improve, which, the next morning over coffee, will have me nodding my head and thinking, "That's a great suggestion," could have me in tears the night of the workshop. So, I take that pile of evaluations and set it aside for the morning. Then I take care of me for the rest of the night by nurturing my body and helping myself wind down. How do you help yourself when you're exhausted and feeling vulnerable?

Treat Yourself the Way You Would Treat Your Best Friend

If you tend to be hard on yourself when you mess up, think about what you'd say to your best friend or do for your best friend if they were in the same situation. Then say that and do that for yourself.

Give Yourself Permission to Fail

Recently, I've gotten into indoor rock climbing. Completing a climb without "falling" (having to take a break or coming off the wall) feels amazing. However, I know that if I never fall, my rate of improvement will be slower than if I push myself to try more challenging climbs and fail. Failure and mistakes are essential to learning and growth. Keep this in mind and give yourself permission to be human, mess up, and learn from your mistakes.

Use Positive Self-Coaching Tips

Unfortunately, negative self-talk ("Ugh! I'm such a loser!") often comes very naturally to people, but positive self-talk ("It's okay; I'm human") doesn't. Think about some positive self-coaching tips that can help you through tough times. Have you ever done something super adventurous or gutsy? Remind yourself of that the next time you're in a situation where you're intimidated. I like to think back to when I went skydiving with my daughter and use this motivator: "Jeannie, you jumped out of a frickin' airplane! Don't let *this* scare you." Is there something a loved one says to you that calms you when you're stressed? Try saying that to yourself when you're in a difficult situation. I'm claustrophobic. I recently got through an hour-long MRI by imagining my husband, Ed, next to me on one side, saying in his calming voice, "You're okay, baby" and my best friend, Pam, on the other side, saying, "You've got this."

Keep a Joy Journal

Tarana Burke, founder of the Me Too movement and author of the book *Un-Bound*, talks about being a "twenty-something-year-old pregnant black girl who had very limited resources"[2] trying to figure out a way to help herself when times got tough. She ended up going to the dollar store, buying a notebook, and writing "Joy" at the top. Then she began to write down everything that brought her joy. In her YouTube video, "Tarana's Toolbox: Joy Journal," she says,

> Over time, my little notebook started filling up. I didn't have to pay for that. You couldn't take that from me. I didn't have to pay $99.99. I didn't have to meditate on it. I didn't have to go to a seminar. I didn't have to listen to a DVD every day. I could laugh with my girlfriends any time I wanted to. I could spend as much time with my baby as I wanted to. And it was *my* joy. And when I felt like, *This is a really tough life* . . . When I felt like, *Why don't I have enough money to pay my rent?*. . . When I felt like, *Why do I feel so unworthy?*. . . When I felt like, whatever the things were that made me feel like draggin' my knuckles, as my girlfriend would say . . . I would pick up my journal to remind myself that there's another part of my life.[3]

Know Your Recipe for Wellness and Follow It

When I travel for work and my usual routine gets thrown out of whack for several days, my recipe for wellness and selfcare involves three things: sleep, exercise, and vegetables. If I consistently get none or only one of these during my travels, I'm in rough shape. Two is significantly better. All three and I am at the top of my game! What's your wellness recipe?

Think about What's Not Wrong

Have you ever noticed that comfort is such a fantastic feeling immediately after a toothache? But do we appreciate comfort on a daily basis? In his book *Peace Is Every Step*, the late Thích Nhất Hạnh, world-renowned Zen master and spiritual leader, wrote about the importance of spending some time thinking about what's *not* wrong in any given moment. He writes, "We often ask, 'What's wrong?' Doing so, we invite painful seeds of sorrow to come up and manifest. We feel suffering, anger, and depression, and produce more such seeds. We would be much happier if we tried to stay in touch with the healthy, joyful seeds inside us and around us. We should learn to ask, 'What's not wrong?' and be in touch with that."[4]

When life gets challenging, I remind myself to focus on what's not wrong. For example:

> *What's wrong:* My car broke down and I'm late for a meeting. Darn it!
> *What's not wrong:* I'm healthy! My family is healthy! Paying for car repairs won't be a huge financial burden for me! The sun is out! I've got a granola bar in my bag! I hate meetings! I don't have to poop! Life is good!

Even during very challenging times, you're likely to find that there is so much more that's not wrong with your life.

PACE YOURSELF

Part of being an effective ally and really sticking with it for the long haul involves figuring out what works for you, what interests you, what you will and won't do, and what reasonably fits into your schedule and lifestyle. My husband, Ed, and I are great about exercising every day, but we have very different strategies for making that work for us. Ed is motivated by his gear and his data. He uses his Garmin watch, his "smart trainer," and the Zwift and Strava apps. He calculates his heart rate, his calories burned, his miles per hour, his pedal revolutions per minute, and I don't know what else. I listen to my music while I plod down the street or I watch a movie while I pedal on my exercise bike. I couldn't care less how fast I'm going, how many calories I'm burning, or whether or not I'm performing better than I did yesterday. If I had to calculate my CPMs, my MPHs, and my RPMs, I simply wouldn't exercise. I'd lie on the couch instead, watching *Star Trek: The Next Generation* reruns.

I've come to learn my strengths and interests as an ally as well. I love having respectful conversations with people who think differently from me. I love creating spaces for individuals to be vulnerable with each other without fear of judgment. I hate talking to politicians. I *really* hate it. Through all of my years volunteering and working at our LGBTQ+ center, I went only once to an LGBTQ+ lobbying day at our state capitol. Does dropping that piece off my plate make me a bad ally? I don't think so. I think the other work I do makes up for the fact that I skip out on a day that will make me completely miserable.

I'm not advocating for never moving out of our comfort zones. I am all about trying new things and challenging ourselves. My point is that we can't do everything, and we should not be expected to. It's not realistic or sustainable to have those expectations. Extreme "lose weight fast" diets don't work. We can't stick with them. Small healthy-eating lifestyle changes do. They're sustainable. Allyship works the same way. Give yourself permission to do the kind of ally work that you love, that fits your personality, and that you're likely to be able to continue to do for the long haul.

CONTINUE YOUR EDUCATION

One very important aspect of being a useful and effective ally is ensuring that we stay current on LGBTQ+ language and topics. This doesn't mean we need to know every single vocabulary word and identity term, but we should work to keep up to date on what's happening within the communities we're advocating for. One way that I do this without becoming overwhelmed is to take words or topics one at a time. If I hear more than once or twice about an issue or an identity that's unfamiliar to me, I investigate it and educate myself. For example, I knew the dictionary definition of the word *asexual*, but I really didn't know much about this identity or community. About twelve years ago, I noticed that workshop participants were suddenly asking questions about asexual people. It was time for me to educate myself. I did some reading, I watched some videos, and I also watched the documentary film (*A*)*sexual*.[5] I learned a lot, and it really helped me understand the differences between sexual attraction and romantic attraction. I became much more proficient at answering questions about the asexual community in a respectful and informed way. And learning should be ongoing, even on topics we've already investigated. More recently, I read the book *Ace: What Asexuality Reveals about Desire, Society, and the Meaning of Sex* by Angela Chen[6] and became even savvier regarding asexuality.

Besides consuming books, blogs, videos, and movies, we can also increase our ally savviness by getting out to events like workshops and conferences. The largest and bestknown LGBTQ+ conference in the United States is Creating Change, an annual conference run by the National LGBTQ Task Force. It takes place in late January or early February in a different city each year. Not only does Creating Change offer a wide range of valuable workshops, but the venue itself turns into "queer planet" for five days. Hotel staff members walk around wearing pronoun pins, people introduce themselves by saying, "Hi! I'm Jeannie—she, her, and hers," and entire floors of restrooms are designated all-gender. It's an extremely cool experience and exposes participants to the most cutting-edge stuff.

EVERY SO OFTEN, RETURN TO "WHY?"

I mentioned in chapter 12 that for eight years I was the coordinator of our agency's bike ride fundraiser. One year, while trying to encourage the riders to get out there and start fundraising, I implemented a "Why I Ride" campaign. I asked riders to snap a picture of themselves holding a sign about why they ride and post it on their social media sites and in their fundraising emails. The results were passionate, moving, and effective.

Six days before that year's ride in June 2016, the Pulse nightclub shooting in Orlando took place. Fifty-three people were wounded and forty-nine were killed. It stands as the deadliest attack ever on the LGBTQ+ communities.

Every year I gave a brief speech before the riders set off, to motivate them for the day ahead. That year, with an extremely heavy heart, I found it more difficult than ever to inspire my crew. I had no words. I agonized for days over what I would say, and, in the end, it was my riders and their "Why I Ride" messages that inspired *me*. Instead of a speech that year, I read their beautiful messages.

Here are a few of the reasons my riders took to the road in June 2016:

Joe: I ride because I don't want my nephew to grow up in a world where people are discriminated against for whom they love and how they identify.

Debbie: I ride for health, because hiding who you are is not healthy.

Pam: I ride for truth. I can't imagine how it must feel to be afraid to let your true self show. And until that fear becomes groundless, I will ride.

Craig: I ride because equality means everyone!

Anastasia: I ride because this is the only world we have and I want it to be a safe zone for everyone. #loveeveryone #somechicksmarrychicks #getoverit #fckh8

Ronald: I ride because LGBT youth and elderly still experience huge injustices.

Rowan: I ride for everyone who never will again. Remember our dead and fight like hell for the living.

Maya: I ride because love and equity are the foundation for happiness.

I told you at the very beginning that this is a book about how to be an ally, not why to be an ally—but pause every once in a while and think about why you're involved as an ally and why this work is important to you. Talk with other allies about what motivates them. It's powerful, restorative, and necessary.

Jeannie: I ride to create a world where everyone can live authentically in all aspects of their lives. I ride to eliminate gender bias and gender policing. I ride to increase the likelihood that everyone will believe that when it comes to their orientations, gender identity, and gender expression, they're perfect just as they are. I ride because if my grandchildren ever ask me if I was involved in the fight for LGBTQ+ rights, I'll get to say, "Hell yeah!"

Enjoy the ride.

NOTES

1. Reprinted with permission from Audre Lorde, *A Burst of Light: And Other Essays* (Mineola, NY: Dover Publications, 1988), 130.

2. Tarana Burke, "Tarana's Toolbox: Joy Journal," YouTube, April 8, 2021, https://www.youtube.com/watch?v=CF_OinWVhOM&ab_channel=TaranaBurke.

3. Ibid.

4. Thích Nhất Hạnh, *Peace Is Every Step: The Path of Mindfulness in Everyday Life* (New York: Bantam Books, 1991), 77.

5. Katy Chevigny, Beth Davenport, and Jolene Pinder (producers) and Angela Tucker (director), *(A)sexual* (New York: FilmBuff, 2012), DVD.

6. Angela Chen, *Ace: What Asexuality Reveals about Desire, Society, and the Meaning of Sex* (Boston: Beacon Press, 2020).

ACKNOWLEDGMENTS

This book would not have been possible without the support, knowledge, time, and generosity of the people below. An *enormous* thank-you goes out to:

Ed Freedman, for encouraging all adventures and for giving the gift that started it all.

Julie Gainsburg, for the many hours you put into editing this book, for all the Oxford commas, and for being there for me no matter what.

Hayden Freedman, for listening to *every* voice and for challenging me to consider things from different perspectives.

Becca Gainsburg, for encouraging me to reach higher and for making me laugh.

Vicki and Roy Gainsburg, for raising me in a household where equality was a no-brainer.

Pam Polashenski, for showing me what badassery truly looks like.

Scott Fearing, for sharing the "assume goodwill" philosophy that is at the heart of this book and for creating a safe space for me to come out as a loud and proud ally.

Noah Wagoner, for being my social justice go-to guy and for being an ally to the world.

The wonderful team at Rowman & Littlefield: Mark Kerr, Sarah Rinehart, Catherine Herman, Courtney Packard, Jessica McCleary, Karin Cholak, and Meghann French.

ACKNOWLEDGMENTS

My personal reviewers, editors, and advisors: Tim Ackroyd, Jeanette Adams-Price, Steve Brosnihan, Julie Buchanan, Karen Catlin, Oona Foxe, Tovia Freedman, Alice Glinert, Shimona Gorelick, Christopher Hennelly, Chris Hinesley, Elizabeth Olson, Cara Pelletier, Anastasia Polashenski, Tallis Polashenski, Walter Polashenski, Bev Mondillo Wright, and Steve Wright.

Everyone else who made this book come alive with their personal stories, insights, and experiences: Jason Ballard, Sam Cappiello, Kelly Clark, Rowan Collins, Maur DeLaney, Joe Doty, Daniel Fox, Todd Gordon, Gabrielle Hermosa, Sean Johnston, Mike Kelly, Matt Krueger, Eridan Maeder, Wanda Martinez-Johncox, Lore McSpadden, Kayden Eli Miller, Dee Murray, Manuel Peña, Patrick Pitoni, Maya Polashenski, Ronald Pratt, Craig Ronald, Gloria Ronga, Susan Rubin, Matt Tappon, Deborah Trubatch, Jonathan Wetherbee, and the Zacharias family.

Carlos the cat, for all the snuggle breaks and for letting me mess with your pronouns.

DISCUSSION GUIDE

Looking for another way to become a savvy ally? Consider hosting a *Savvy Ally* book club and using these questions to guide your discussion. You can download a copy of this discussion guide at www.savvyallyaction.com.

PART I: BECOMING KNOWLEDGEABLE ALLIES

- In chapter 2, Gainsburg writes about the common question "Why do there have to be so many identities?" She states that typically this question comes from people who have figured out their identity and have their word or words locked in place. Words are created when there's a need. Are there aspects of your identity for which you haven't found quite the right word?

- Are there identities of yours that you've hidden or avoided answering questions about? What influenced you in deciding to hide those identities? How did that make you feel about yourself and your environment?

- In chapter 3, Gainsburg introduces Jacob Tobia's new metaphor for coming out, using a snail rather than a closet. Did this make you think differently about the coming-out experience and the role that allies can play to support LGBTQ+ folks who feel unsafe at work or school? If yes, in what ways?

- Did the diagram of sex, gender, and sexuality, discussed in chapter 4, cause you to reflect on yourself in a new way? If so, what was the impact?

- Gainsburg writes about the problematic issue of people confusing attraction and behavior and how this issue lies at the heart of many misunderstandings about LGBTQ+ people and inclusion efforts. Have you experienced people confusing attraction and behavior in your workplace, school, or faith community? If so, what did this look like? What was the impact or response?

PART II: BUILDING SKILLS FOR HAVING RESPECTFUL CONVERSATIONS

- Were you sharing your pronouns in your email signature and/or on video conferencing platforms before you read *The Savvy Ally*? If so, what motivated you to do so. If not, are you likely to do it now? Why or why not?
- In chapter 5, Gainsburg asserts that the best way to gather information about how to respectfully refer to people is to establish systems where you're gathering the information from *everyone* who wants to share. Which techniques mentioned in this book for gathering pronouns are ones that could be implemented in your workplace, school, or faith community?
- Are there LGBTQ+ etiquette language tips or ally actions, shared in chapter 6, that you're likely to embrace after reading this book? Which will be the most challenging and why?
- Did any of the bloopers in chapter 6 surprise you? What bloopers have you made or heard others make? What bloopers do people make when referring to parts of your identity? How have you corrected people when they have made bloopers about your identity?
- Chapter 7 begins with a quote from Sam Killermann about your "You Soup" ingredient list. Which of your "ingredients" do people tend to focus on? What parts of your identity are important to you that others don't see or tend to overlook?
- Gainsburg shares that myths and stereotypes about straight cisgender allies had held her back from being vocal and active as an ally for many years. Have any of those myths or stereotypes held you back from taking a more active role as an ally? If you were able to overcome these myths and stereotypes, what helped?
- In chapter 8, Gainsburg states that humans are naturally resistant learners. Have you experienced yourself being a resistant learner? What helps you overcome your resistance to learning new ideas that conflict with old ones?
- Have you ever let someone know that their language or behavior is problematic? Have you ever informed someone that they misgendered some-

one else by using the wrong name, pronoun, or gendered word, like *Sir*? If so, what was the interaction like? Do you think it was effective? What was the other person's reaction? Now that you've read about the effective educator tips in chapter 8, are there things you would do differently next time? If so, how would you alter your approach?

- Discuss a recent experience in which you saw discriminatory or inappropriate behavior and didn't step in or speak up. What held you back? Did you learn anything from the book that better equips you to intervene now?

PART III: TAKING ACTION TO CREATE MORE INCLUSIVE SPACES

- Which of the common questions in chapter 9 have you been asked? How did you respond? Would you change your response based on what you learned in this book? If so, how would you change it? Are there other questions you've fielded about the LGBTQ+ communities that you didn't know how to respond to? Discuss with your group some savvy ways to respond to these.
- Have you ever experienced receiving equal treatment when what you needed was equitable treatment (i.e., where one-size-fits-all didn't fit you)? If so, how did that make you feel?
- What actions stood out to you in chapter 10, "Duct Tape Patch-Up Jobs and Big Fixes"? Would you say your workplace, school, and/or faith community has applied more duct tape patch-up jobs or big fixes when it comes to creating more inclusive spaces? What further changes can you see implementing or advocating for in these spaces?
- Gainsburg notes that when LGBTQ+ people enter a space (i.e., a health center, a business, a faith community), they look for specific indicators that they will be welcome there. What do LGBTQ+ people see when they enter your workplace, school, or faith community, or look at your organization's website?
- In chapter 13, Gainsburg mentions that some people are taught that saying *Sir* and *Ma'am* is a sign of respect and others believe that applying gendered words like *Sir* and *Ma'am* to strangers is problematic. How do you make decisions about whether to use gendered or gender-neutral words for strangers? How do you navigate a situation where you need to use a pronoun to refer to someone, but you don't know what it is? How do you reply to an email sent from someone who's given you no information about how to respectfully refer to them?

PART IV: ALLYING RESPONSIBLY

- Do you allow yourself to be raggedy? Do you forgive yourself when you mess up? If not, what gets in your way? Have you ever experienced positive outcomes after messing up? If so, what were they?
- In chapter 14, Gainsburg shares some strategies for "getting it right the next time" after you've accidentally misgendered someone. What strategies for remembering people's names and pronouns have worked for you?
- Have you experienced any of the backlash against allies discussed in chapter 15? Have you ever been in a situation where you tried to do "the right thing" as an ally, only to be called out and told you did it wrong? If so, how did you recover from that situation? What did you learn from that experience?
- Have you seen or heard the words *accomplice*, *advocate*, and *co-conspirator* that some folks think should replace the word *ally* or should be used to show different levels of support? What are your thoughts on this?
- In the final chapter, Gainsburg pushes back on putting a heavy focus on ally accountability. She writes about encountering daunting lists of expectations for allies and unforgiving attitudes when allies mess up. Instead, she promotes forgiveness, sustainability, and self-care. What are your thoughts on this approach? Have you found that a focus on ally accountability motivates you or does it make you feel like you'll never be "ally enough"?
- What are some ally actions that you can take that are a good fit for your personality and skill set and are also sustainable? Are there any ally actions that aren't a good fit for your personality and skill set that you would prefer to avoid or drop off your plate?
- Gainsburg asserts that allies should always be learning and growing. What are your favorite sources for keeping up to date with LGBTQ+ topics? What concepts or identities are you interested in learning more about?
- In the "Take Care of Yourself" section in chapter 16, Gainsburg shares her recipe for wellness (i.e., sleep, exercise, and vegetables). What's your wellness recipe? What self-care strategies do you implement when you're feeling exhausted or vulnerable?
- At the very end of the book, Gainsburg encourages you to think about what motivates you as an ally. What's your "Why"?

GLOSSARY

WARNING: IDENTITIES BEING DEFINED!

Cultural words and identity words vary in meaning with the user. They also change over time. This glossary should be used as a tool for basic reference. It should never be used to label others. Proceed with caution!

affectional orientation: The part of an individual's identity that describes to whom they are romantically attracted. It is also known as *romantic orientation.*

agender: Relating to an individual who has no gender.

ally: A person who is not a part of a particular marginalized group but who stands up and advocates for the rights of people in that group.

androgynous: A gender expression that is neither feminine nor masculine. It is sometimes defined as a blending of both masculinity and femininity.

aromantic: Relating to an individual with a low or absent romantic attraction. This word is also used as an umbrella term for a spectrum of identities. A few of the many identities under the aromantic umbrella are *demiromantic* and *grayromantic.*

asexual: Relating to an individual with a low or absent sexual attraction. This word is also used as an umbrella term for a spectrum of identities. A few of the many identities under the asexual umbrella are *demisexual* and *graysexual. Asexual* is sometimes shortened to *ace.*

binary: Relating to two things or two options. Individuals who are either *men* or *women* (whether they're transgender or cisgender) fit into the gender binary.

biological sex: A categorization of an individual that is based on their reproductive system and secondary sex characteristics: genitalia, chromosomes, hormones, etc.

biphobia: Fear, intolerance, or hatred of people who are, or who are perceived to be, bisexual or pansexual.

biromantic: Relating to an individual who is romantically attracted to both men and women or to people regardless of their gender.

bisexual: Relating to an individual who is sexually attracted to both men and women or to people regardless of their gender.

cisgender: Relating to an individual whose gender identity matches the sex they were assigned at birth; someone who is not transgender. *Cisgender* is sometimes shortened to *cis*.

cisnormativity: The assumption that everyone is cisgender or that being cisgender is the "right" way to be.

cross-dresser: An individual who, for comfort, enjoyment, and/or self-expression, wears clothing that has been designated by society as inappropriate for their gender.

demiromantic: Relating to an individual who experiences romantic or affectional attraction to a person only after they've developed a close emotional bond with them.

demisexual: Relating to an individual who experiences sexual attraction to a person only after they've developed a close emotional bond with them.

drag king: An entertainer whose act features wearing men's clothing, facial makeup, and facial hair in order to impersonate a man.

drag queen: An entertainer whose act features wearing women's clothing, a wig, and makeup in order to impersonate a woman.

gay: Relating to an individual who is sexually attracted only to people of the same gender. Traditionally a term used only by men, the term *gay* is now embraced by some others as well.

gender expansive: Relating to an individual whose gender expression or gender identity does not fit into society's binary expectations. Some people prefer this term to *gender nonconforming*.

gender expression: The way an individual expresses their gender to the outside world, through clothing, hairstyles, interests, mannerisms, and movements. The typical categories of gender expression are *masculine*, *feminine*, and *androgynous*.

gender-fluid: Relating to an individual whose gender identity regularly fluctuates.

gender identity: An individual's sense of their own gender. The typical categories of gender identity are *man, woman,* and *nonbinary.*

gender nonconforming: Relating to an individual whose gender expression or gender identity does not fit into society's binary expectations. Some people prefer this term to *gender expansive.*

gender policing: The societal enforcement of binary gender roles and expectations.

genderqueer: Relating to an individual whose gender identity is neither man nor woman.

grayromantic: Relating to an individual who experiences romantic attraction rarely or with low intensity.

graysexual: Relating to an individual who experiences sexual attraction rarely or with low intensity. *Graysexual* is sometimes shortened to *gray-A or gray-ace.*

heteronormativity: The assumption that everyone is heterosexual or that being heterosexual is the "right" way to be.

heteroromantic: Relating to a man who is romantically attracted only to women or a woman who is romantically attracted only to men.

heterosexual: Relating to a man who is sexually attracted only to women or a woman who is sexually attracted only to men; also known as *straight.*

homophobia: Fear, intolerance, or hatred of people who are, or who are perceived to be, gay or lesbian.

homoromantic: Relating to an individual who is romantically attracted only to people of the same gender.

homosexual: An outdated term relating to an individual who is sexually attracted only to people of the same gender. The words *gay* and *lesbian* are more respectful terms.

intersectionality: The complex and overlapping ways that an individual's many identities (sexual orientation, gender, race, ethnicity, ability, socioeconomic status, immigration status, language, size, religion, etc.) come together and shape their experiences and social interactions. The prejudice and discrimination related to these overlapping identities are unique and are different from the prejudice and discrimination faced by people with each individual identity.

intersex: Relating to an individual whose biological sex characteristics (i.e., genitals, reproductive organs, chromosomes, and/or hormones) do not fit typical binary notions of male or female bodies.

intimate behaviors: Sexual and/or romantic activities.

lesbian: Relating to a woman who is sexually attracted only to women.

LGBTQ+: One of the many initialisms created to refer to all sexual and gender minorities. It stands for lesbian, gay, bisexual, transgender, queer and/or questioning, plus so much more!

microaggression: A commonplace comment or behavior toward a person from a historically marginalized community that is hurtful, insulting, or demeaning. The comment may or may not be intentionally insulting.

misgender: To use a gendered term, like *Sir* or *Ma'am*, incorrectly when referring to someone.

MSM: An abbreviation for "men who have sex with men." This term was created to acknowledge and offer appropriate health care to men who don't use the terms *gay, bisexual,* or *pansexual* to refer to themselves, but who are engaging in sexual activities with men.

Mx: A gender-neutral title that can be used to replace gendered titles, such as *Mr., Mrs., Ms.,* and *Miss.*

neopronoun: A new, not officially recognized gender-neutral pronoun. Some examples are: *xe, ze,* and *ey.*

nonbinary: Relating to an individual whose gender identity is neither man nor woman. This word can be used as an umbrella term that includes many identities, such as *agender, gender expansive, gender-fluid, genderqueer,* and *Two-Spirit. Nonbinary* is sometimes shortened to *NB* or *enby.*

panromantic: Relating to an individual who is romantically attracted to people regardless of their gender.

pansexual: Relating to an individual who is sexually attracted to people regardless of their gender.

polyamorous: Relating to an individual who engages in more than one sexual and/or romantic relationship at a time, with the knowledge and consent of all involved.

QPOC: An initialism that stands for queer people of color.

QTPOC: An initialism that stands for queer and/or transgender people of color.

queer: A reclaimed term that is liked by some and disliked by others. It can be used to define any orientation that is not straight and/or any gender that is not cisgender.

questioning: Relating to an individual who is currently unsure of or exploring their orientation and/or gender identity.

romantic orientation: The part of an individual's identity that describes to whom they are romantically attracted. It is also known as *affectional orientation.*

sexual orientation: The part of an individual's identity that describes to whom they are sexually attracted.

SGM: An initialism that stands for sexual and gender minority. This initialism is used in some healthcare and academic settings as a replacement for the terms *LGBTQ+* and *queer.*

straight: Relating to a man who is sexually attracted only to women or a woman who is sexually attracted only to men; also known as *heterosexual.*

TGX: An initialism that stands for transgender and gender expansive.

transfeminine: Relating to an individual, typically one who was assigned male at birth, whose gender identity or expression falls in the woman or feminine area of the gender spectrum.

transgender: Relating to an individual whose sex assigned at birth does not match their gender identity. This word can be used as an individual's identity term or as an umbrella term that includes many identities, such as *genderqueer, nonbinary, trans man,* and *trans woman. Transgender* is sometimes shortened to *trans.*

transition: Changing from one state to another. Often used to refer to the process by which a transgender individual takes steps to align their body with their gender identity.

trans man: Relating to an individual who was assigned female at birth, but whose gender identity is man.

transmasculine: Relating to an individual, typically one who was assigned female at birth, whose gender identity or expression falls in the man or masculine area of the gender spectrum.

transphobia: Fear, intolerance, or hatred of people who are, or who are perceived to be, transgender.

transsexual: An outdated term relating to an individual who uses medical and/or surgical treatments to help align their body with their gender identity by transitioning from the sex they were assigned at birth. The newer word, *transgender,* is more commonly used, whether a person undergoes a medical or surgical transition or not.

trans woman: Relating to an individual who was assigned male at birth, but whose gender identity is woman.

Two-Spirit: A modern term, used by some Indigenous North Americans, to describe people who have the spirit of both man and woman or are a third gender. It is embraced by some Indigenous North Americans and rejected by others.

BIBLIOGRAPHY

AAA Project Visibility. *Project Visibility.* Boulder, CO: Boulder County Area Agency on Aging, 2004. DVD.

ACLU. "Four Myths about Trans Athletes, Debunked." April 30, 2020. https://www .aclu.org/news/lgbtq-rights/four-vennmyths-about-trans-athletes-debunked/.

ACLU. "Legislation Affecting LGBTQ Rights across the Country." https://www.aclu .org/legislation-affecting-lgbtq-rights-across-country.

Airton, Lee. *Gender: Your Guide: A Gender-Friendly Primer on What to Know, What to Say, and What to Do in the New Gender Culture.* Avon, MA: Adams Media, 2018.

American Civil Liberty Union. "Know Your Rights: Students' Rights." https://www .aclu.org/know-your-rights/students-rights/.

American Progress. "Health Disparities in LGBT Communities of Color." January 15, 2010. https://www.americanprogress.org/article/health-disparities-in-lgbt-communi ties-of-color/.

Amnesty International. "Safety during Protest" [flyer]. https://www.amnestyusa.org /pdfs/SafeyDuringProtest_F.pdf.

Austen, Jane. *Emma.* London: John Murray, 1815.

Baynton, Douglas. "Language Matters: Handicapping an Affliction." Disability History Museum. https://www.disabilitymuseum.org/dhm/edu/essay.html?id=30.

Beckham, Ash. "Ash Beckham at Ignite Boulder 20." Filmed March 2, 2013, at Ignite Conference, Boulder, CO. YouTube. https://www.youtube.com/watch?v =Gxs78C3XGok.

Beckham, Ash. "We're All Hiding Something. Let's Find the Courage to Open Up." TED, February 21, 2014. https://www.youtube.com/watch?v=uq83lU6nuS8&ab _channel=TED.

Berger, Miriam. "A Guide to How Gender-Neutral Language Is Developing around the World." *Washington Post*, December 15, 2019. https://www.washingtonpost

.com/world/2019/12/15/guide-how-gender-neutral-language-is-developing-around
-world/.

Bi, Stephani, Scott C. Cook, and Marshall H. Chin. "Improving Care of LGBTQ People of Color." *AFT Health Care*, Fall 2021. https://www.aft.org/hc/fall2021/bi_cook_chin.

Burke, Tarana. "Tarana's Toolbox: Joy Journal." YouTube, April 8, 2021. https://www.youtube.com/watch?v=CF_OinWVhOM&ab_channel=TaranaBurke.

Burroughs, Nannie Helen. *The 12 Things the Negro Must Do for Himself.* Circa early 1900s.

Bustos, Valeria P., Samyd S. Bustos, Andres Mascaro et al. "Regret after Gender-Affirmation Surgery: A Systematic Review and Meta-Analysis of Prevalence." *Plastic and Reconstructive Surgery Global Open* 9, no. 3 (March 2021): e3477. https://www.ncbi.nlm.nih.gov/pmc/articles/PMC8099405/.

Butler, Kelsey. "Anti-LGBTQ Proposals Are Flooding U.S. State Legislatures at a Record Pace." *Bloomberg*, April 8, 2022. https://www.bloomberg.com/news/articles/2022-04-08/mapping-the-anti-lgbtq-proposals-flooding-u-s-state-legislatures.

Calico, Hippie. "Asexuality: The Invisible Orientation." YouTube, April 12, 2020. https://www.youtube.com/watch?v=R9tSal4YyII&ab_channel=HippieCalico.

Carpenter, Megan. "Get It Wrong for Me: What I Need from Allies." LinkedIn, May 28, 2020. https://www.linkedin.com/pulse/get-wrong-me-what-i-need-from-allies-megan-carpenter/.

Cass, Vivienne. "Homosexual Identity Formation: A Theoretical Model." *Journal of Homosexuality* 4, no. 3 (spring 1979): 219–35.

Catlin, Karen. *Better Allies: Everyday Actions to Create Inclusive, Engaging Workplaces.* Second Ed. Better Allies Press, 2021.

Chemaly, Soraya. "How Women and Minorities Are Claiming Their Right to Rage." *The Guardian*, May 11, 2019. https://www.theguardian.com/lifeandstyle/2019/may/11/women-and-minorities-claiming-right-to-rage.

Chen, Angela. *Ace: What Asexuality Reveals about Desire, Society, and the Meaning of Sex.* Boston: Beacon Press, 2020.

Chescaleigh. "Sometimes You're a Caterpillar." YouTube, March 24, 2015. https://www.youtube.com/watch?v=hRiWgx4sHGg&ab_channel=chescaleigh.

Chescaleigh. "Getting Called Out: How to Apologize." YouTube, September 6, 2013. https://www.youtube.com/watch?v=C8xJXKYL8pU&ab_channel=chescaleigh.

Chevigny, Katy, Beth Davenport, and Jolene Pinder, producers, and Angela Tucker, director. *(A)sexual.* New York: FilmBuff, 2012. DVD.

Choi, Soon Kyu, and Ilan H. Meyer. *LGBT Aging: A Review of Research Findings, Needs, and Policy Implications.* Los Angeles: The Williams Institute, 2016. file:///C:/Users/jgain/Documents/Savvy%20Ally%20Action/Resources/Older%20Adults/LGBT-Aging-A-Review%202016.pdf.

Clarey, Christopher. "Gender Test after a Gold-Medal Finish." *New York Times*, August 19, 2009. https://www.nytimes.com/2009/08/20/sports/20runner.html.

CNBC. "'Bathroom Bill' to Cost North Carolina $3.76 Billion." March, 27, 2017. https://
www.cnbc.com/2017/03/27/bathroom-bill-to-cost-north-carolina-376-billion
.html.

Colapinto, John. *As Nature Made Him: The Boy Who Was Raised as a Girl.* New York:
HarperCollins, 2000.

Cox, Josie. "Pride Pays: LGBT-Friendly Businesses Are More Profitable, Research
Shows." *Forbes*, May 24, 2021. https://www.forbes.com/sites/josiecox/2021/05/24
/pride-pays-lgbt-friendly-businesses-are-more-profitable-research-shows/.

Crenshaw, Kimberlé. "The Urgency of Intersectionality." TEDWomen 2016, December 7, 2016. https://www.ted.com/talks/kimberle_crenshaw_the_urgency_of
_intersectionality?language=en.

Doyle, Glennon. "Playing Our Roles: How Does Culture's Invention of Gender Typecast Every Last One of Us?" *We Can Do Hard Things with Glennon Doyle*, August
24, 2021. https://momastery.com/blog/episode-20/.

Fearing, Scott. *Successful LGBT Education: A Manual.* Minneapolis: OutFront Minnesota, 1996.

Fitzsimons, Tim. "Puberty Blockers Linked to Lower Suicide Risk for Transgender
People." CBS News, January 24, 2020. https://www.nbcnews.com/feature/nbc-out
/puberty-blockers-linked-lower-suicide-risk-transgender-people-n1122101.

Fox, Morgan Jon. "The One You Never Forget." YouTube, August 25, 2020. https://www
.youtube.com/watch?v=1aa9SttW0zk&ab_channel=MorganJonFox.

GLSEN. "Transgender Inclusion in High School Athletics." July 2019. https://www
.glsen.org/sites/default/files/2019-10/GLSEN-Transgender-Inclusion-High-School
-Athletics.pdf.

Goldberg, Susan. "School Forms: What Happens When Both Parents Are Mother."
Today's Parent, St. Joseph Communications, December 31, 2013. https://www
.todaysparent.com/family/what-happens-when-both-parents-are-mother/.

Griffin, Pat, and Helen J. Carroll. "On the Team: Equal Opportunity for Transgender Student Athletes." October 4, 2010. https://www.nclrights.org/wp-content/up
loads/2013/07/TransgenderStudentAthleteReport.pdf.

Gutierrez-Morfin, Noel. "NIH Recognizes LGBTQ Community as 'Health Disparity
Population.'" NBC News, October 7, 2016. https://www.nbcnews.com/feature/nbc
-out/nih-recognizes-lgbtq-community-health-disparity-population-n661161.

Hagen, Sofie. *Happy Fat: Taking Up Space in a World That Wants to Shrink You.*
London: 4th Estate, 2019.

Hanna, Jason, Madison Park, and Elliott C. McLaughlin. "North Carolina Repeals
'Bathroom Bill.'" CNN Politics, March 30, 2017. https://www.cnn.com/2017/03/30
/politics/north-carolina-hb2-agreement/index.html.

Hida. "How Common Is Intersex? An Explanation of the Stats." Intersex Campaign
for Equality, April 1, 2015. https://www.intersexequality.com/how-common-is
-intersex-in-humans/.

Human Rights Campaign. "QTBIPOC Mental Health and Well-Being." https://www
.hrc.org/resources/qtbipoc-mental-health-and-well-being.

Human Rights Campaign. "The Cost of the Closet and the Rewards of Inclusion:
Why the Workplace Environment for LGBT People Matters to Employers." https://
assets2.hrc.org/files/assets/resources/Cost_of_the_Closet_May2014.pdf.

Human Rights Campaign. "The Lies and Dangers of Efforts to Change Sexual Orientation or Gender Identity." Accessed October 21, 2019. https://www.hrc.org
/resources/the-lies-and-dangers-of-reparative-therapy.

Human Rights Campaign. "Violence against the Transgender Community in 2018."
https://www.hrc.org/resources/violence-against-the-transgender-community
-in-2018.

Human Rights Campaign. "Workplace Gender Transition Guidelines." https://www
.hrc.org/resources/workplace-gender-transition-guidelines.

Human Rights Campaign. *A Workplace Divided: Understanding the Climate for LGBTQ
Workers Nationwide.* https://www.hrc.org/resources/a-workplace-divided-under
standing-the-climate-for-lgbtq-workers-nationwide.

Human Rights Campaign. *Corporate Equality Index 2019.* Last updated April 4,
2019. https://assets2.hrc.org/files/assets/resources/CEI-2019-FullReport.pdf?
_ga=2.72494480.2003376306.1571331256-1109047636.1571331256.

Intrepid Guide, The. "10 Proven Memory Hacks: How to Remember New Vocabulary
Faster." August 30, 2020. https://www.theintrepidguide.com/memory-hacks-how
-to-memorize-vocabulary-faster/.

James, S. E., J. L. Herman, S. Rankin et al. *The Report of the 2015 U.S. Transgender
Survey.* Washington, DC: National Center for Transgender Equality, 2016. https://
transequality.org/sites/default/files/docs/usts/USTS-Full-Report-Dec17.pdf.

Joint Commission. *Advancing Effective Communication, Cultural Competence, and
Patient- and Family-Centered Care for the Lesbian, Gay, Bisexual, and Transgender (LGBT) Community: A Field Guide.* Oak Brook, IL: Joint Commission, 2011.
https://www.jointcommission.org/-/media/tjc/documents/resources/patient-safety
-topics/health-equity/lgbtfieldguide_web_linked_verpdf.pdf?db=web&hash=FD72
5DC02CFE6E4F21A35EBD839BBE97&hash=FD725DC02CFE6E4F21A35EB
D839BBE97.

Kann, Laura, Emily O'Malley Olsen, Tim McManus et al. "Sexual Identity, Sex of
Sexual Contacts, and Health-Related Behaviors among Students in Grades 9–12—
United States and Selected Sites, 2015." *Center for Disease Control and Prevention
Morbidity and Mortality Weekly Report, Surveillance Summaries* 65, no. 9 (August
12, 2016): 19–22.

Karslake, Daniel G., director. *For They Know Not What They Do.* DK Works, April 25,
2019.

Keir, John, producer, and Lahood Grant, director. *Intersexion: Gender Ambiguity Unveiled.* Kilbirnie, Wellington, New Zealand: Ponsonby Production Limited, 2012.
DVD.

Kellaway, Mitch. "Trans Folks Respond to 'Bathroom Bills' with #WeJustNeedToPee Selfies." *Advocate*, March 14, 2015. https://www.advocate.com/politics/transgender /2015/03/14/trans-folks-respond-bathroom-bills-wejustneedtopee-selfies.

Keneally, Thomas. *Schindler's List*. New York: Simon & Schuster, 1994.

Kennedy, John F. A written message to the 14th Annual Convention of Americans for Democratic Action, May 11, 1961. https://www.jfklibrary.org/asset-viewer /archives/JFKWHCFCHRON/002/JFKWHCFCHRON-002-008?image _identifier=JFKWHCFCHRON-002-008-p0069.

Killermann, Sam. *A Guide to Gender: The Social Justice Advocate's Handbook*, rev. and updated ed. Austin, TX: Impetus Books, 2017.

Killermann, Sam. "You Soup: Understanding Diversity and the Intersections of Identity." It's Pronounced Metrosexual, October 2012. https://www.itspronouncedmetro sexual.com/2012/10/individual-difference-and-group-similiarity/.

Kosciw, Joseph G., Caitlin M. Clark, and Leesh Menard. "The 2021 National School Climate Survey." GLSEN. https://www.glsen.org/sites/default/files/2022-10/NSCS -2021-Full-Report.pdf.

Lorde, Audre. *A Burst of Light: And Other Essays*. Mineola, NY: Dover Publications, 1988.

Lynn, Sydney. "The A Stands for Asexuality: Putting the A in the LGBTQA+ Community." *Thought Catalog*, April 3, 2015. https://thoughtcatalog.com/sydney lynn/2015/04/the-a-stands-for-asexualityputtingthea-in-lgbtqa-community/.

Maglaty, Jeanne. "When Did Girls Start Wearing Pink?" *Smithsonian Magazine*, April 7, 2011. https://www.smithsonianmag.com/arts-culture/when-did-girls-start -wearing-pink-1370097/.

McKenzie, Mia. *Black Girl Dangerous: On Race, Queerness, Class and Gender*. Oakland, CA: BGD Press, 2014.

McNaught, Brian. *Brian McNaught's Guide to LGBTQ Issues in the Workplace*. Independently published, November 2017.

McWhorter, John. "How 'Woke' Became an Insult." *New York Times*, August 17, 2021. https://www.nytimes.com/2021/08/17/opinion/woke-politically-correct.html?action =click&module=RelatedLinks&pgtype=Article.

Medical Accident Group. "Do You Regret Having Cosmetic Surgery?" https:// www.medicalaccidentgroup.co.uk/news/do-you-regret-having-cosmetic-surgery /#:~:text=Many%20people%20regret%20having%20had,very%20happy%20 with%20its%20results.

Meleen, Michele. "42 Everyday Gender-Neutral Terms to Use." YourDictionary.com. https://grammar.yourdictionary.com/style-and-usage/30-everyday-gender-neutral -terms-to-use.html.

Michelson, Noah. "More Americans Claim to Have Seen a Ghost than Have Met a Trans Person." *HuffPost*, December, 21, 2015. https://www.huffpost.com/entry /more-americans-claim-to-have-seen-a-ghost-than-have-met-a-trans-person_n_5677 fee5e4b014efe0d5ed62.

Moskowitz, Clara. "When Teachers Highlight Gender, Kids Pick Up Stereotypes." *Live Science*, November 16, 2010. https://www.livescience.com/8966-teachers -highlight-gender-kids-pick-stereotypes.html.

Movement Advancement Project and SAGE. "*Improving the Lives of LGBT Older Adults*." March 2010. https://www.lgbtmap.org/improving-the-lives-of-lgbt-older -adults.

Movement Advancement Project. "Nondiscrimination Laws." https://www.lgbtmap.org /equality-maps/non_discrimination_laws.

Mozilla. "Mozilla Workplace Transition Policy Guidelines." https://blog.mozilla.org /careers/mozilla-workplace-transition-policy-guidelines/.

Myers, Alex. "Why We Need More Queer Identity Labels, Not Fewer." *Slate*, January 16, 2018. https://slate.com/human-interest/2018/01/lgbtq-people-need-more-labels -not-fewer.html.

National LGBTQIA+ Health Education Center. "Focus on Forms and Policy: Creating an Inclusive Environment for LGBT Patients." August 7, 2017. https://www .lgbthealtheducation.org/wp-content/uploads/2017/08/Forms-and-Policy-Brief.pdf.

NCAA. *NCAA Inclusion of Transgender Student-Athletes Handbook*. August 2010. https://ncaaorg.s3.amazonaws.com/inclusion/lgbtq/INC_TransgenderHandbook .pdf.

News 18. "Did You Know Men Were the First to Wear High-heeled Shoes?" *Smithsonian Magazine*, September 16, 2020. https://www.news18.com/news/lifestyle/did -you-know-men-were-the-first-to-wear-high-heel-shoes-2881163.html.

Nhất Hạnh, Thích. *Peace Is Every Step: The Path of Mindfulness in Everyday Life*. New York: Bantam Books, 1991.

Ochs, Robyn. "It's I-dentity Not You-dentity." RobynOchs.com. WordPress, April 27, 2021. https://robynochs.com/2021/04/27/its-i-dentity-not-you-dentity/.

Orr, Asaf, and Joel Baum. "Schools in Transition: A Guide for Supporting Transgender Students in K–12 Schools." https://www.aclu.org/sites/default/files/field_document /schools.in_.transition.2015.pdf.

Owens-Reid, Dannielle, and Kristin Russo. *This Is a Book for Parents of Gay Kids*. San Francisco: Chronicle Books, 2014.

Palmer, Amanda. "The Art of Asking." TED2013, February 2013. https://www.ted .com/talks/amanda_palmer_the_art_of_asking?language=en.

Palmer, Amanda. *The Art of Asking: Or How I Learned to Stop Worrying and Let People Help*. New York: Grand Central, 2014.

Parry, Madeleine, and John Olb, directors. *Hannah Gadsby: Nanette*. Netflix, 2018. 1 hr., 9 min. https://www.netflix.com/title/80233611.

Patterson, Don. "40 Keys to Volleyball Greatness." *VolleyballUSA* (summer 2014): 39.

Pendharkar, Eesha. "Pride Flags and Black Lives Matter Signs in the Classroom: Supportive Symbols or Propaganda?" *Education Week*, January 25, 2022. https://www .edweek.org/leadership/pride-flags-and-black-live-matters-signs-in-the-classroom -supportive-symbols-or-propaganda/2022/01.

PFLAG. "Advocacy One-Pagers." https://pflag.org/resource/advocacy-one-pagers.

Pizzo, Presley. "Boots & Sandals: How to Handle Mistakes." Guide to Allyship. https:// guidetoallyship.com/#THE-WORK-OF-ALLYSHIP.

POPSUGAR. "What It Means to Be Intersex with Emily Quinn." YouTube, June 14, 2017. https://www.youtube.com/watch?v=FwnfOnUweew&ab_channel =POPSUGAR.

Powell, John. *The Secret of Staying in Love*. RCL Benziger, 1974.

Prager, Sarah. "When the Forms Don't Fit Your Family." *New York Times*, September 1, 2020. https://www.nytimes.com/2020/09/01/parenting/lgbtq-family-paperwork .html.

RadioTimes. "*Orange Is the New Black*'s Wonder Woman Laverne Cox on Being a Transgender Trailblazer." July 26, 2015. https://www.radiotimes.com/news/2015 -07-26/orange-is-the-new-blacks-wonder-woman-laverne-cox-on-being-a-transgen der-trailblazer/.

Rafferty, Jason. "Gender Development in Children." American Academy of Pediatrics, September 18, 2018. https://www.healthychildren.org/English/ages-stages/grade school/Pages/Gender-Identity-and-Gender-Confusion-In-Children.aspx.

Real Families. "Gender Neutral Education: Can Our Kids Go Gender Free." You-Tube, November 3, 2018. https://www.youtube.com/watch?v=3Y4lgKnmWSk&ab _channel=RealFamilies.

Reality Check team. "Homosexuality: The Countries Where It Is Illegal to Be Gay." BBC News, May 12, 2021. https://www.bbc.com/news/world-43822234.

Sadowski, Michael. *Safe Is Not Enough: Better Schools for LGBTQ Students*. Cambridge, MA: Harvard Education Press, 2016.

Savvy Ally Action. "Why Share Pronouns?" YouTube, October 18, 2022. https://youtu .be/h0a2sdBKRpU.

Scott, C. E., C. R. Howie, D. MacDonald et al. "Predicting Dissatisfaction Following Total Knee Replacement: A Prospective Study of 1217 Patients." *Journal of Bone & Joint Surgery*, September 2010, 92(9): 1253–58. https://pubmed.ncbi.nlm.nih .gov/20798443/.

Shively, Michael G., and John P. DeCecco. "Components of Sexual Identity." *Journal of Homosexuality* 3, no. 1 (1977): 41–48. https://www.tandfonline.com/doi /abs/10.1300/J082v03n01_04.

Sterling, Penny. "Coffeeshop." Penny Sterling (blog), February 9, 2018. https://www .penny-sterling.com/post/im-in-this-coffeeshop-see.

Tackenberg, Rich, director. *Coming Out Party*. Studio City, CA: Ariztical Entertain-ment, 2003. DVD.

Timsit, Annabelle. "The Push to Make French Gender-Neutral." *The Atlantic*, Novem-ber 24, 2017. https://www.theatlantic.com/international/archive/2017/11/inclusive -writing-france-feminism/545048/.

Ting, Jasmine. "Disney Parks Switch to More Inclusive Messages." Paper Magazine, July 3, 2021. https://www.papermag.com/disney-parks-inclusion-2653650433.html ?rebellitiem=5#rebelltitem5.

Tobia, Jacob. *Sissy: A Coming-of-Gender Story*. New York: G. P. Putnam's Sons, 2019.

Transgender Law Center. "CA Governor Signs 'All-Gender' Restroom Bill." September 29, 2016. https://transgenderlawcenter.org/archives/13317.

Trevor Project, The. "Pronoun Usage among LGBTQ Youth." July 29, 2020. https://www.thetrevorproject.org/research-briefs/pronouns-usage-among-lgbtq-youth/.

Valdes, Roberto. "I'm a Queer Man of Color. Here's How Intersectionality Impacts Me." *WHYY*, February 26, 2020. https://whyy.org/articles/im-a-queer-man-of-color -heres-how-intersectionality-impacts-me.

Venn-Brown, Anthony. *A Life of Unlearning: A Preacher's Struggle with His Homosexuality, Church, and Faith*, 3rd ed. Australia: Ambassadors & Bridge Builders International, 2015.

Viverito, CV. "Nonbinary Gender Identities: A Diverse Global History." Out & Equal Workplace Advocates. https://outandequal.org/wp-content/uploads/2021/02 /Nonbinary-History.pdf.

Wade, Lisa. "The Manly Origins of Cheerleading." *HuffPost*, December 31, 2021 (updated March 2, 2013). https://www.huffpost.com/entry/cheerleading -history_b_2372103.

What We Know: The Public Policy Research Project. "What Does the Scholarly Research Say about the Effect of Gender Transition on Transgender Well-Being?" (online literature review). Cornell University, 2018. https://whatweknow.inequality .cornell.edu/topics/lgbt-equality/what-does-the-scholarly-research-say-about-the -well-being-of-transgender-people/.

Wicks, Amanda. "More Republican Legislators Arrested for Bathroom Misconduct than Trans People." Complex, March 2016. https://www.complex.com/life /2016/03/republican-legislators-arrested-for-bathroom-misconduct.

Wikipedia. "LGBT Rights by Country or Territory." https://en.wikipedia.org/wiki /LGBT_rights_by_country_or_territory.

Wikipedia. "Microaggression." https://en.wikipedia.org/wiki/Microaggression.

Williams, David R., and Toni D. Rucker. "Understanding and Addressing Racial Disparities in Health Care." *Health Care Financing Review* 21, no. 4 (Summer 2000): 75–90. https://www.ncbi.nlm.nih.gov/pmc/articles/PMC4194634/.

Wilson, Lena. "What Are Puberty Blockers?" *New York Times*, May 11, 2021. https://www.nytimes.com/2021/05/11/well/family/what-are-puberty-blockers .html#:~:text=Puberty%20blockers%20are%20medications%20that,align%20 with%20their%20gender%20identities.

Witz, Billy. "As Lia Thomas Swims, Debate about Transgender Athletes Swirls." *New York Times*, January 24, 2022. https://www.nytimes.com/2022/01/24/sports/lia -thomas-transgender-swimmer.html.

Yoshino, Kenji. *Covering: The Hidden Assault on Our Civil Rights.* New York: Random House, 2006.

5 Calls. "How to Call Your Representative with 5calls.org." YouTube, April 13, 2017. https://www.youtube.com/watch?v=N62ViRRn61I&ab_channel=5Calls.

INDEX